A
MARVEL COMICS
PRESENTATION

CIVIL WAR WITHDRAWN
MS. MARVEL

WRITER
BRIAN REED

PENCILERS
ROBERTO DE LA TORRE (#6-8),
MIKE WIERINGO (#9-10) &
GIUSEPPE CAMUNCOLI (SPECIAL #1)

INKERS
JON SIBAL (#6-8),
WADE VON GRAWBADGER (#9-10)
& LORENZO RUGGIERO (SPECIAL #1)

COLORIST
CHRIS SOTOMAYOR

LETTERER
DAVE SHARPE

COVER ART
DAVID MACK (#6-8),
MIKE WIERINGO (#9-10) &
GIUSEPPE CAMUNCOLI (SPECIAL #1)

ASSISTANT EDITOR
DANIEL KETCHUM

EDITOR
ANDY SCHMIDT

COLLECTION EDITOR
JENNIFER GRÜNWALD

ASSISTANT EDITOR
SARAH BRUNSTAD

ASSOCIATE MANAGING EDITOR
ALEX STARBUCK

EDITOR, SPECIAL PROJECTS
MARK D. BEAZLEY

SENIOR EDITOR,
SPECIAL PROJECTS
JEFF YOUNGQUIST

SVP PRINT, SALES & MARKETING
DAVID GABRIEL

EDITOR IN CHIEF
AXEL ALONSO

CHIEF CREATIVE OFFICER
JOE QUESADA

PUBLISHER
DAN BUCKLEY

EXECUTIVE PRODUCER
ALAN FINE

CIVIL WAR: MS. MARVEL. Contains material originally published in magazine form as MS. MARVEL #6-10 and MS. MARVEL SPECIAL. First printing 2015. ISBN# 978-0-7851-9813-0. Published by MARVEL WORLDWIDE, INC., a subsidiary of MARVEL ENTERTAINMENT, LLC. OFFICE OF PUBLICATION: 135 West 50th Street, New York, NY 10020. Copyright © 2015 MARVEL No similarity between any of the names, characters, persons, and/or institutions in this magazine with those of any living or dead person or institution is intended, and any such similarity which may exist is purely coincidental. Printed in Canada. ALAN FINE, President, Marvel Entertainment; DAN BUCKLEY, President, TV, Publishing and Brand Management; JOE QUESADA, Chief Creative Officer; TOM BREVOORT, SVP of Publishing; DAVID BOGART, SVP of Operations & Procurement, Publishing; C.B. CEBULSKI, VP of International Development & Brand Management; DAVID GABRIEL, SVP Print, Sales & Marketing; JIM O'KEEFE, VP of Operations & Logistics; DAN CARR, Executive Director of Publishing Technology; SUSAN CRESPI, Editorial Operations Manager; ALEX MORALES, Publishing Operations Manager; STAN LEE, Chairman Emeritus. For information regarding advertising in Marvel Comics or on Marvel.com, please contact Jonathan Rheingold, VP of Custom Solutions & Ad Sales, at jrheingold@marvel.com. For Marvel subscription inquiries, please call 800-217-9158. Manufactured between 4/27/2015 and 5/4/2015 by SOLISCO PRINTERS, SCOTT, QC, CANADA.

10987654321

PREVIOUSLY

STAMFORD, CONNECTICUT — After a terrible accident involving the super-hero team NEW WARRIORS results in the deaths of hundreds of schoolchildren, the long-debated Superhuman Registration Act is finally made law.

Heroes must register their identities with the government and be trained as proper law enforcement officers. Failure to register is a crime, punishable by incarceration.

Heroes have divided into two camps — those allied with Iron Man, who supports the law, and those who follow Captain America, who has moved underground to fight back against a government that has turned its back on him.

And so begins the CIVIL WAR...

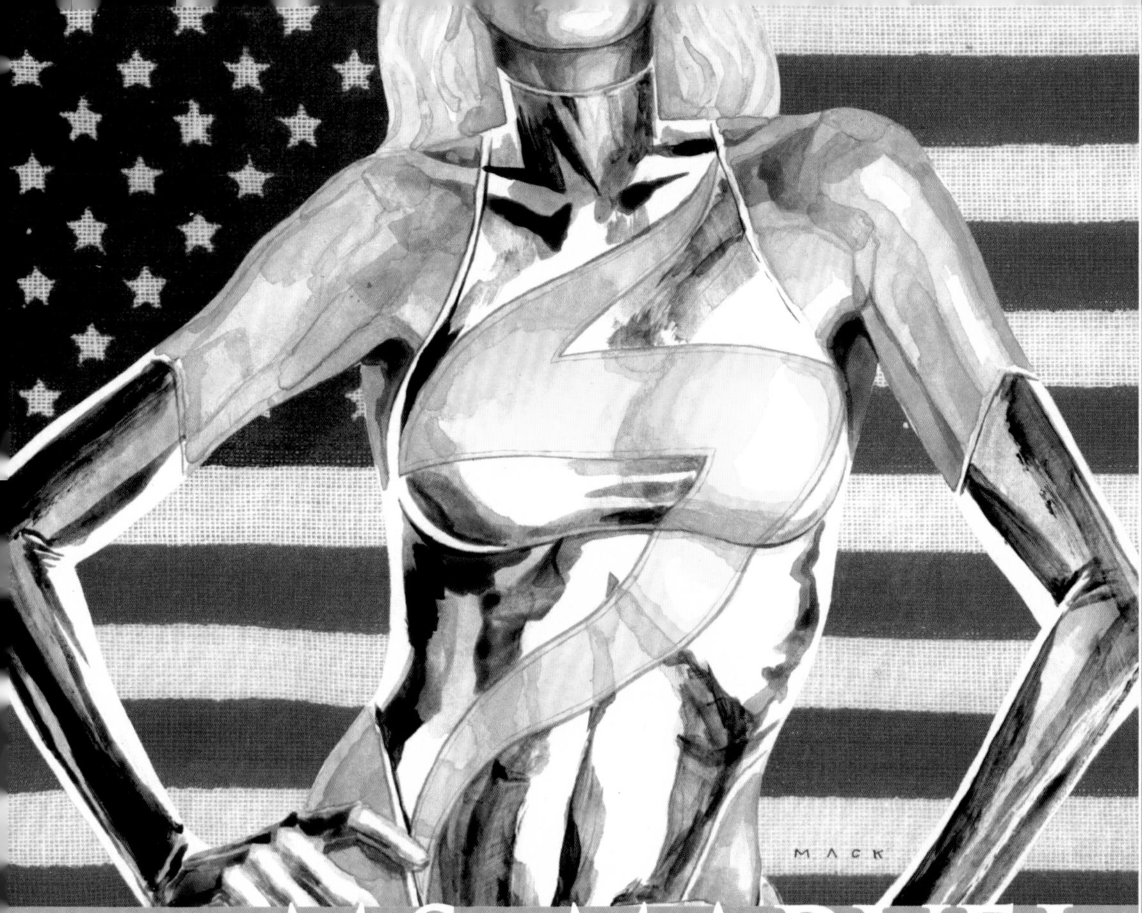
MACK

MS. MARVEL

A MARVEL COMICS EVENT

CIVIL WAR

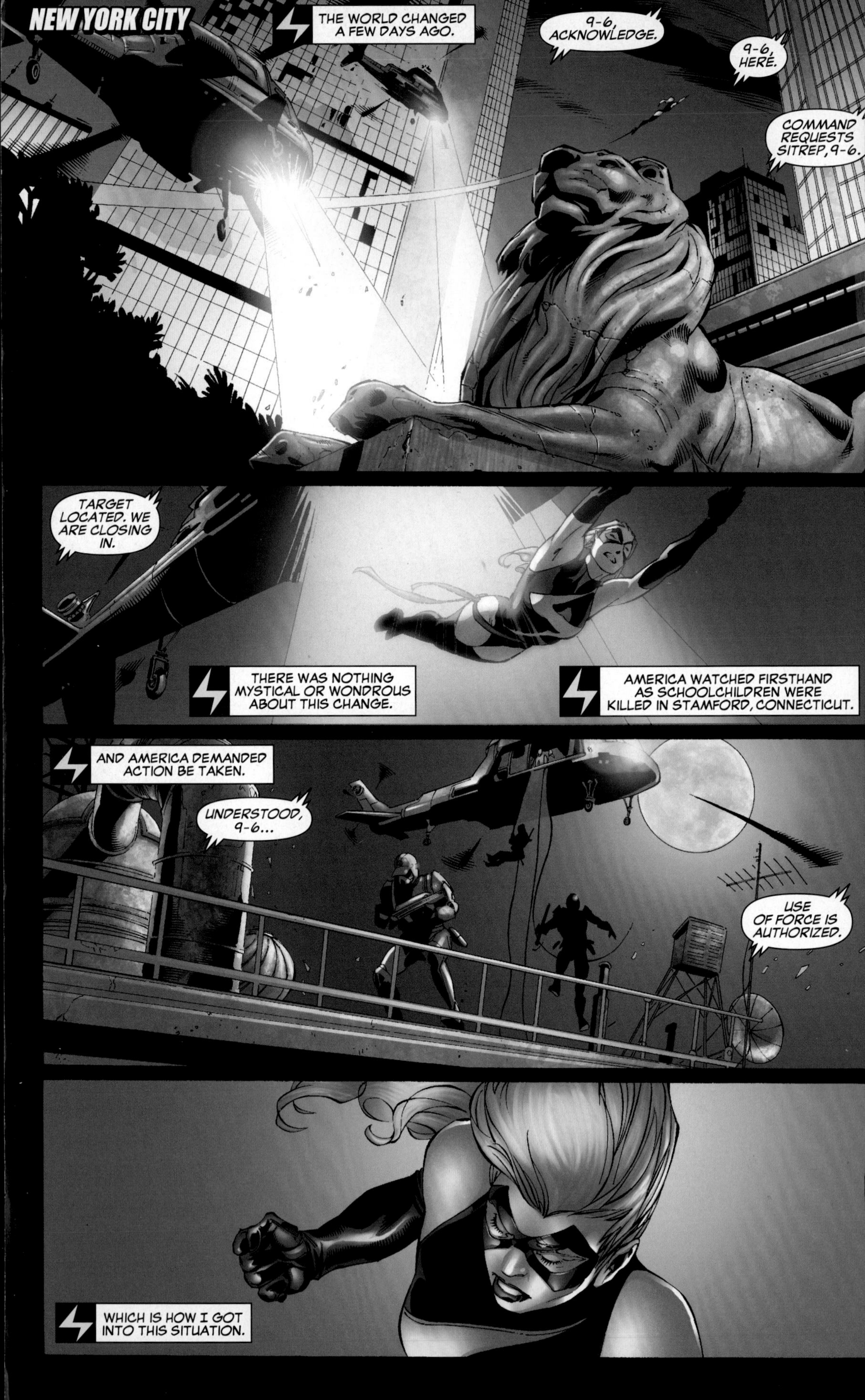
NEW YORK CITY
THE WORLD CHANGED A FEW DAYS AGO.
9-6, ACKNOWLEDGE.
9-6, HERE.
COMMAND REQUESTS SITREP, 9-6.
TARGET LOCATED. WE ARE CLOSING IN.
THERE WAS NOTHING MYSTICAL OR WONDROUS ABOUT THIS CHANGE.
AMERICA WATCHED FIRSTHAND AS SCHOOLCHILDREN WERE KILLED IN STAMFORD, CONNECTICUT.
AND AMERICA DEMANDED ACTION BE TAKEN.
UNDERSTOOD, 9-6...
USE OF FORCE IS AUTHORIZED.
WHICH IS HOW I GOT INTO THIS SITUATION.

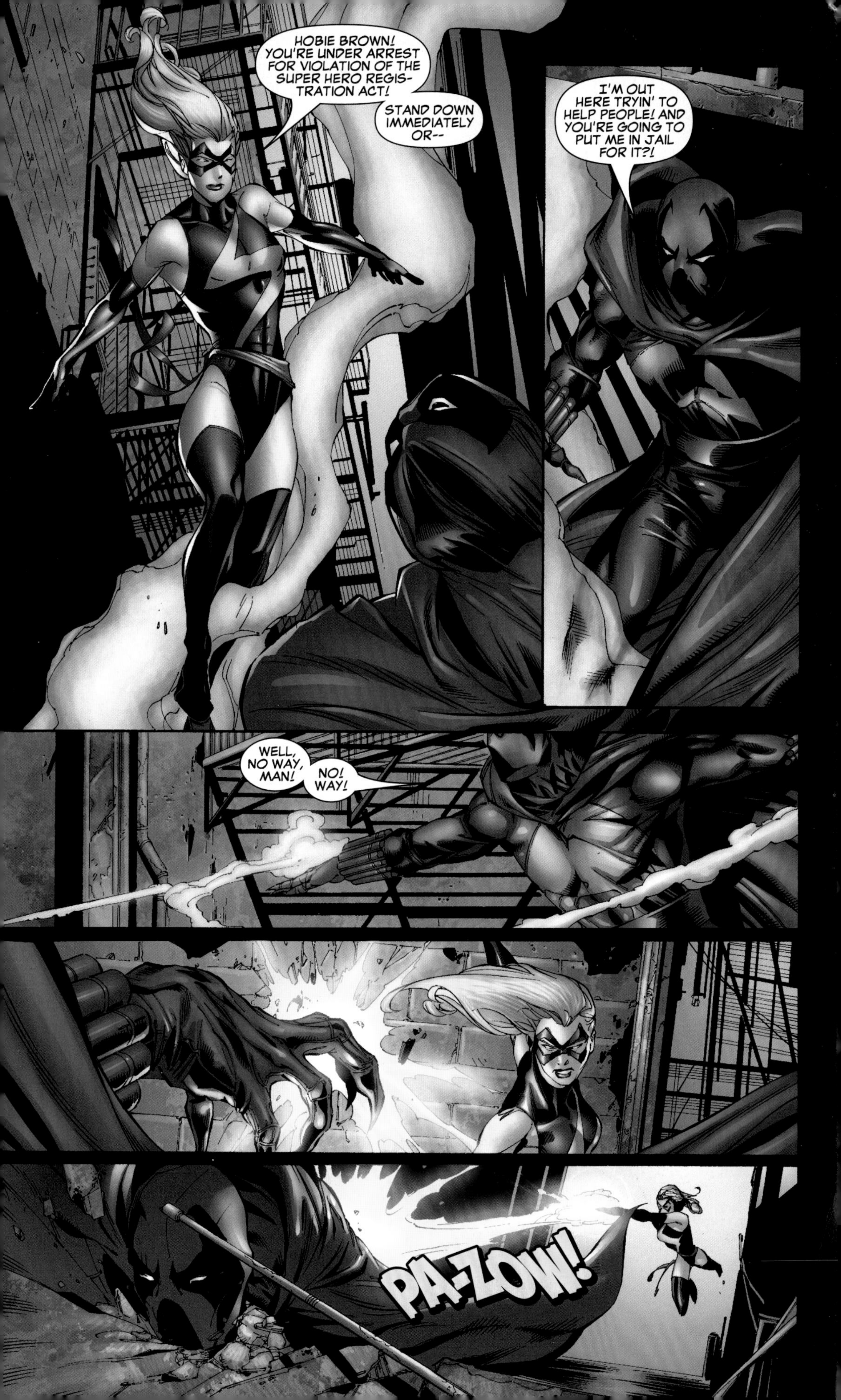
HOBIE BROWN! YOU'RE UNDER ARREST FOR VIOLATION OF THE SUPER HERO REGISTRATION ACT!
STAND DOWN IMMEDIATELY OR--
I'M OUT HERE TRYIN' TO HELP PEOPLE! AND YOU'RE GOING TO PUT ME IN JAIL FOR IT?!
WELL, NO WAY, MAN!
NO! WAY!
PA-ZOW!

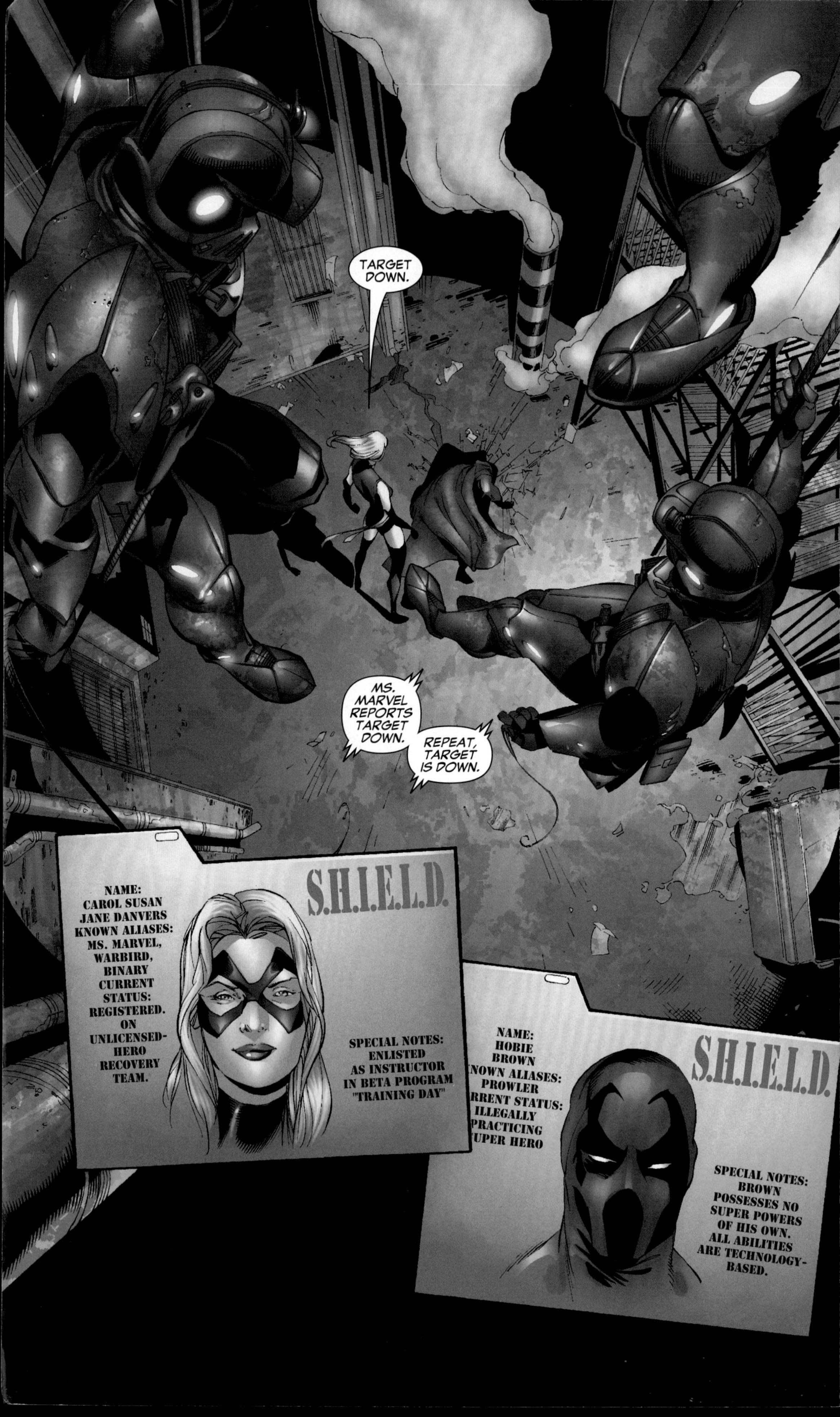
TARGET DOWN.
MS. MARVEL REPORTS TARGET DOWN.
REPEAT, TARGET IS DOWN.
S.H.I.E.L.D.
NAME: CAROL SUSAN JANE DANVERS
KNOWN ALIASES: MS. MARVEL, WARBIRD, BINARY
CURRENT STATUS: REGISTERED. ON UNLICENSED-HERO RECOVERY TEAM.
SPECIAL NOTES: ENLISTED AS INSTRUCTOR IN BETA PROGRAM "TRAINING DAY"
S.H.I.E.L.D.
NAME: HOBIE BROWN
KNOWN ALIASES: PROWLER
CURRENT STATUS: ILLEGALLY PRACTICING SUPER HERO
SPECIAL NOTES: BROWN POSSESSES NO SUPER POWERS OF HIS OWN. ALL ABILITIES ARE TECHNOLOGY-BASED.

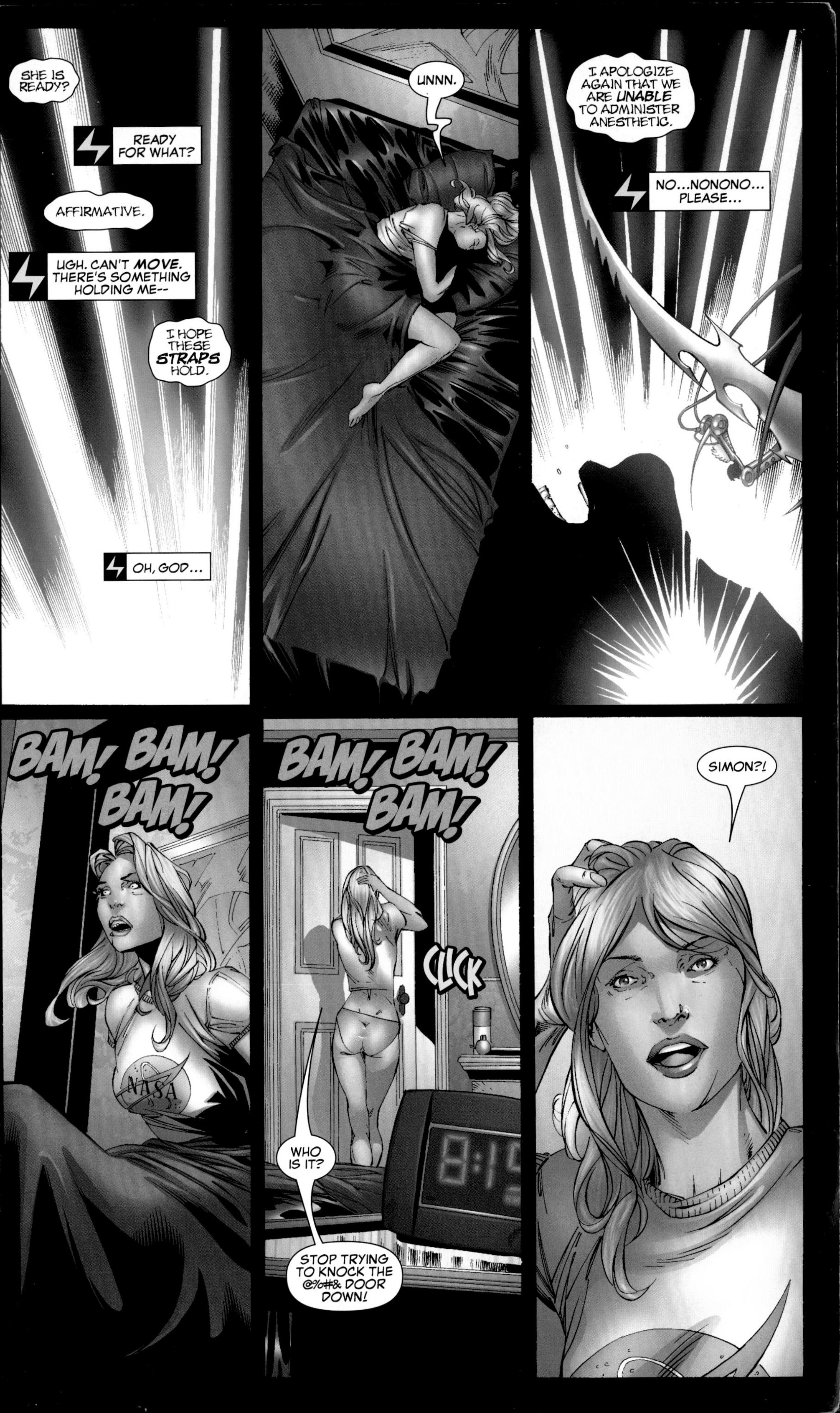
SHE IS READY?
READY FOR WHAT?
AFFIRMATIVE.
UGH. CAN'T MOVE. THERE'S SOMETHING HOLDING ME--
I HOPE THESE STRAPS HOLD.
OH, GOD...
UNNN.
I APOLOGIZE AGAIN THAT WE ARE UNABLE TO ADMINISTER ANESTHETIC.
NO...NONONO... PLEASE...
BAM! BAM! BAM!
BAM! BAM! BAM!
CLICK
WHO IS IT?
STOP TRYING TO KNOCK THE @%#& DOOR DOWN!
SIMON?!

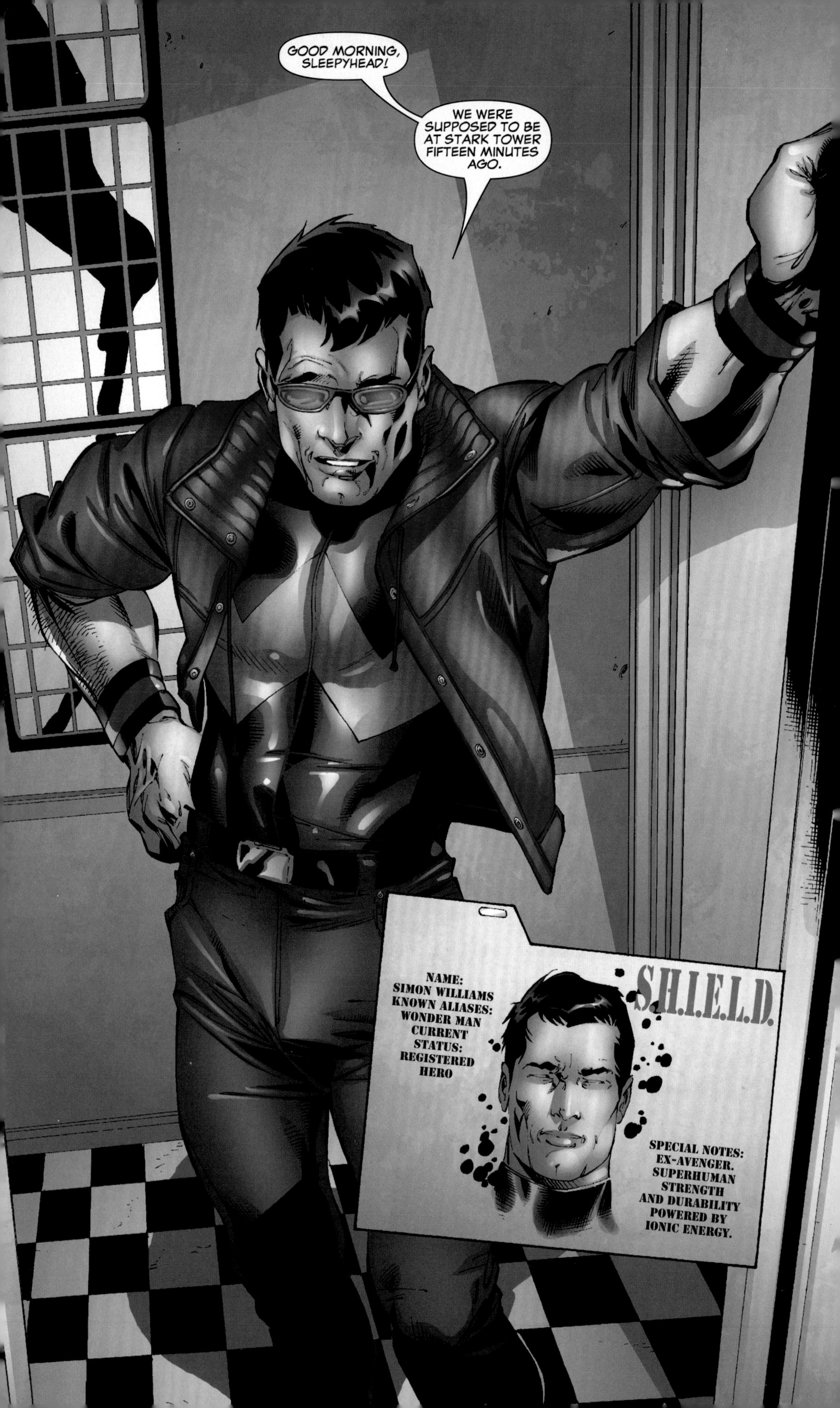
GOOD MORNING, SLEEPYHEAD!
WE WERE SUPPOSED TO BE AT STARK TOWER FIFTEEN MINUTES AGO.
S.H.I.E.L.D.
NAME: SIMON WILLIAMS
KNOWN ALIASES: WONDER MAN
CURRENT STATUS: REGISTERED HERO
SPECIAL NOTES: EX-AVENGER. SUPERHUMAN STRENGTH AND DURABILITY POWERED BY IONIC ENERGY.

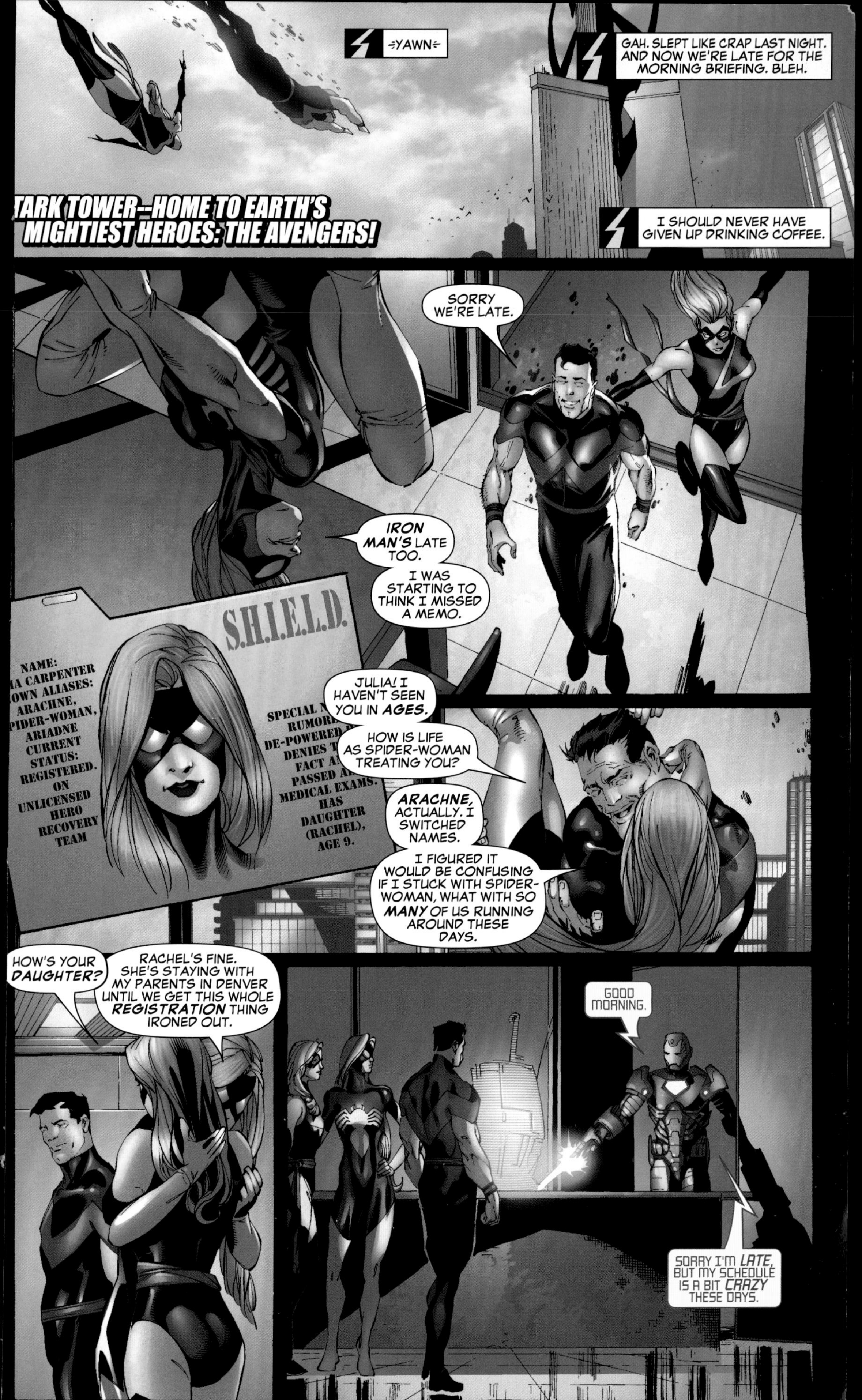

=YAWN=
GAH. SLEPT LIKE CRAP LAST NIGHT. AND NOW WE'RE LATE FOR THE MORNING BRIEFING. BLEH.
TARK TOWER--HOME TO EARTH'S MIGHTIEST HEROES: THE AVENGERS!
I SHOULD NEVER HAVE GIVEN UP DRINKING COFFEE.
SORRY WE'RE LATE.
IRON MAN'S LATE TOO.
I WAS STARTING TO THINK I MISSED A MEMO.
S.H.I.E.L.D.
NAME: MA CARPENTER OWN ALIASES: ARACHNE, PIDER-WOMAN, ARIADNE CURRENT STATUS: REGISTERED. ON UNLICENSED HERO RECOVERY TEAM
SPECIAL N RUMORE DE-POWERED DENIES T FACT A PASSED A MEDICAL EXAMS. HAS DAUGHTER (RACHEL), AGE 9.
JULIA! I HAVEN'T SEEN YOU IN AGES.
HOW IS LIFE AS SPIDER-WOMAN TREATING YOU?
ARACHNE, ACTUALLY. I SWITCHED NAMES.
I FIGURED IT WOULD BE CONFUSING IF I STUCK WITH SPIDER-WOMAN, WHAT WITH SO MANY OF US RUNNING AROUND THESE DAYS.
HOW'S YOUR DAUGHTER?
RACHEL'S FINE. SHE'S STAYING WITH MY PARENTS IN DENVER UNTIL WE GET THIS WHOLE REGISTRATION THING IRONED OUT.
GOOD MORNING.
SORRY I'M LATE, BUT MY SCHEDULE IS A BIT CRAZY THESE DAYS.

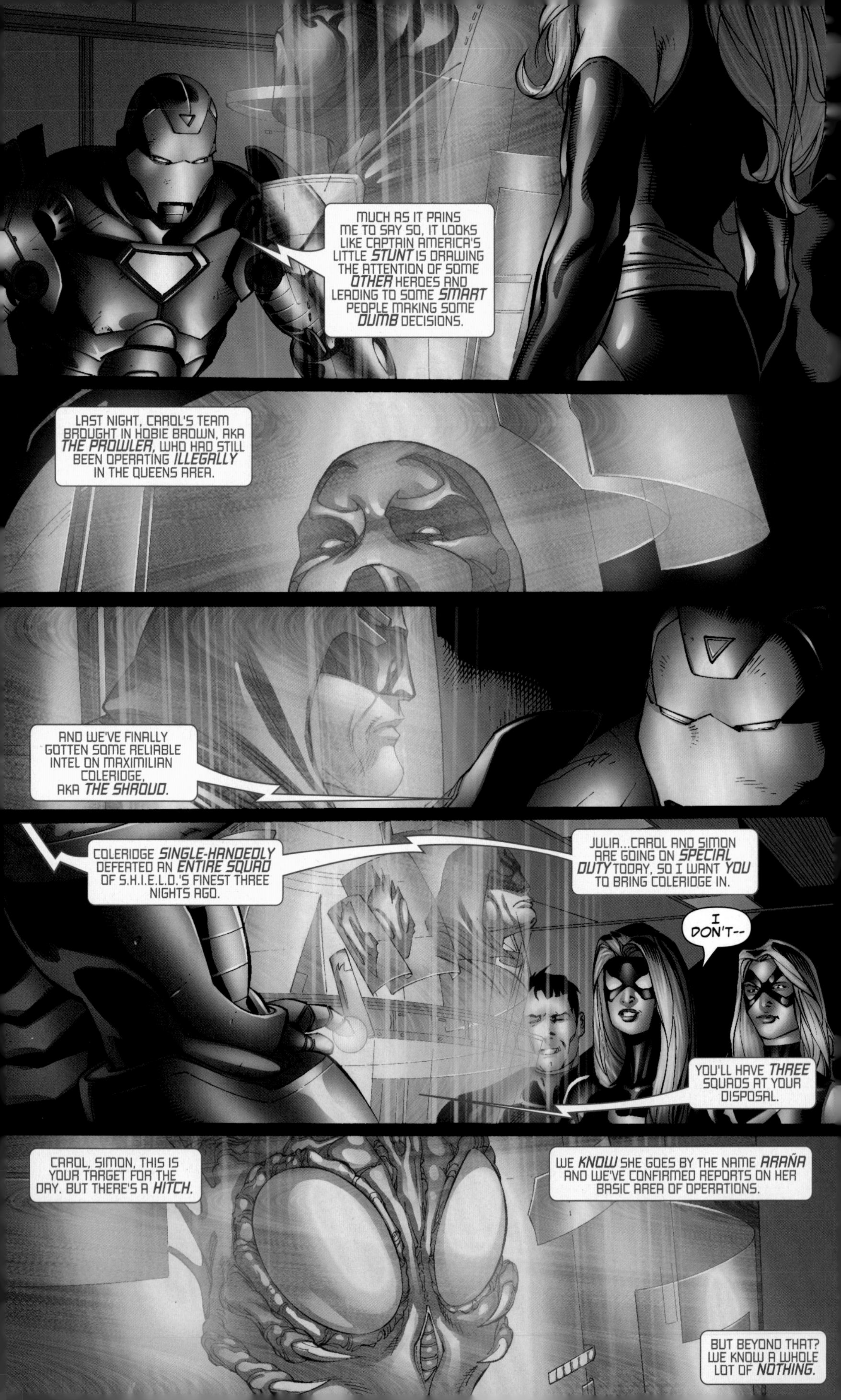

MUCH AS IT PAINS ME TO SAY SO, IT LOOKS LIKE CAPTAIN AMERICA'S LITTLE STUNT IS DRAWING THE ATTENTION OF SOME OTHER HEROES AND LEADING TO SOME SMART PEOPLE MAKING SOME DUMB DECISIONS.
LAST NIGHT, CAROL'S TEAM BROUGHT IN HOBIE BROWN, AKA THE PROWLER, WHO HAD STILL BEEN OPERATING ILLEGALLY IN THE QUEENS AREA.
AND WE'VE FINALLY GOTTEN SOME RELIABLE INTEL ON MAXIMILIAN COLERIDGE, AKA THE SHROUD.
COLERIDGE SINGLE-HANDEDLY DEFEATED AN ENTIRE SQUAD OF S.H.I.E.L.D.'S FINEST THREE NIGHTS AGO.
JULIA...CAROL AND SIMON ARE GOING ON SPECIAL DUTY TODAY, SO I WANT YOU TO BRING COLERIDGE IN.
I DON'T--
YOU'LL HAVE THREE SQUADS AT YOUR DISPOSAL.
CAROL, SIMON, THIS IS YOUR TARGET FOR THE DAY. BUT THERE'S A HITCH.
WE KNOW SHE GOES BY THE NAME ARAÑA AND WE'VE CONFIRMED REPORTS ON HER BASIC AREA OF OPERATIONS.
BUT BEYOND THAT? WE KNOW A WHOLE LOT OF NOTHING.

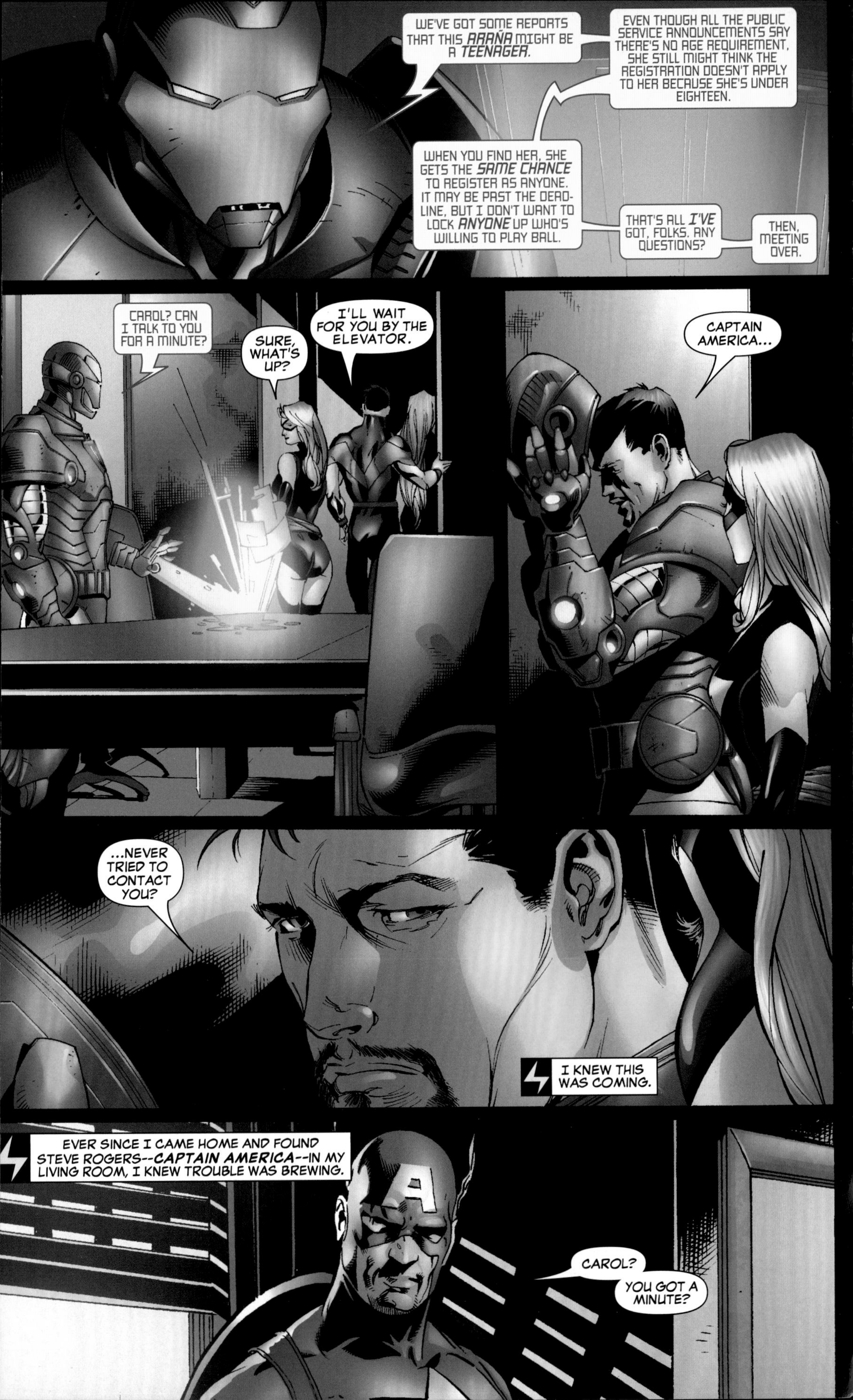
WE'VE GOT SOME REPORTS THAT THIS ARAÑA MIGHT BE A TEENAGER.
EVEN THOUGH ALL THE PUBLIC SERVICE ANNOUNCEMENTS SAY THERE'S NO AGE REQUIREMENT, SHE STILL MIGHT THINK THE REGISTRATION DOESN'T APPLY TO HER BECAUSE SHE'S UNDER EIGHTEEN.
WHEN YOU FIND HER, SHE GETS THE SAME CHANCE TO REGISTER AS ANYONE. IT MAY BE PAST THE DEADLINE, BUT I DON'T WANT TO LOCK ANYONE UP WHO'S WILLING TO PLAY BALL.
THAT'S ALL I'VE GOT, FOLKS. ANY QUESTIONS?
THEN, MEETING OVER.
CAROL? CAN I TALK TO YOU FOR A MINUTE?
SURE, WHAT'S UP?
I'LL WAIT FOR YOU BY THE ELEVATOR.
CAPTAIN AMERICA...
...NEVER TRIED TO CONTACT YOU?
I KNEW THIS WAS COMING.
EVER SINCE I CAME HOME AND FOUND STEVE ROGERS--CAPTAIN AMERICA--IN MY LIVING ROOM, I KNEW TROUBLE WAS BREWING.
CAROL?
YOU GOT A MINUTE?

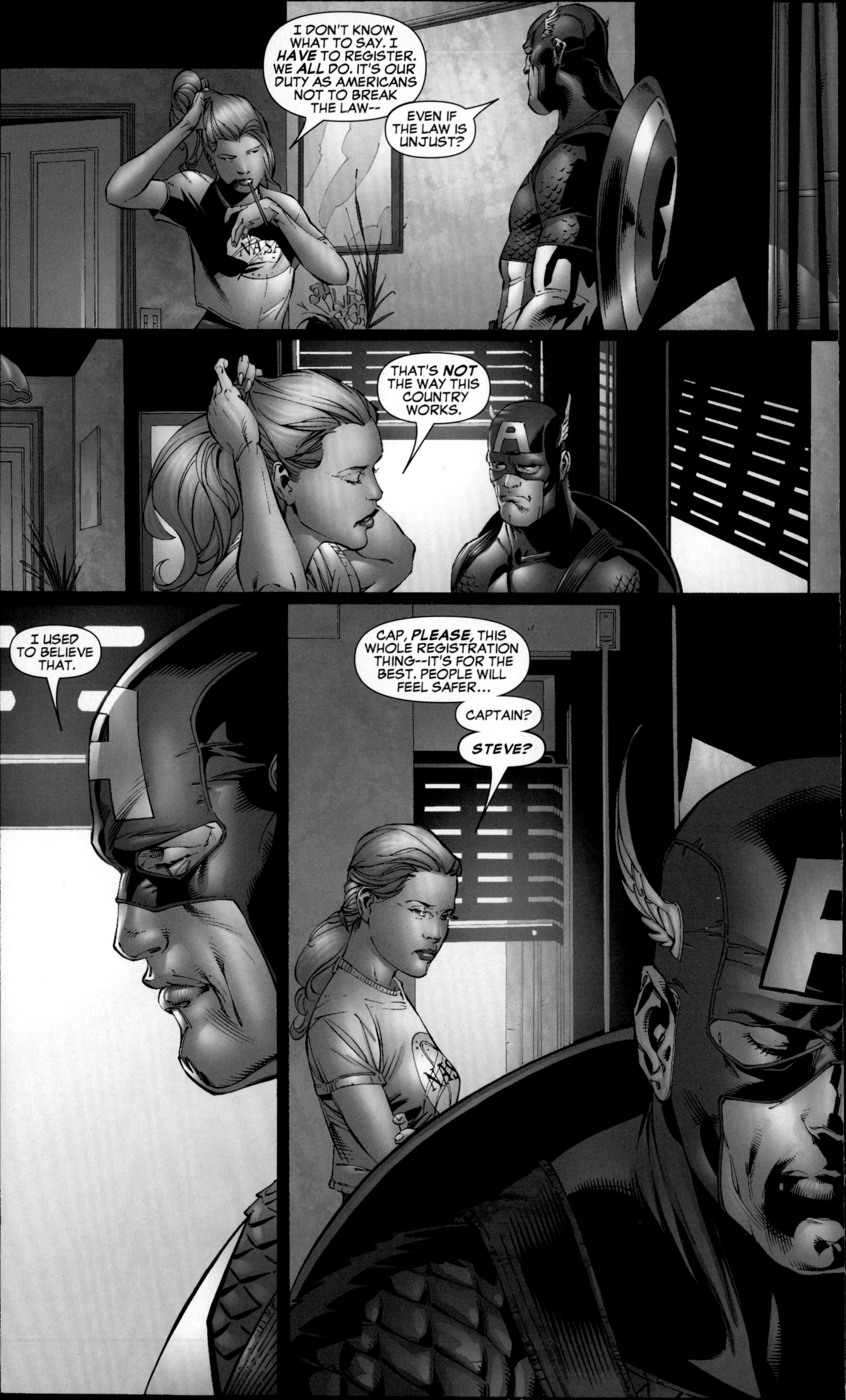
I DON'T KNOW WHAT TO SAY. I *HAVE* TO REGISTER. WE *ALL* DO. IT'S OUR DUTY AS AMERICANS NOT TO BREAK THE LAW--
EVEN IF THE LAW IS UNJUST?
THAT'S *NOT* THE WAY THIS COUNTRY WORKS.
I USED TO BELIEVE THAT.
CAP, *PLEASE*, THIS WHOLE REGISTRATION THING--IT'S FOR THE BEST. PEOPLE WILL FEEL SAFER...
CAPTAIN?
STEVE?

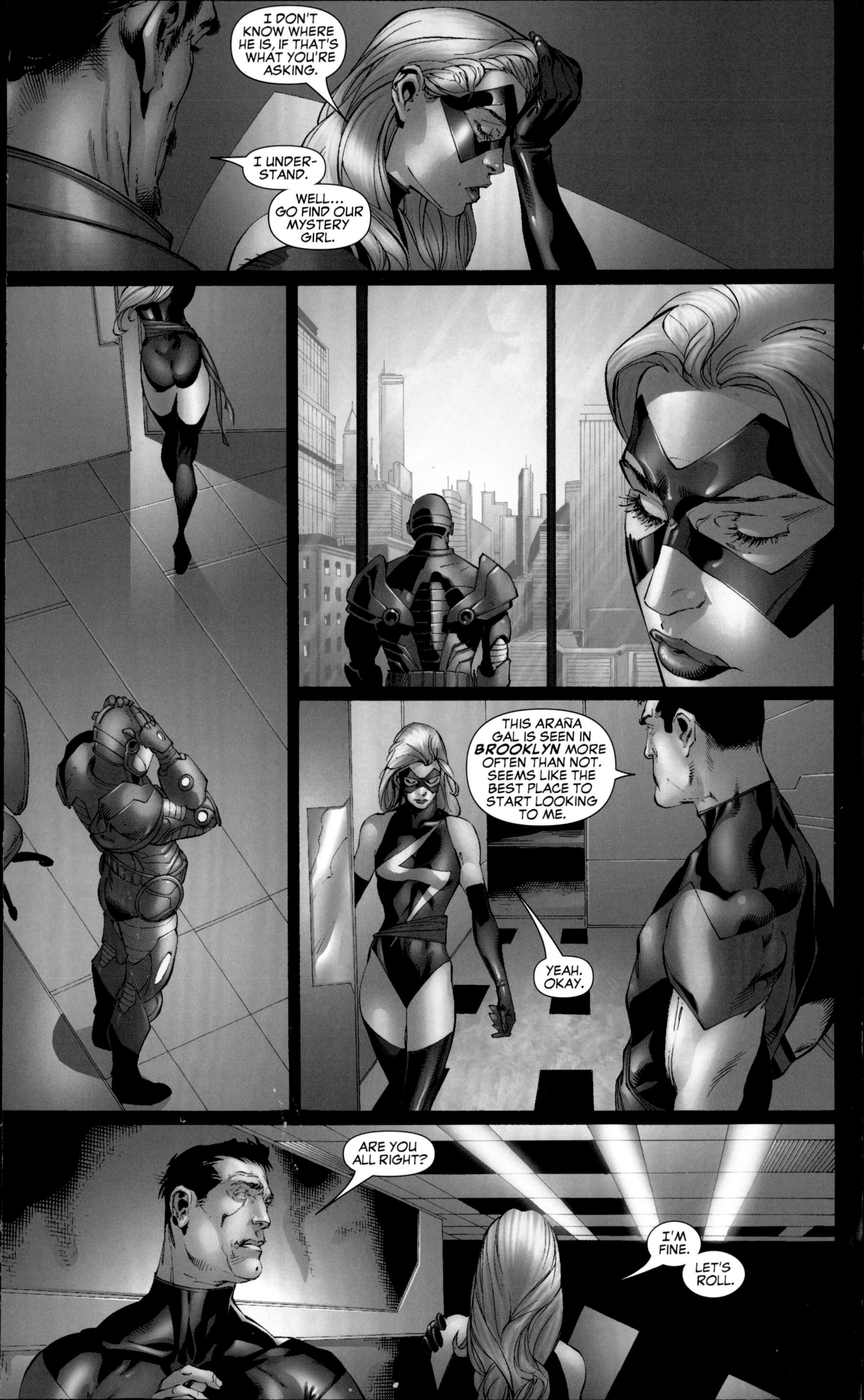
I DON'T KNOW WHERE HE IS, IF THAT'S WHAT YOU'RE ASKING.
I UNDER-STAND.
WELL... GO FIND OUR MYSTERY GIRL.
THIS ARAÑA GAL IS SEEN IN BROOKLYN MORE OFTEN THAN NOT. SEEMS LIKE THE BEST PLACE TO START LOOKING TO ME.
YEAH. OKAY.
ARE YOU ALL RIGHT?
I'M FINE.
LET'S ROLL.

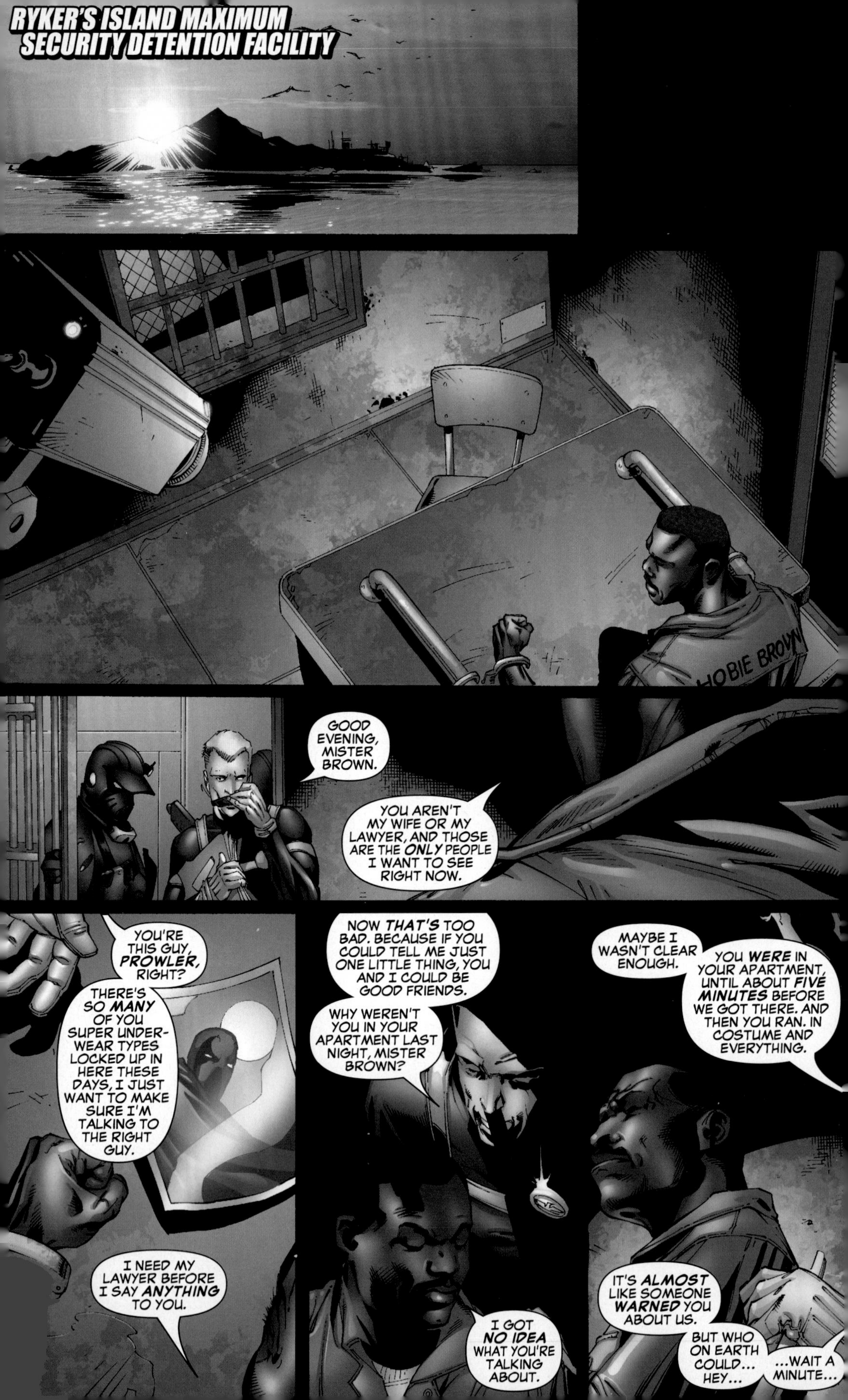
RYKER'S ISLAND MAXIMUM SECURITY DETENTION FACILITY
HOBIE BROWN
GOOD EVENING, MISTER BROWN.
YOU AREN'T MY WIFE OR MY LAWYER, AND THOSE ARE THE ONLY PEOPLE I WANT TO SEE RIGHT NOW.
YOU'RE THIS GUY, PROWLER, RIGHT?
THERE'S SO MANY OF YOU SUPER UNDER-WEAR TYPES LOCKED UP IN HERE THESE DAYS, I JUST WANT TO MAKE SURE I'M TALKING TO THE RIGHT GUY.
I NEED MY LAWYER BEFORE I SAY ANYTHING TO YOU.
NOW THAT'S TOO BAD. BECAUSE IF YOU COULD TELL ME JUST ONE LITTLE THING, YOU AND I COULD BE GOOD FRIENDS.
WHY WEREN'T YOU IN YOUR APARTMENT LAST NIGHT, MISTER BROWN?
I GOT NO IDEA WHAT YOU'RE TALKING ABOUT.
MAYBE I WASN'T CLEAR ENOUGH.
YOU WERE IN YOUR APARTMENT, UNTIL ABOUT FIVE MINUTES BEFORE WE GOT THERE. AND THEN YOU RAN. IN COSTUME AND EVERYTHING.
IT'S ALMOST LIKE SOMEONE WARNED YOU ABOUT US.
BUT WHO ON EARTH COULD... HEY...
...WAIT A MINUTE...

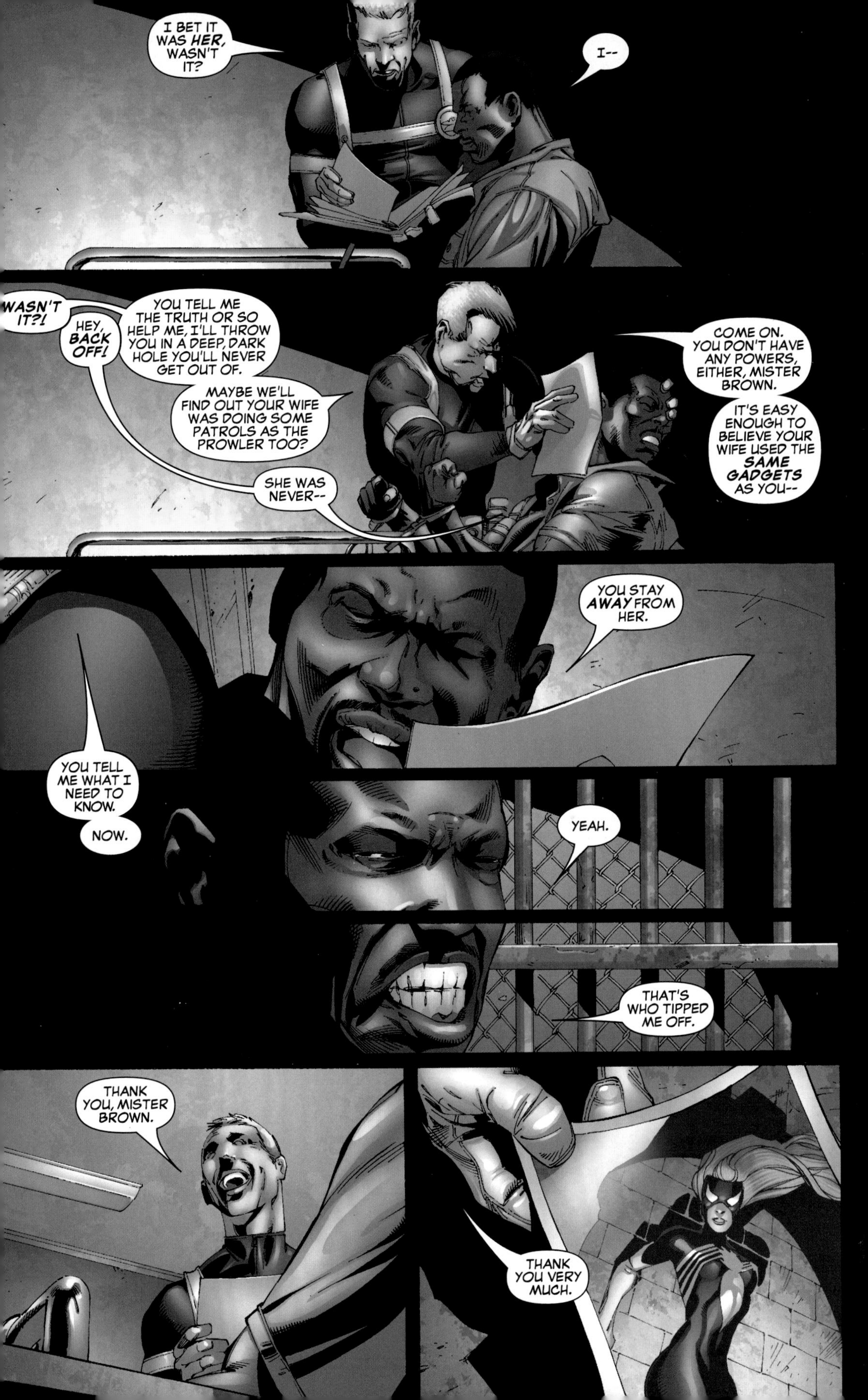
I BET IT WAS HER, WASN'T IT?
I--
WASN'T IT?!
YOU TELL ME THE TRUTH OR SO HELP ME, I'LL THROW YOU IN A DEEP, DARK HOLE YOU'LL NEVER GET OUT OF.
MAYBE WE'LL FIND OUT YOUR WIFE WAS DOING SOME PATROLS AS THE PROWLER TOO?
HEY, BACK OFF!
SHE WAS NEVER--
COME ON. YOU DON'T HAVE ANY POWERS, EITHER, MISTER BROWN.
IT'S EASY ENOUGH TO BELIEVE YOUR WIFE USED THE SAME GADGETS AS YOU--
YOU STAY AWAY FROM HER.
YOU TELL ME WHAT I NEED TO KNOW.
NOW.
YEAH.
THAT'S WHO TIPPED ME OFF.
THANK YOU, MISTER BROWN.
THANK YOU VERY MUCH.

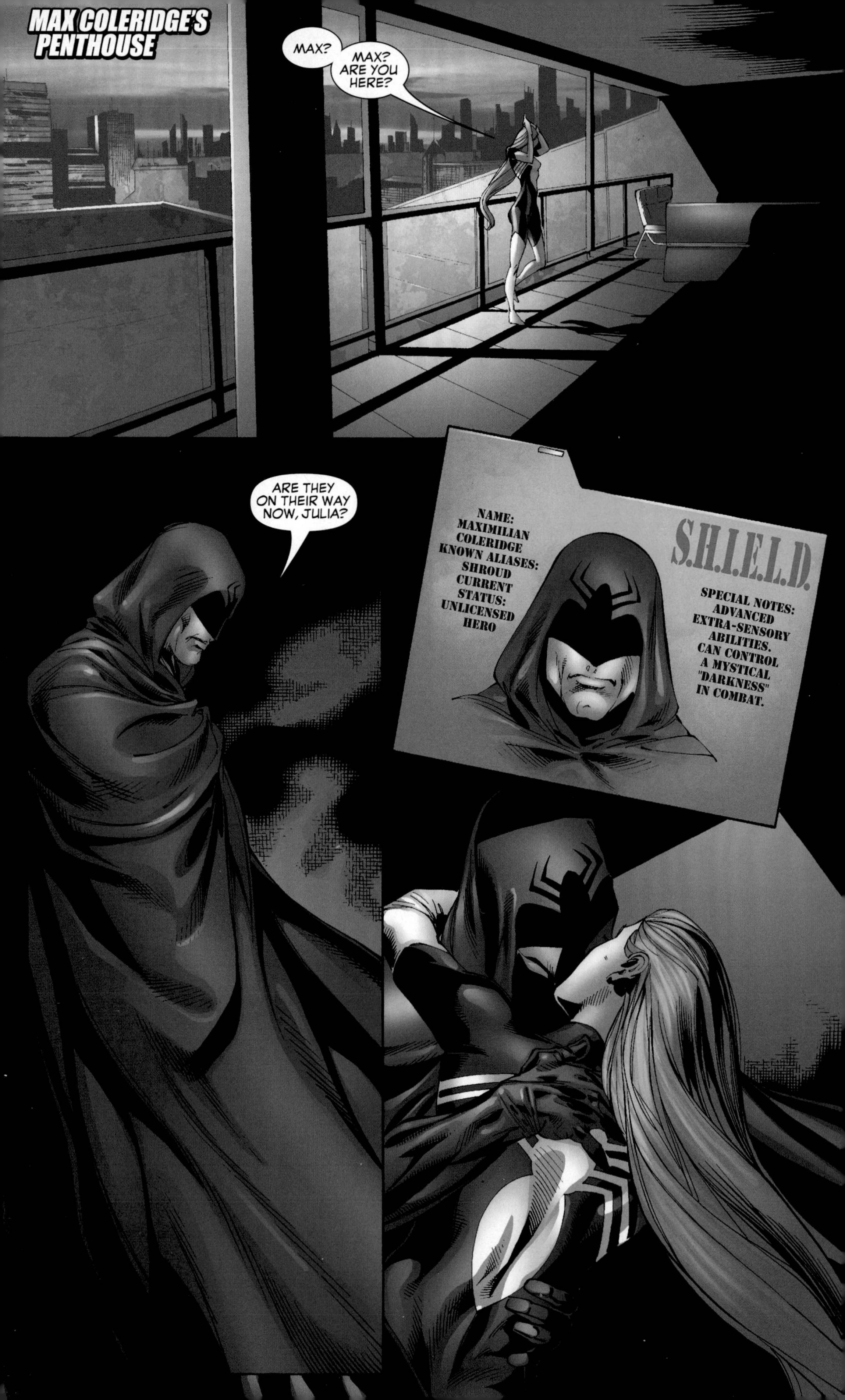
MAX COLERIDGE'S PENTHOUSE
MAX?
MAX? ARE YOU HERE?
ARE THEY ON THEIR WAY NOW, JULIA?
S.H.I.E.L.D.
NAME: MAXIMILIAN COLERIDGE
KNOWN ALIASES: SHROUD
CURRENT STATUS: UNLICENSED HERO
SPECIAL NOTES: ADVANCED EXTRA-SENSORY ABILITIES. CAN CONTROL A MYSTICAL "DARKNESS" IN COMBAT.

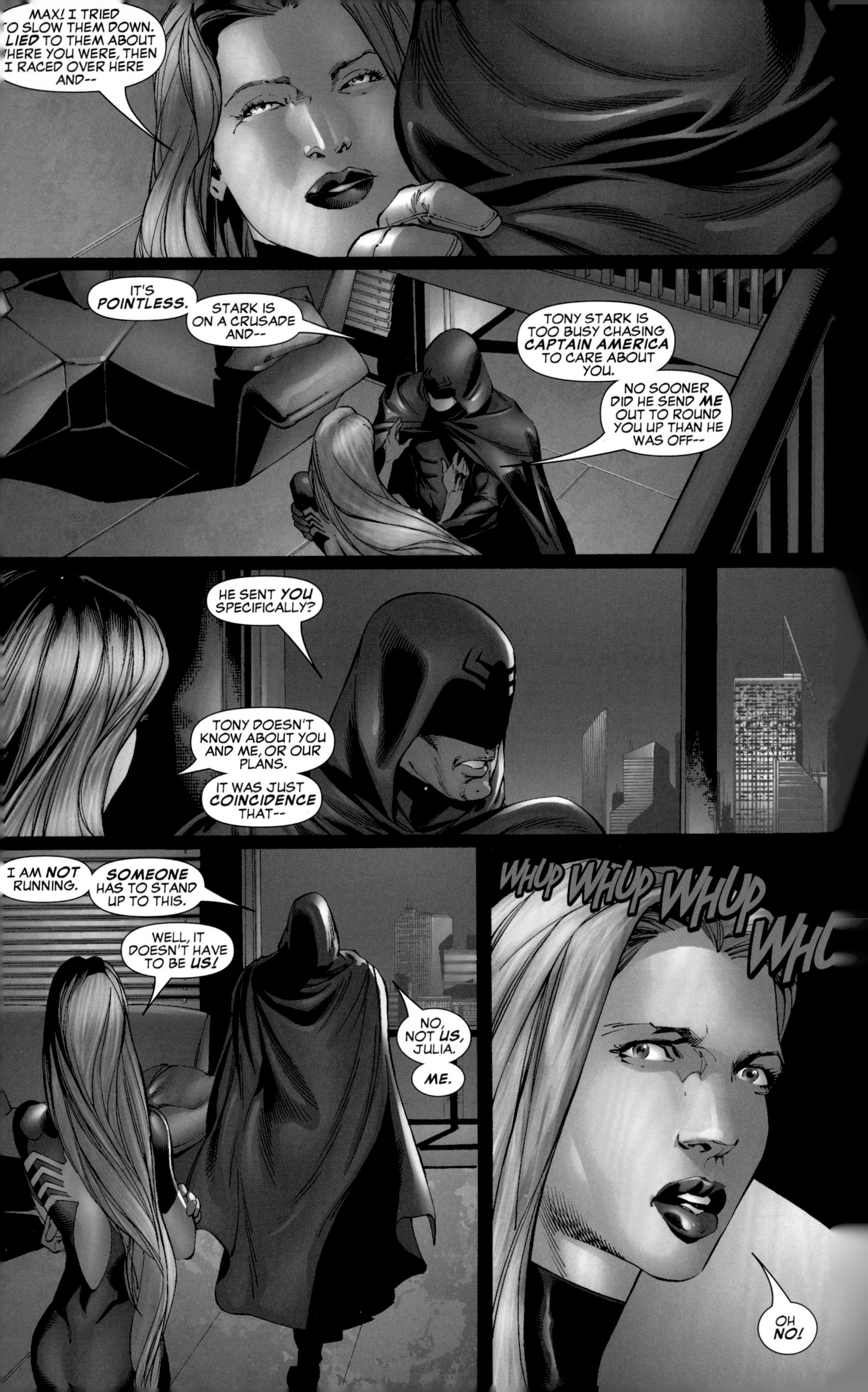
MAX! I TRIED TO SLOW THEM DOWN. LIED TO THEM ABOUT WHERE YOU WERE, THEN I RACED OVER HERE AND--
IT'S POINTLESS.
STARK IS ON A CRUSADE AND--
TONY STARK IS TOO BUSY CHASING CAPTAIN AMERICA TO CARE ABOUT YOU.
NO SOONER DID HE SEND ME OUT TO ROUND YOU UP THAN HE WAS OFF--
HE SENT YOU SPECIFICALLY?
TONY DOESN'T KNOW ABOUT YOU AND ME, OR OUR PLANS.
IT WAS JUST COINCIDENCE THAT--
I AM NOT RUNNING.
SOMEONE HAS TO STAND UP TO THIS.
WELL, IT DOESN'T HAVE TO BE US!
NO, NOT US, JULIA.
ME.
WHUP WHUP WHUP
OH NO!

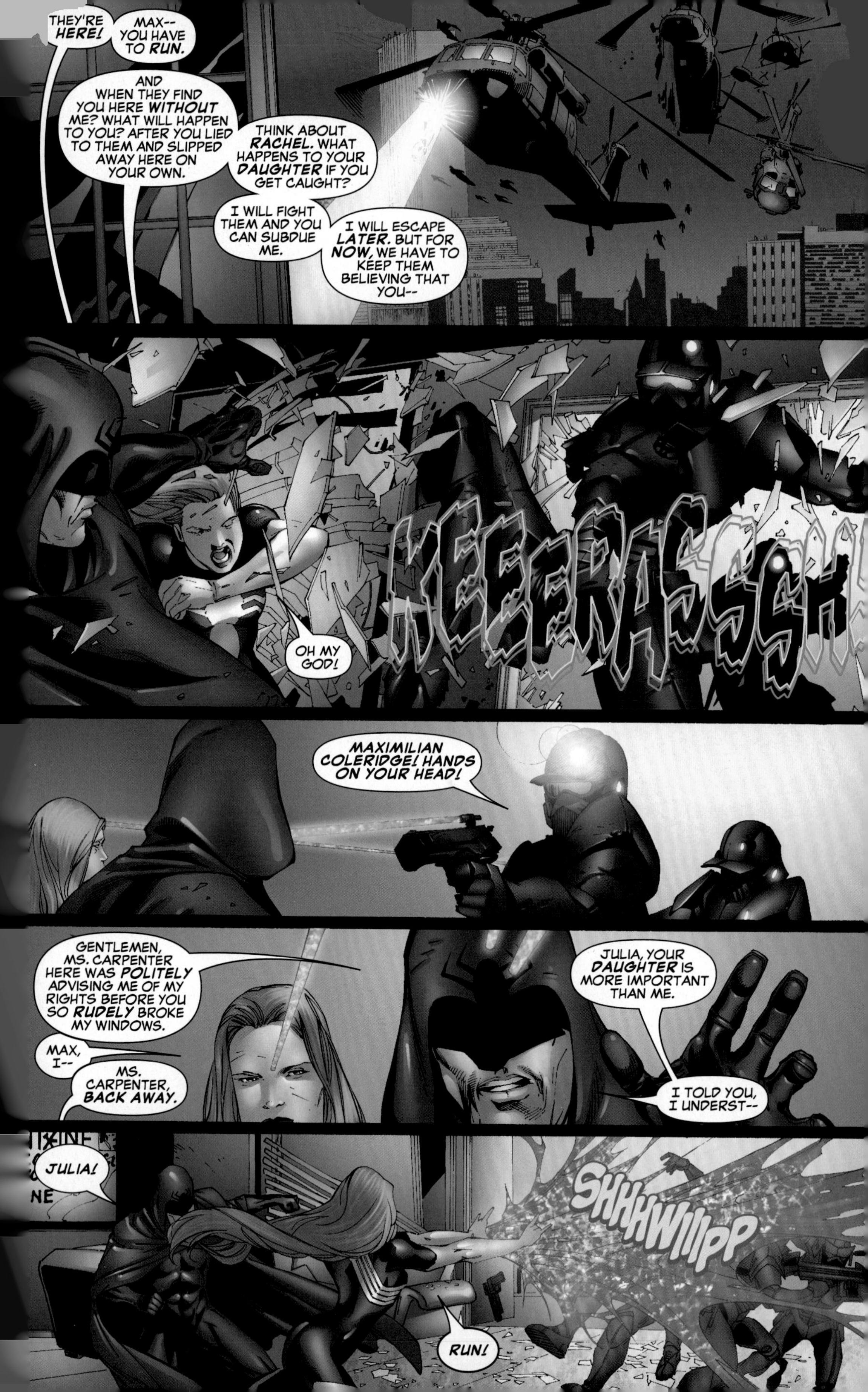

THEY'RE HERE!
MAX-- YOU HAVE TO RUN.
AND WHEN THEY FIND YOU HERE WITHOUT ME? WHAT WILL HAPPEN TO YOU? AFTER YOU LIED TO THEM AND SLIPPED AWAY HERE ON YOUR OWN.
THINK ABOUT RACHEL. WHAT HAPPENS TO YOUR DAUGHTER IF YOU GET CAUGHT?
I WILL FIGHT THEM AND YOU CAN SUBDUE ME.
I WILL ESCAPE LATER. BUT FOR NOW, WE HAVE TO KEEP THEM BELIEVING THAT YOU--
KEEERASSCH
OH MY GOD!
MAXIMILIAN COLERIDGE! HANDS ON YOUR HEAD!
GENTLEMEN, MS. CARPENTER HERE WAS POLITELY ADVISING ME OF MY RIGHTS BEFORE YOU SO RUDELY BROKE MY WINDOWS.
MAX, I--
MS. CARPENTER, BACK AWAY.
JULIA, YOUR DAUGHTER IS MORE IMPORTANT THAN ME.
I TOLD YOU, I UNDERST--
JULIA!
SHHHWIIIPP
RUN!

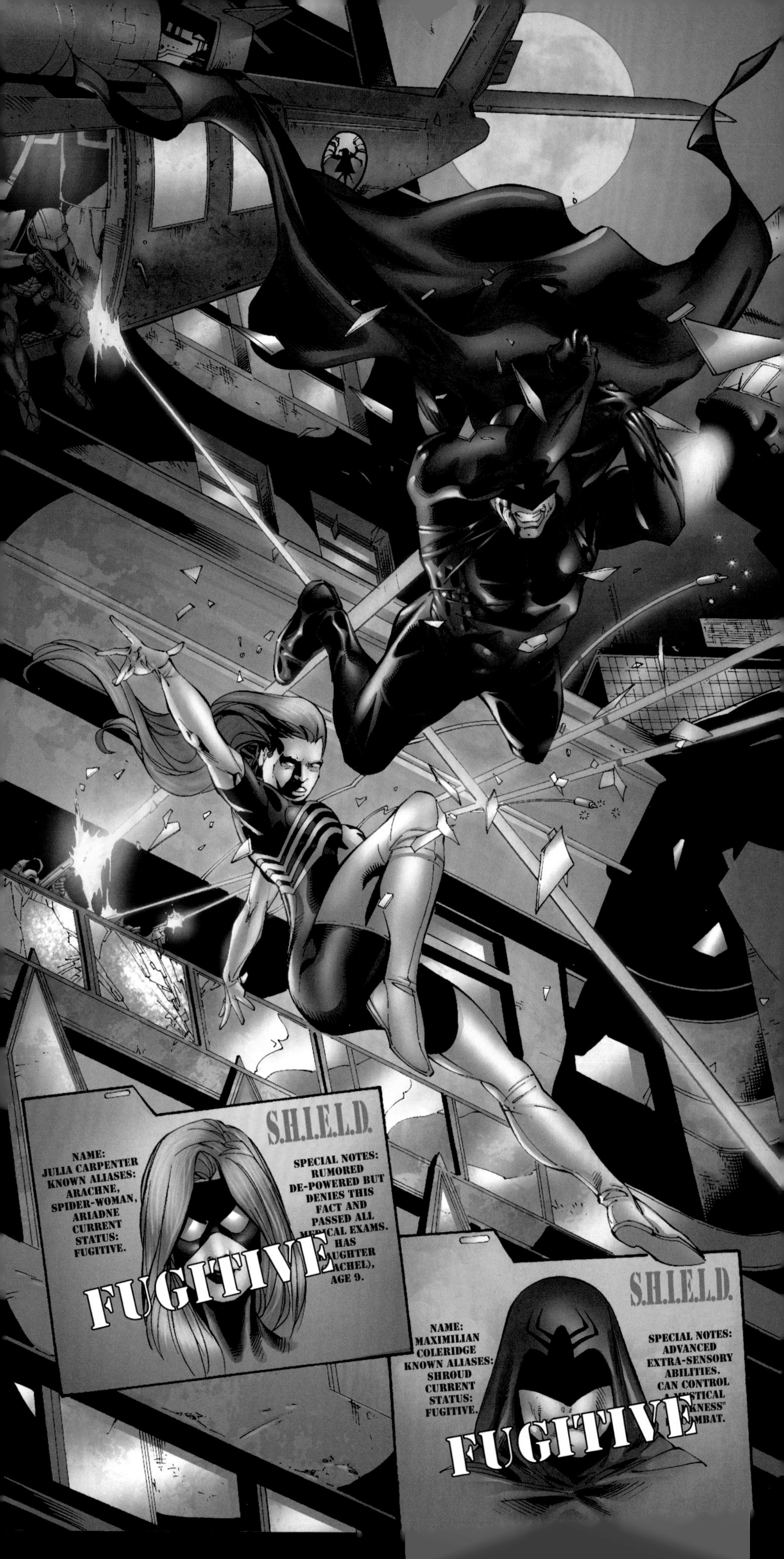

S.H.I.E.L.D.
NAME: JULIA CARPENTER KNOWN ALIASES: ARACHNE, SPIDER-WOMAN, ARIADNE CURRENT STATUS: FUGITIVE.
SPECIAL NOTES: RUMORED DE-POWERED BUT DENIES THIS FACT AND PASSED ALL
HAS
AGE 9.
FUGITIVE
S.H.I.E.L.D.
NAME: MAXIMILIAN COLERIDGE KNOWN ALIASES: SHROUD CURRENT STATUS: FUGITIVE.
SPECIAL NOTES: ADVANCED EXTRA-SENSORY ABILITIES. CAN CONTROL
FUGITIVE

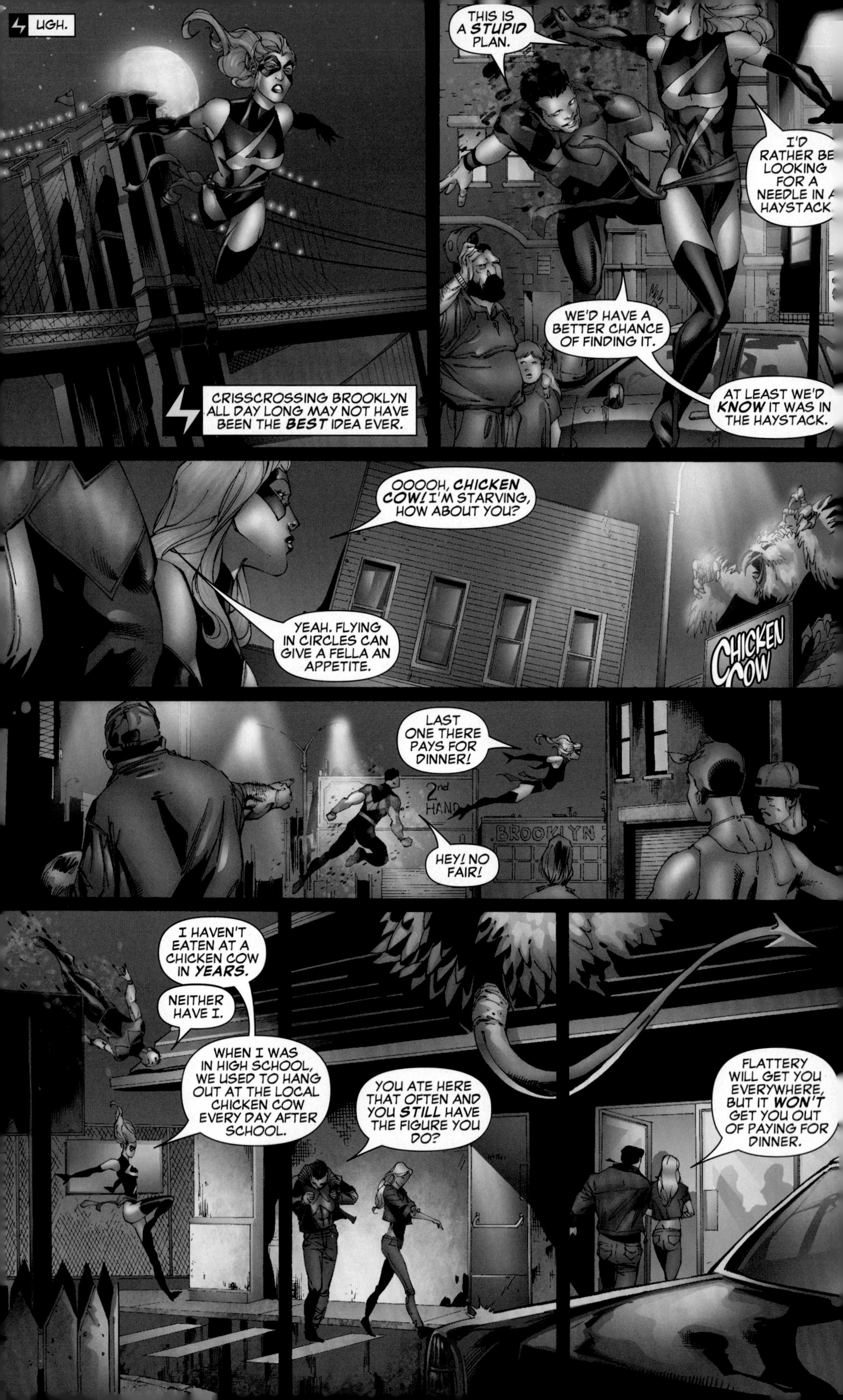
UGH.
CRISSCROSSING BROOKLYN ALL DAY LONG MAY NOT HAVE BEEN THE BEST IDEA EVER.
THIS IS A STUPID PLAN.
I'D RATHER BE LOOKING FOR A NEEDLE IN A HAYSTACK.
WE'D HAVE A BETTER CHANCE OF FINDING IT.
AT LEAST WE'D KNOW IT WAS IN THE HAYSTACK.
OOOOH, CHICKEN COW! I'M STARVING, HOW ABOUT YOU?
YEAH. FLYING IN CIRCLES CAN GIVE A FELLA AN APPETITE.
CHICKEN COW
LAST ONE THERE PAYS FOR DINNER!
2nd HAND
BROOKLYN
HEY! NO FAIR!
I HAVEN'T EATEN AT A CHICKEN COW IN YEARS.
NEITHER HAVE I.
WHEN I WAS IN HIGH SCHOOL, WE USED TO HANG OUT AT THE LOCAL CHICKEN COW EVERY DAY AFTER SCHOOL.
YOU ATE HERE THAT OFTEN AND YOU STILL HAVE THE FIGURE YOU DO?
FLATTERY WILL GET YOU EVERYWHERE, BUT IT WON'T GET YOU OUT OF PAYING FOR DINNER.

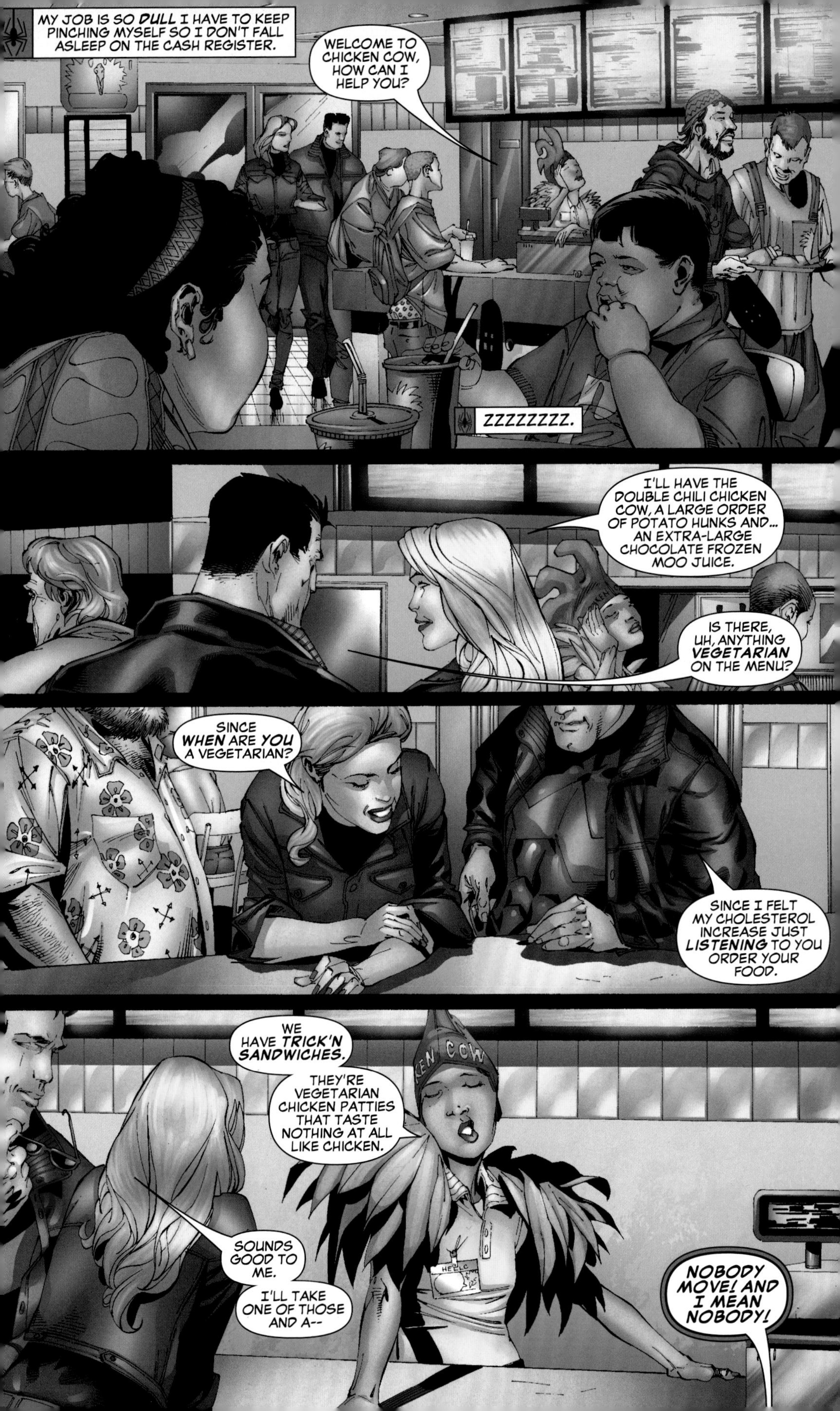
MY JOB IS SO DULL I HAVE TO KEEP PINCHING MYSELF SO I DON'T FALL ASLEEP ON THE CASH REGISTER.
WELCOME TO CHICKEN COW, HOW CAN I HELP YOU?
ZZZZZZZZ.
I'LL HAVE THE DOUBLE CHILI CHICKEN COW, A LARGE ORDER OF POTATO HUNKS AND... AN EXTRA-LARGE CHOCOLATE FROZEN MOO JUICE.
IS THERE, UH, ANYTHING VEGETARIAN ON THE MENU?
SINCE WHEN ARE YOU A VEGETARIAN?
SINCE I FELT MY CHOLESTEROL INCREASE JUST LISTENING TO YOU ORDER YOUR FOOD.
WE HAVE TRICK'N SANDWICHES.
THEY'RE VEGETARIAN CHICKEN PATTIES THAT TASTE NOTHING AT ALL LIKE CHICKEN.
SOUNDS GOOD TO ME.
I'LL TAKE ONE OF THOSE AND A--
NOBODY MOVE! AND I MEAN NOBODY!

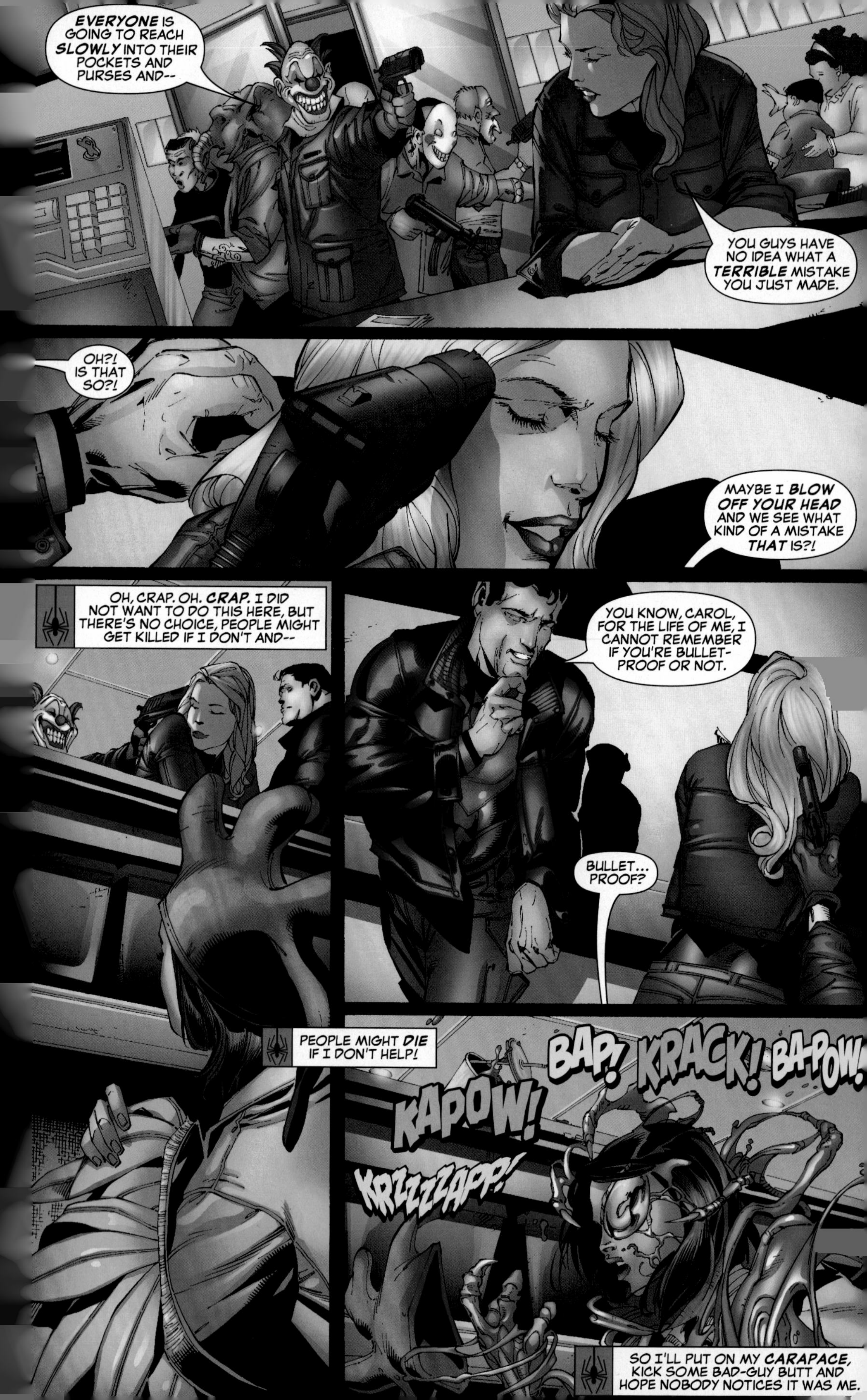

EVERYONE IS GOING TO REACH SLOWLY INTO THEIR POCKETS AND PURSES AND--
YOU GUYS HAVE NO IDEA WHAT A TERRIBLE MISTAKE YOU JUST MADE.
OH?! IS THAT SO?!
MAYBE I BLOW OFF YOUR HEAD AND WE SEE WHAT KIND OF A MISTAKE THAT IS?!
OH, CRAP. OH. CRAP. I DID NOT WANT TO DO THIS HERE, BUT THERE'S NO CHOICE, PEOPLE MIGHT GET KILLED IF I DON'T AND--
YOU KNOW, CAROL, FOR THE LIFE OF ME, I CANNOT REMEMBER IF YOU'RE BULLET-PROOF OR NOT.
BULLET... PROOF?
PEOPLE MIGHT DIE IF I DON'T HELP!
BAP! KRACK! BA-POW!
KAPOW!
KRZZZZAPP!
SO I'LL PUT ON MY CARAPACE, KICK SOME BAD-GUY BUTT AND HOPE NOBODY NOTICES IT WAS ME.

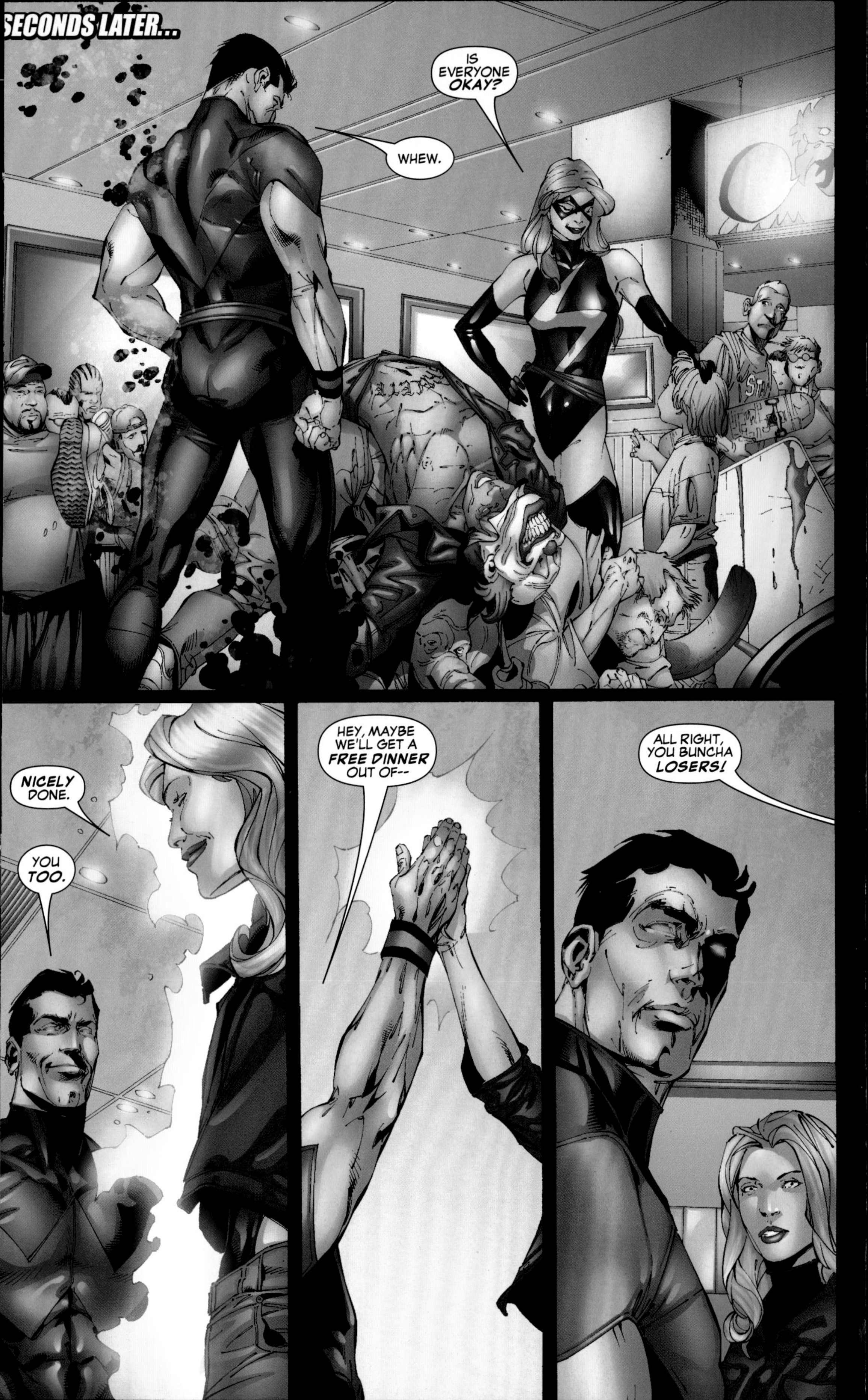
SECONDS LATER...
WHEW.
IS EVERYONE OKAY?
NICELY DONE.
YOU TOO.
HEY, MAYBE WE'LL GET A FREE DINNER OUT OF--
ALL RIGHT, YOU BUNCHA LOSERS!

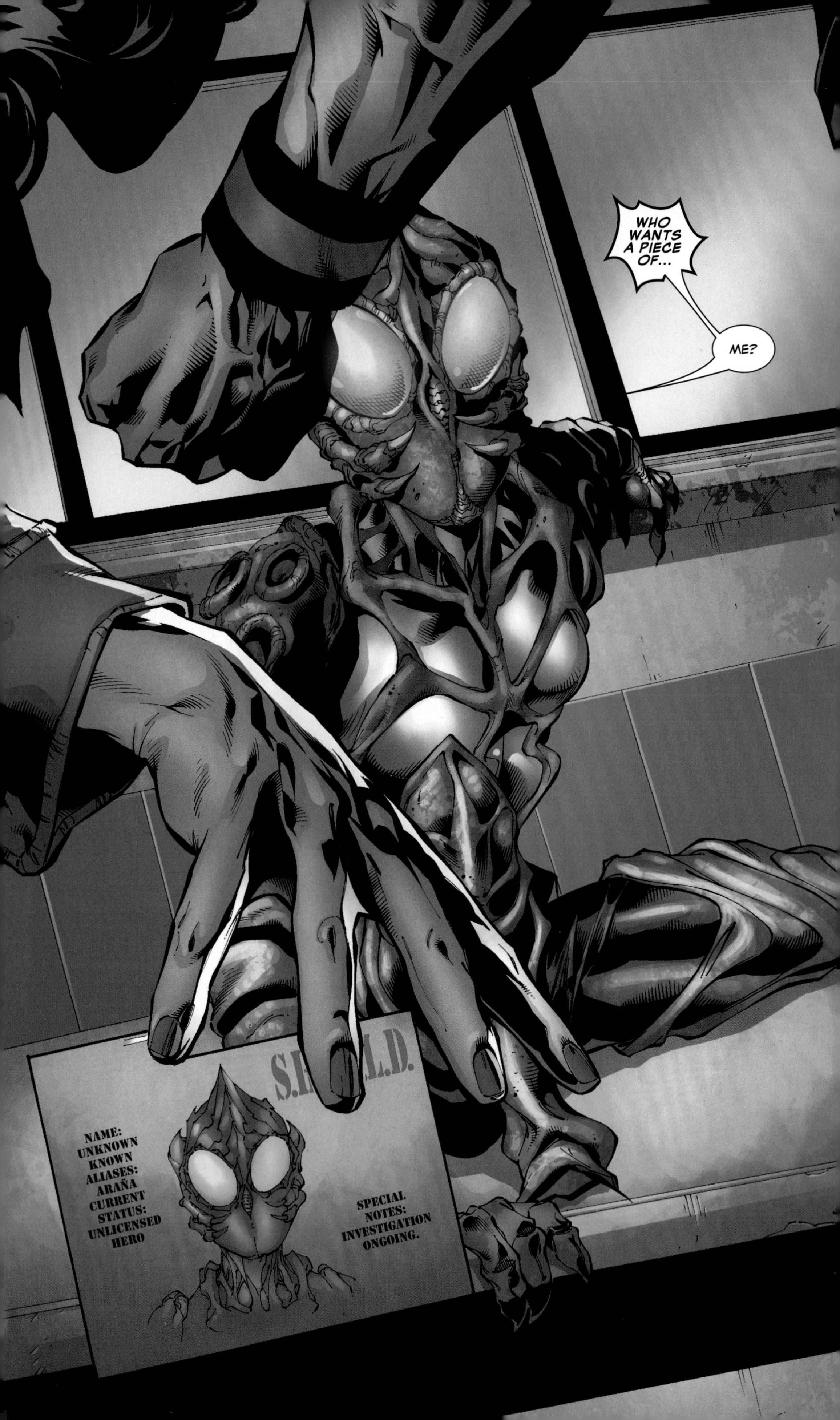
WHO WANTS A PIECE OF...
ME?
NAME: UNKNOWN
KNOWN ALIASES: ARAÑA
CURRENT STATUS: UNLICENSED HERO
SPECIAL NOTES: INVESTIGATION ONGOING.

MS. MARVEL
A MARVEL COMICS EVENT

CIVIL
WAR

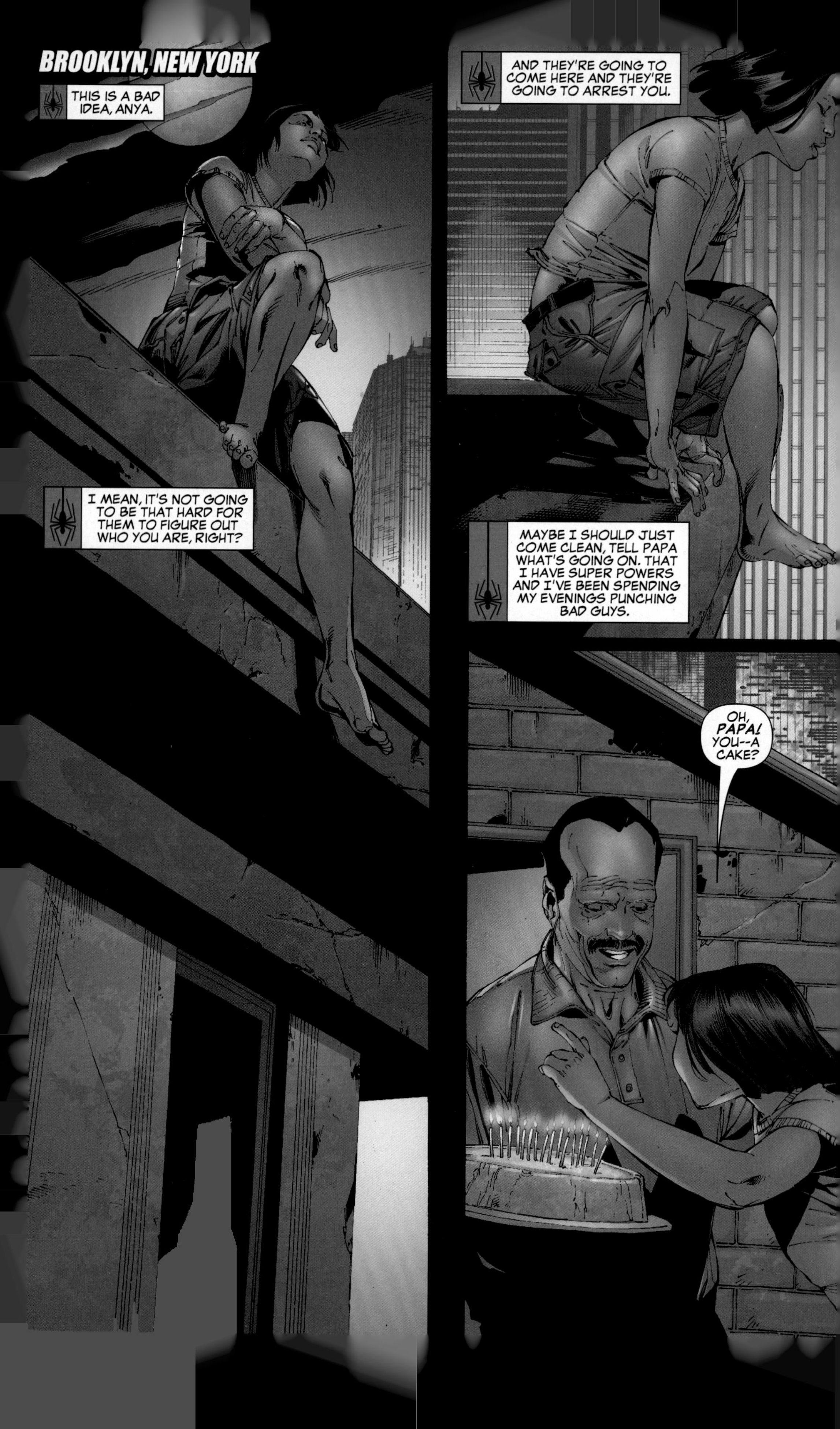
BROOKLYN, NEW YORK
THIS IS A BAD IDEA, ANYA.
I MEAN, IT'S NOT GOING TO BE THAT HARD FOR THEM TO FIGURE OUT WHO YOU ARE, RIGHT?
AND THEY'RE GOING TO COME HERE AND THEY'RE GOING TO ARREST YOU.
MAYBE I SHOULD JUST COME CLEAN, TELL PAPA WHAT'S GOING ON. THAT I HAVE SUPER POWERS AND I'VE BEEN SPENDING MY EVENINGS PUNCHING BAD GUYS.
OH, PAPA! YOU--A CAKE?

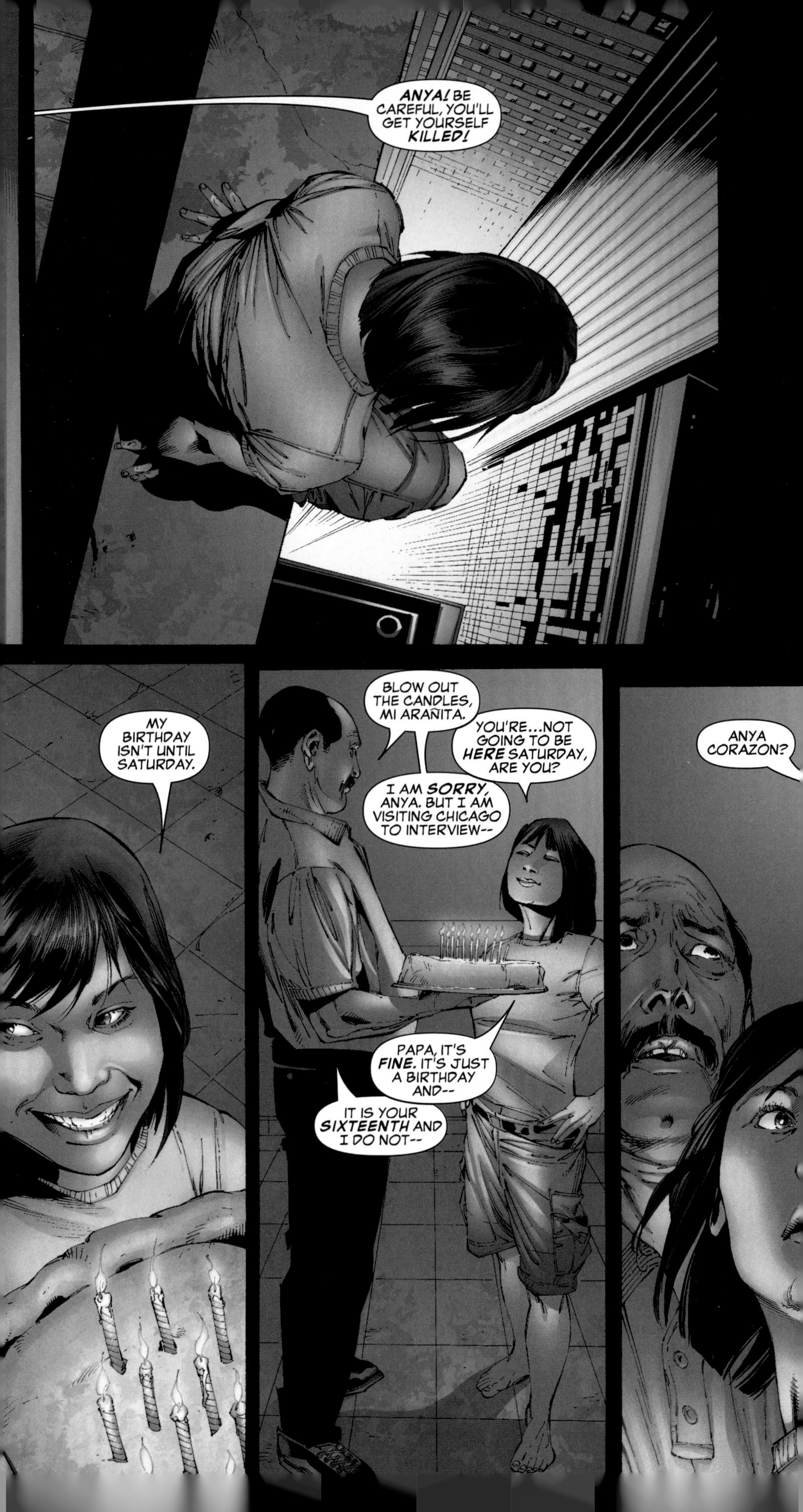
ANYA! BE CAREFUL, YOU'LL GET YOURSELF KILLED!
MY BIRTHDAY ISN'T UNTIL SATURDAY.
BLOW OUT THE CANDLES, MI ARAÑITA.
YOU'RE...NOT GOING TO BE HERE SATURDAY, ARE YOU?
I AM SORRY, ANYA. BUT I AM VISITING CHICAGO TO INTERVIEW--
PAPA, IT'S FINE. IT'S JUST A BIRTHDAY AND--
IT IS YOUR SIXTEENTH AND I DO NOT--
ANYA CORAZON?

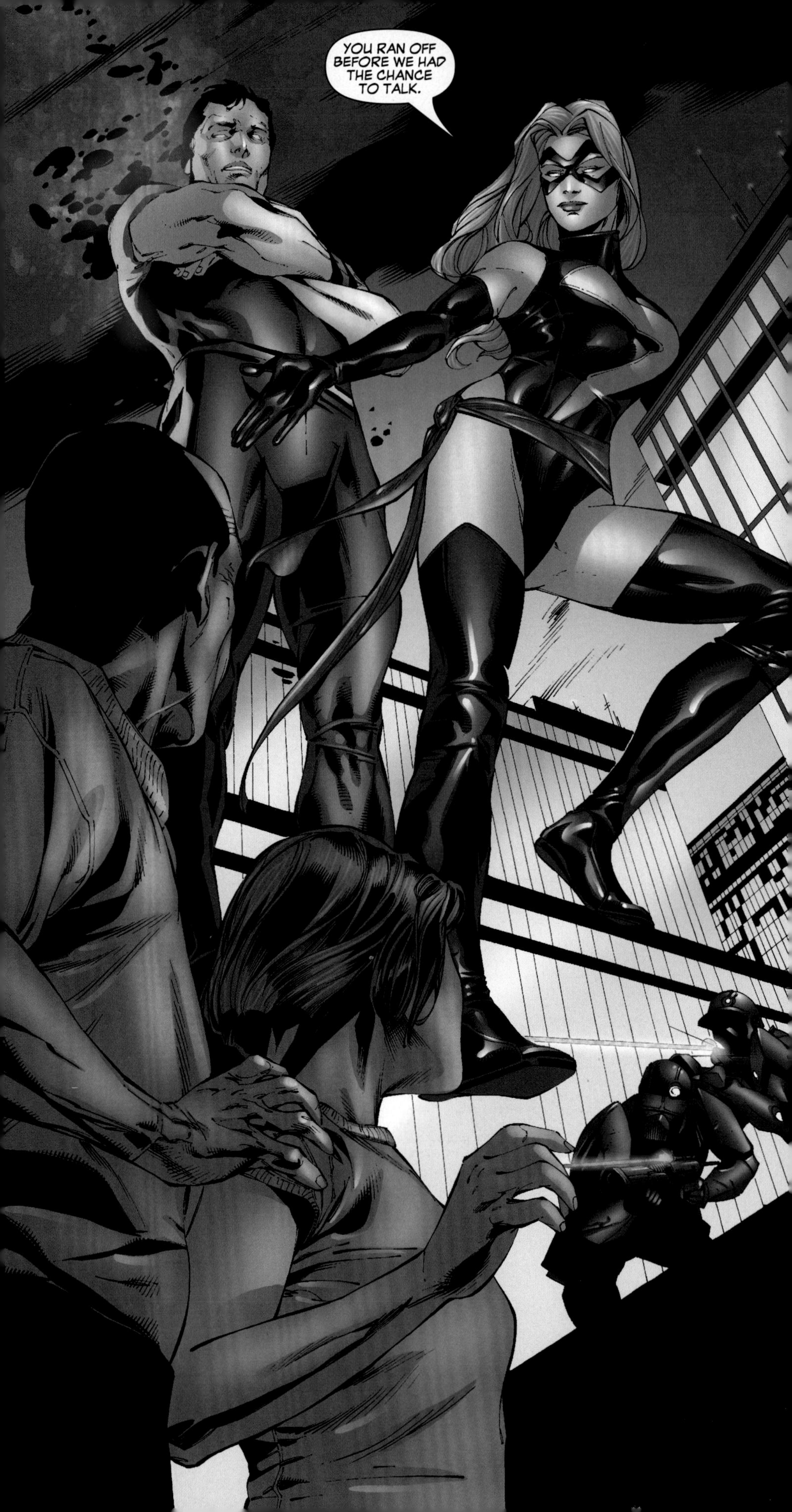
YOU RAN OFF BEFORE WE HAD THE CHANCE TO TALK.

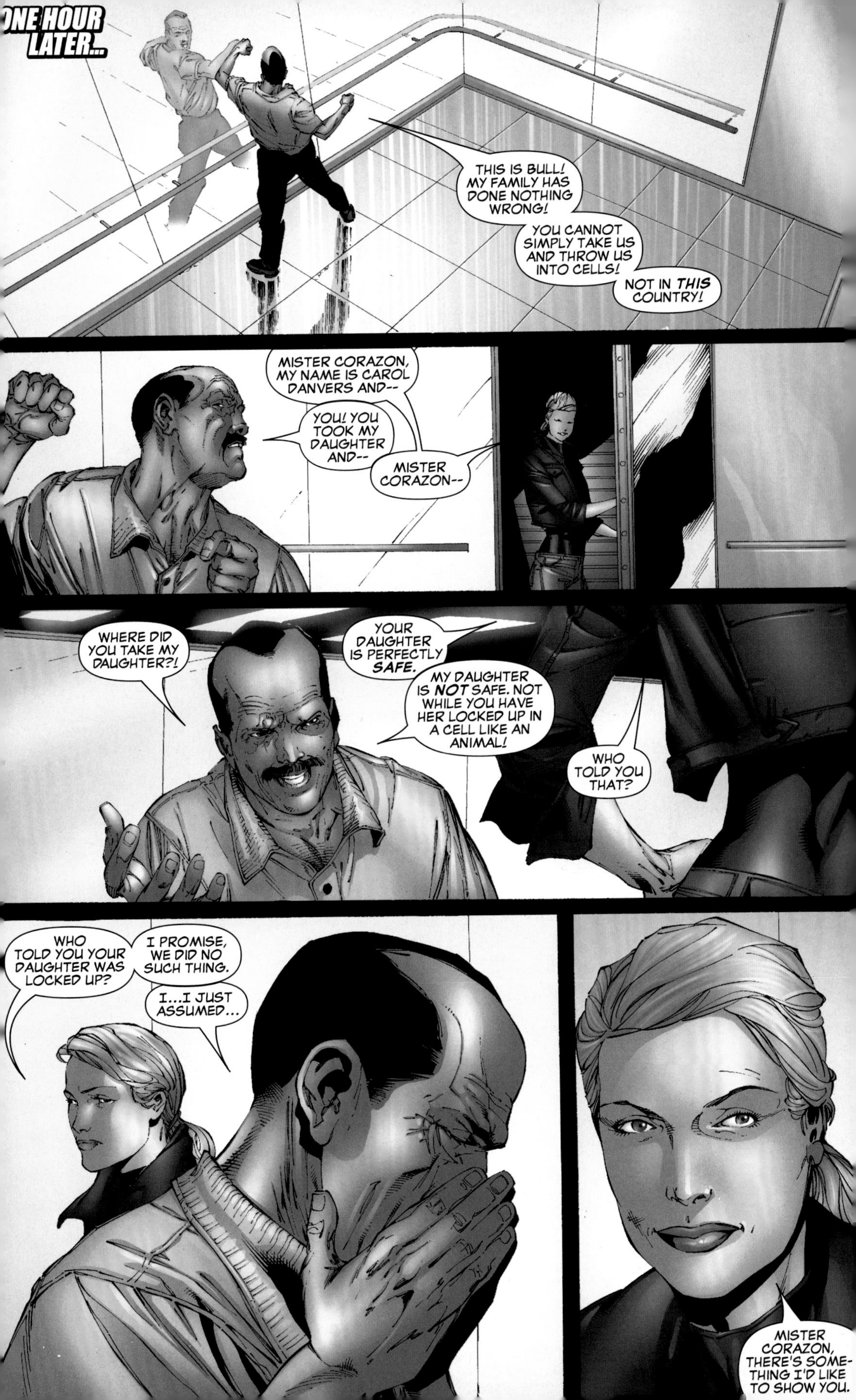
ONE HOUR LATER...
THIS IS BULL! MY FAMILY HAS DONE NOTHING WRONG!
YOU CANNOT SIMPLY TAKE US AND THROW US INTO CELLS!
NOT IN THIS COUNTRY!
MISTER CORAZON, MY NAME IS CAROL DANVERS AND--
YOU! YOU TOOK MY DAUGHTER AND--
MISTER CORAZON--
WHERE DID YOU TAKE MY DAUGHTER?!
YOUR DAUGHTER IS PERFECTLY SAFE.
MY DAUGHTER IS NOT SAFE. NOT WHILE YOU HAVE HER LOCKED UP IN A CELL LIKE AN ANIMAL!
WHO TOLD YOU THAT?
WHO TOLD YOU YOUR DAUGHTER WAS LOCKED UP?
I PROMISE, WE DID NO SUCH THING.
I...I JUST ASSUMED...
MISTER CORAZON, THERE'S SOMETHING I'D LIKE TO SHOW YOU.

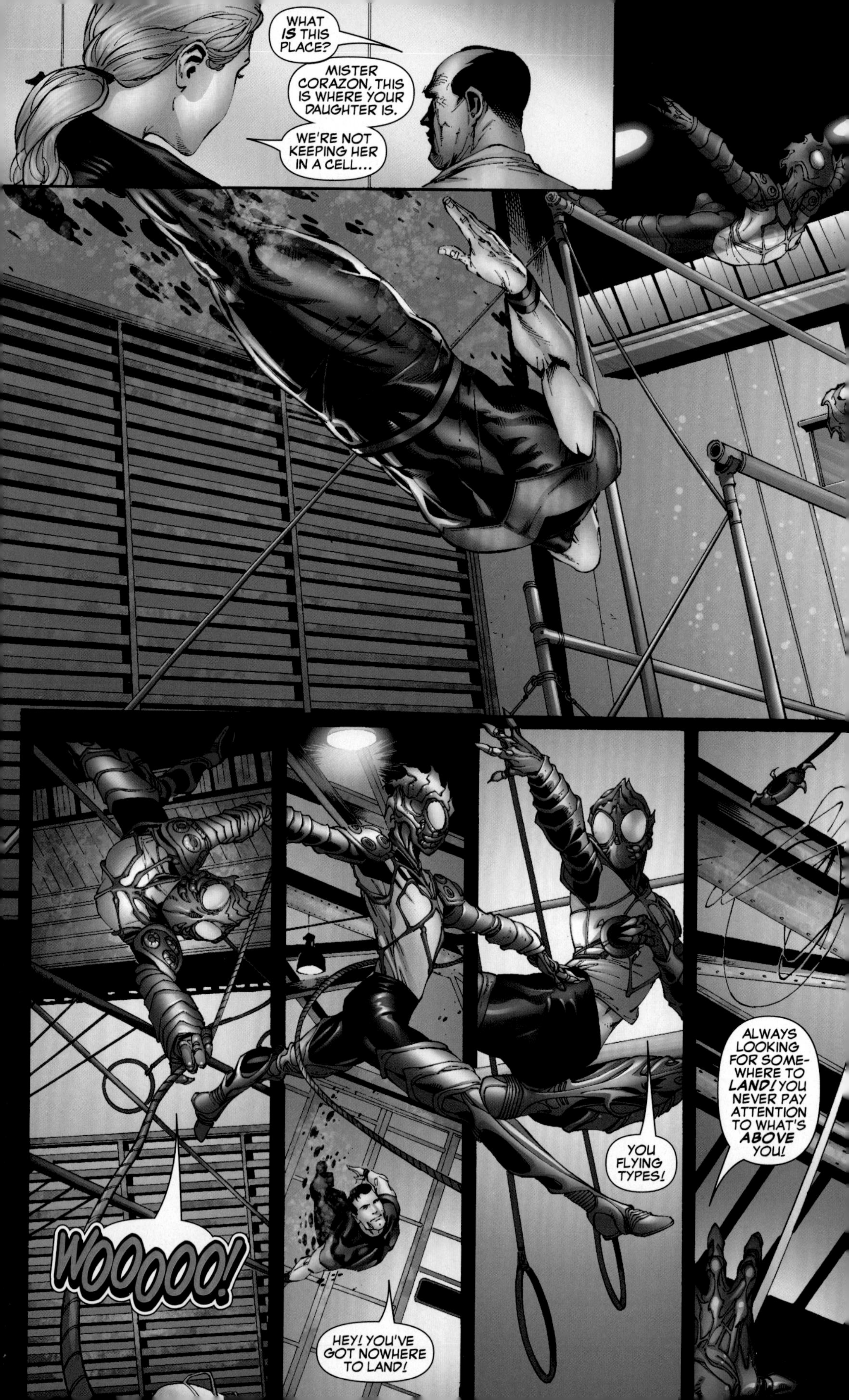
WHAT IS THIS PLACE?
MISTER CORAZON, THIS IS WHERE YOUR DAUGHTER IS.
WE'RE NOT KEEPING HER IN A CELL...
WOOOOO!
HEY! YOU'VE GOT NOWHERE TO LAND!
YOU FLYING TYPES!
ALWAYS LOOKING FOR SOMEWHERE TO LAND! YOU NEVER PAY ATTENTION TO WHAT'S ABOVE YOU!

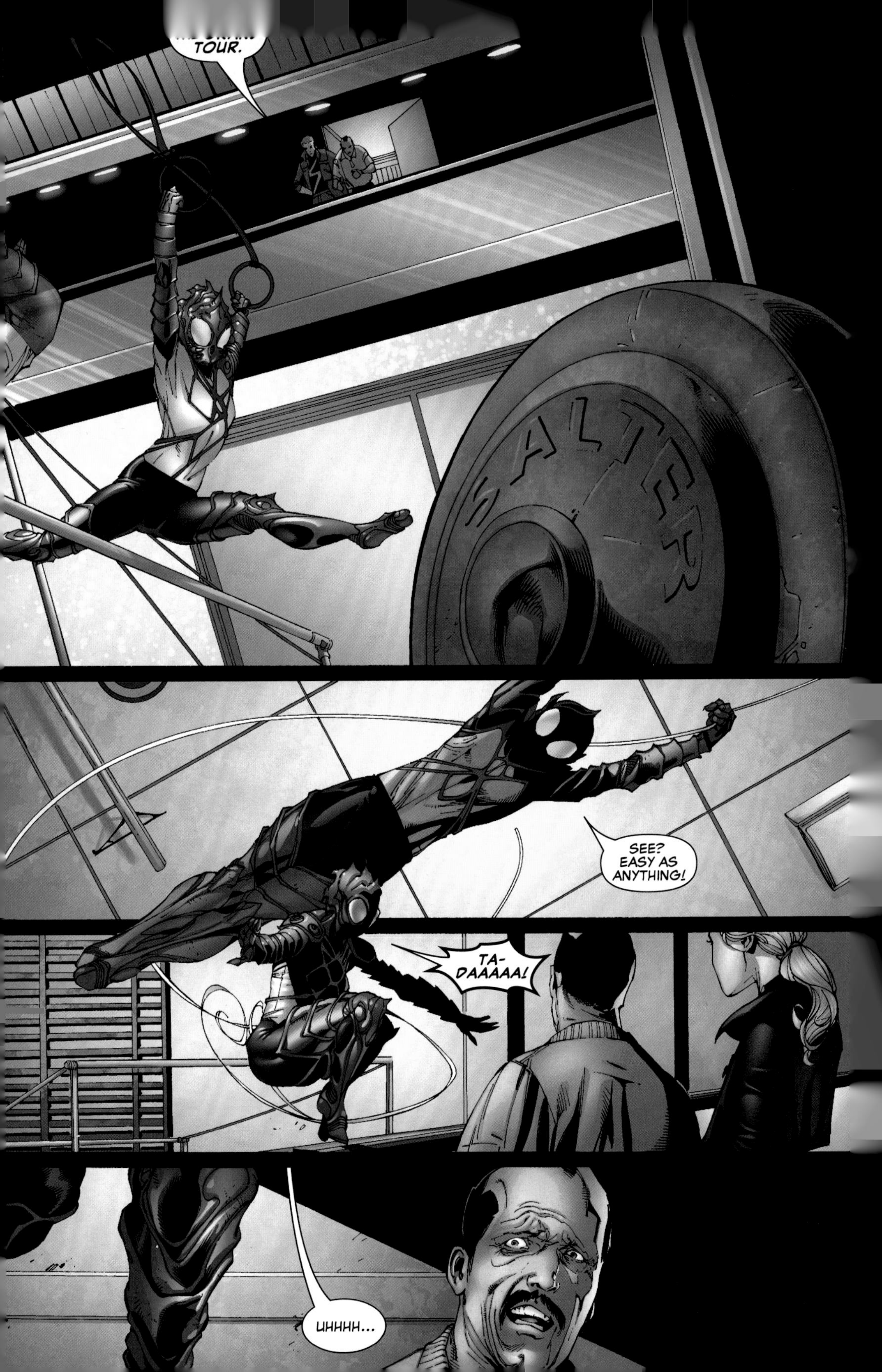
TOUR.
SALTER
SEE? EASY AS ANYTHING!
TA-DAAAAA!
UHHHH...

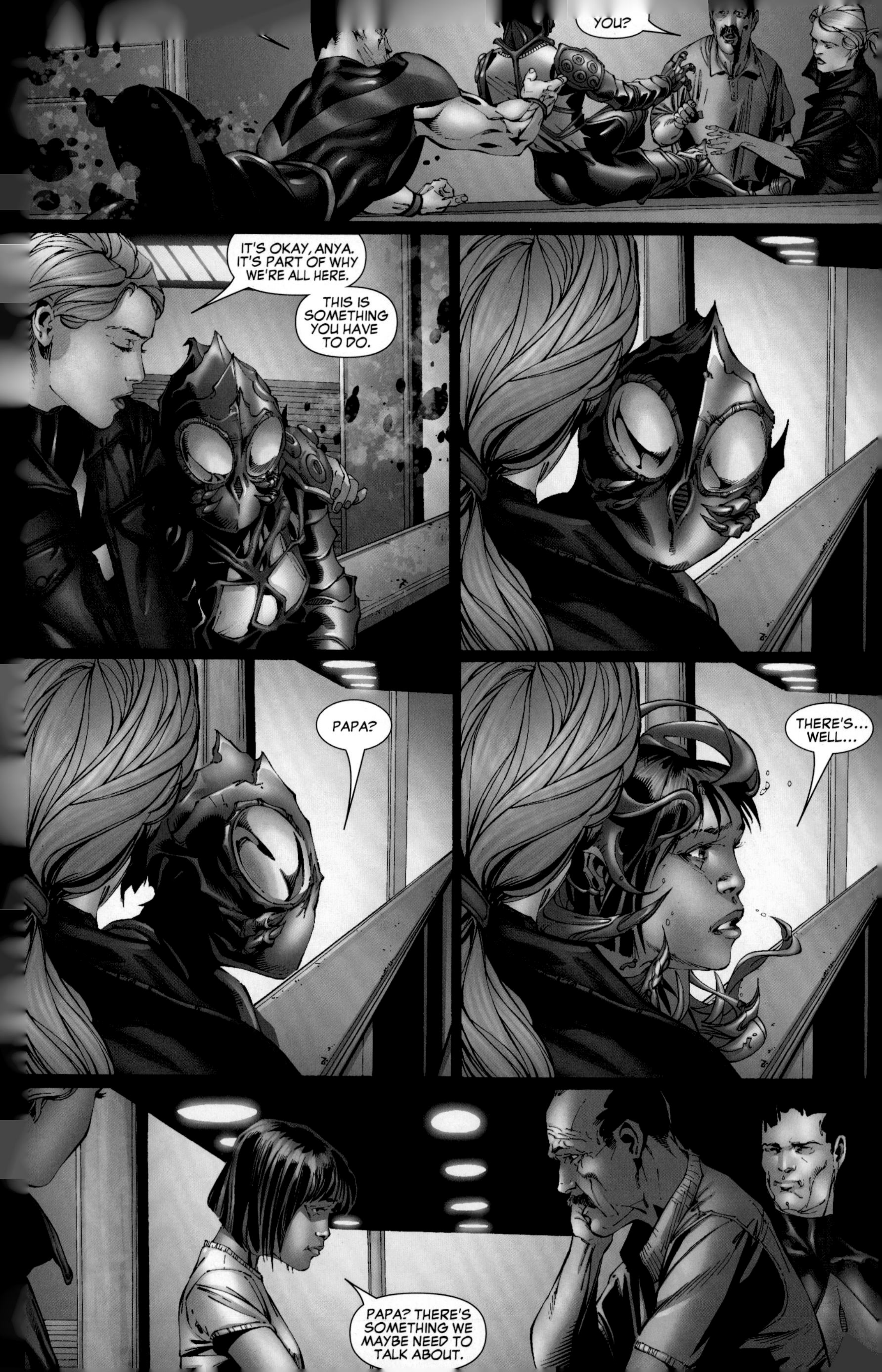
YOU?
IT'S OKAY, ANYA. IT'S PART OF WHY WE'RE ALL HERE.
THIS IS SOMETHING YOU HAVE TO DO.
PAPA?
THERE'S... WELL...
PAPA? THERE'S SOMETHING WE MAYBE NEED TO TALK ABOUT.

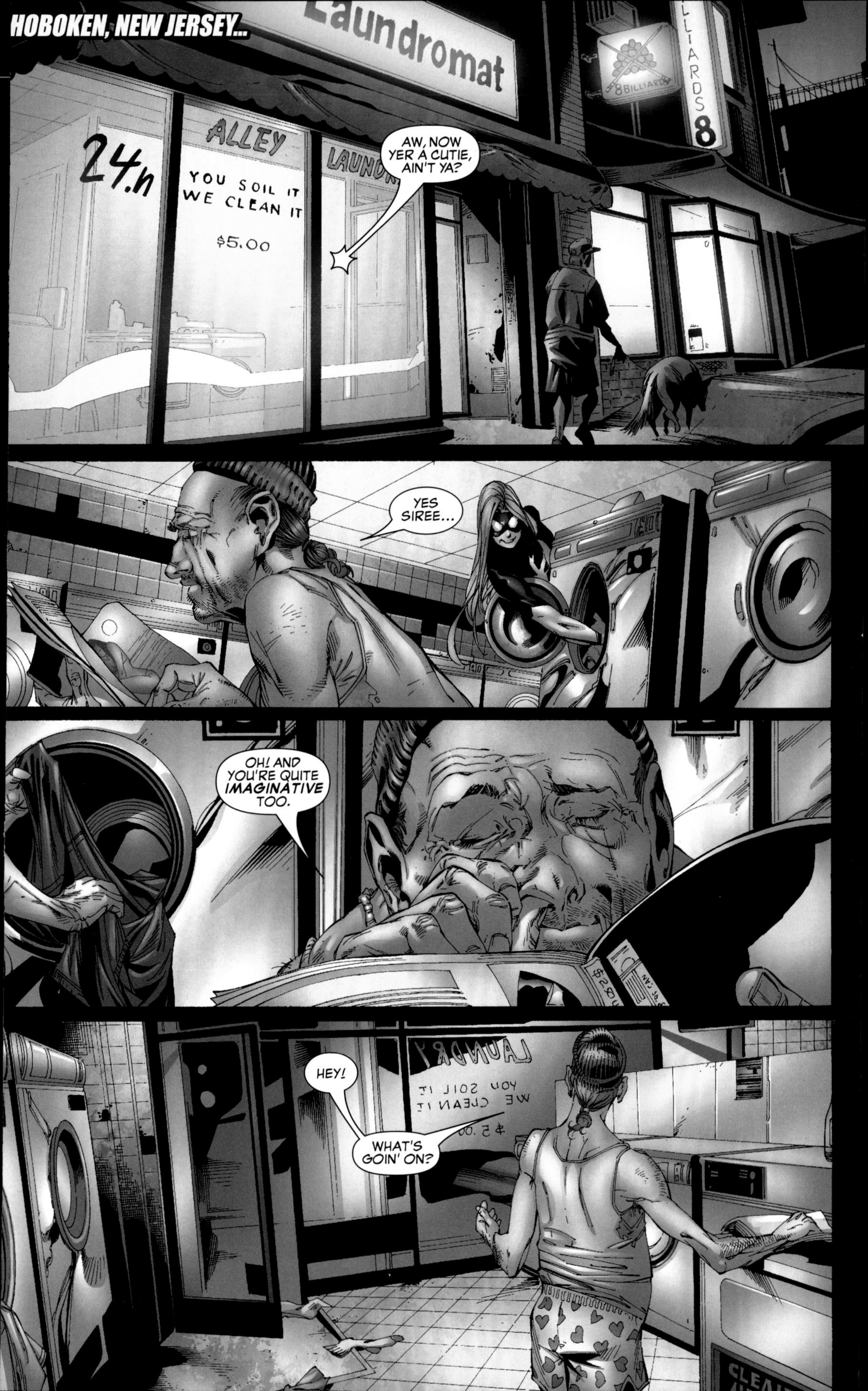
HOBOKEN, NEW JERSEY...
Laundromat
8 BILLIARDS
BILLIARDS 8
24.h
ALLEY
LAUNDRY
YOU SOIL IT
WE CLEAN IT
$5.00
AW, NOW YER A CUTIE, AIN'T YA?
YES SIREE...
OH! AND YOU'RE QUITE IMAGINATIVE TOO.
HEY!
WHAT'S GOIN' ON?

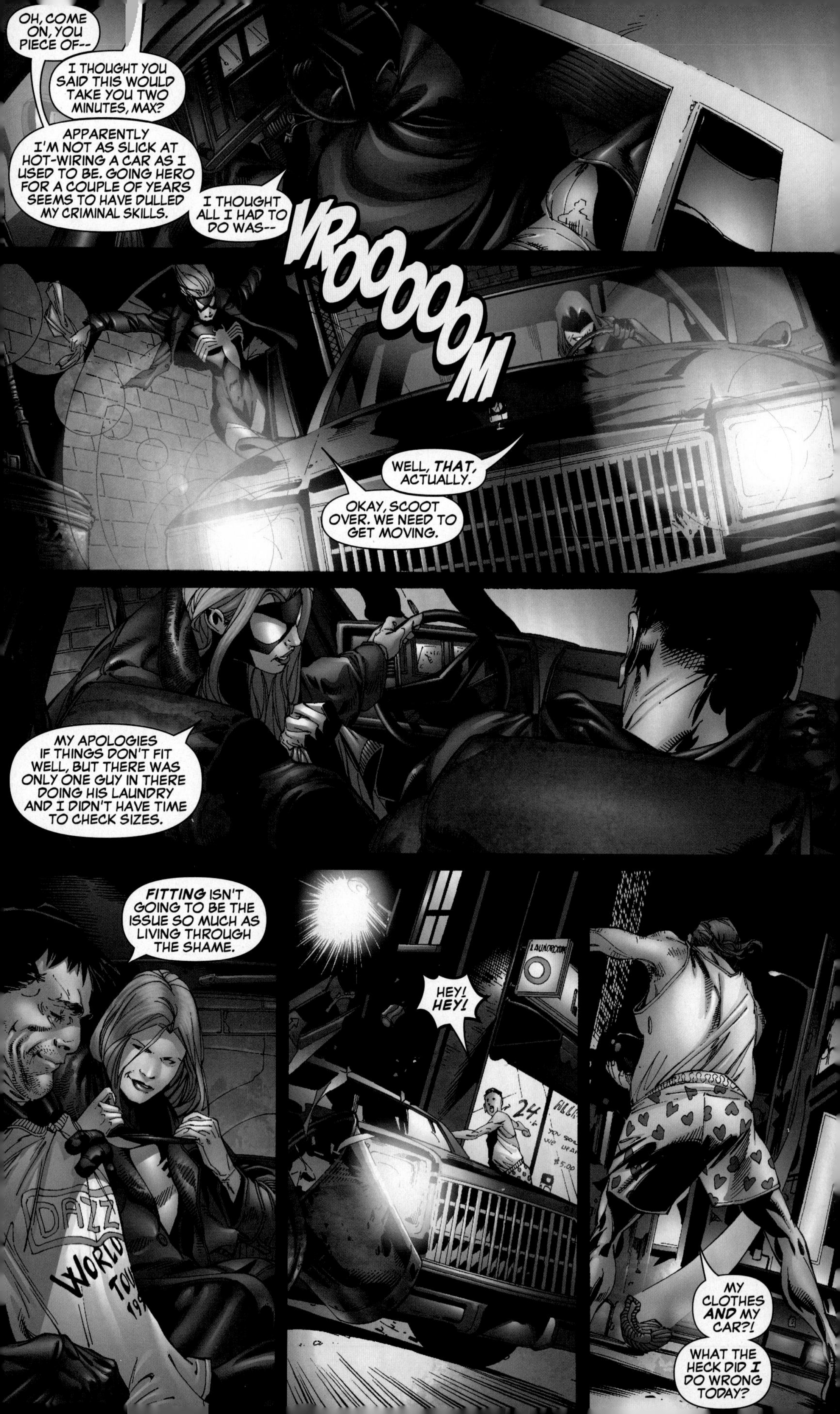

OH, COME ON, YOU PIECE OF--
I THOUGHT YOU SAID THIS WOULD TAKE YOU TWO MINUTES, MAX?
APPARENTLY I'M NOT AS SLICK AT HOT-WIRING A CAR AS I USED TO BE. GOING HERO FOR A COUPLE OF YEARS SEEMS TO HAVE DULLED MY CRIMINAL SKILLS.
I THOUGHT ALL I HAD TO DO WAS--
VROOOOOM
WELL, THAT, ACTUALLY.
OKAY, SCOOT OVER. WE NEED TO GET MOVING.
MY APOLOGIES IF THINGS DON'T FIT WELL, BUT THERE WAS ONLY ONE GUY IN THERE DOING HIS LAUNDRY AND I DIDN'T HAVE TIME TO CHECK SIZES.
FITTING ISN'T GOING TO BE THE ISSUE SO MUCH AS LIVING THROUGH THE SHAME.
HEY! HEY!
MY CLOTHES AND MY CAR?!
WHAT THE HECK DID I DO WRONG TODAY?

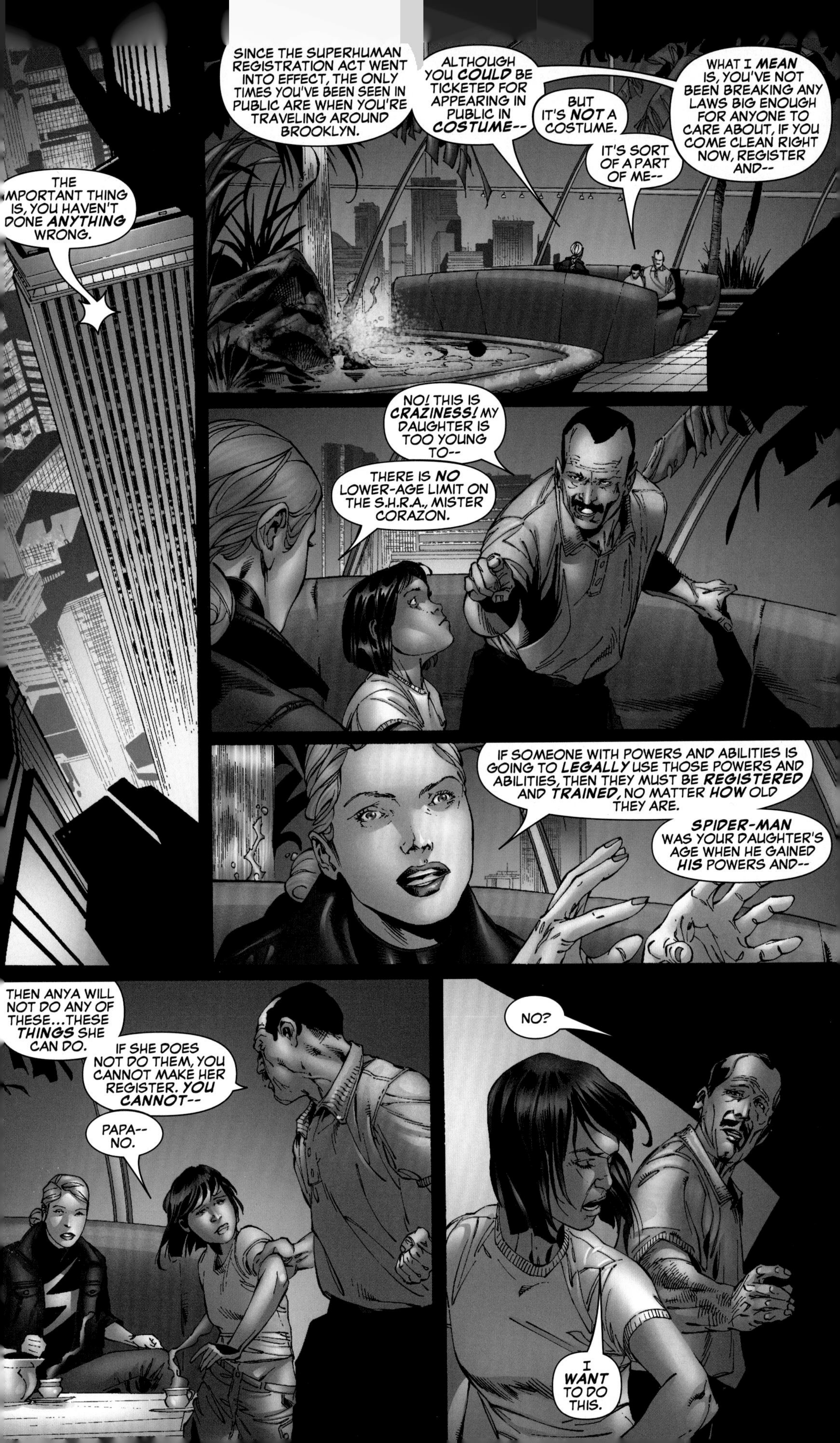
THE IMPORTANT THING IS, YOU HAVEN'T DONE ANYTHING WRONG.
SINCE THE SUPERHUMAN REGISTRATION ACT WENT INTO EFFECT, THE ONLY TIMES YOU'VE BEEN SEEN IN PUBLIC ARE WHEN YOU'RE TRAVELING AROUND BROOKLYN.
ALTHOUGH YOU COULD BE TICKETED FOR APPEARING IN PUBLIC IN COSTUME--
BUT IT'S NOT A COSTUME.
IT'S SORT OF A PART OF ME--
WHAT I MEAN IS, YOU'VE NOT BEEN BREAKING ANY LAWS BIG ENOUGH FOR ANYONE TO CARE ABOUT, IF YOU COME CLEAN RIGHT NOW, REGISTER AND--
NO! THIS IS CRAZINESS! MY DAUGHTER IS TOO YOUNG TO--
THERE IS NO LOWER-AGE LIMIT ON THE S.H.R.A., MISTER CORAZON.
IF SOMEONE WITH POWERS AND ABILITIES IS GOING TO LEGALLY USE THOSE POWERS AND ABILITIES, THEN THEY MUST BE REGISTERED AND TRAINED, NO MATTER HOW OLD THEY ARE.
SPIDER-MAN WAS YOUR DAUGHTER'S AGE WHEN HE GAINED HIS POWERS AND--
THEN ANYA WILL NOT DO ANY OF THESE...THESE THINGS SHE CAN DO.
IF SHE DOES NOT DO THEM, YOU CANNOT MAKE HER REGISTER. YOU CANNOT--
PAPA-- NO.
NO?
I WANT TO DO THIS.

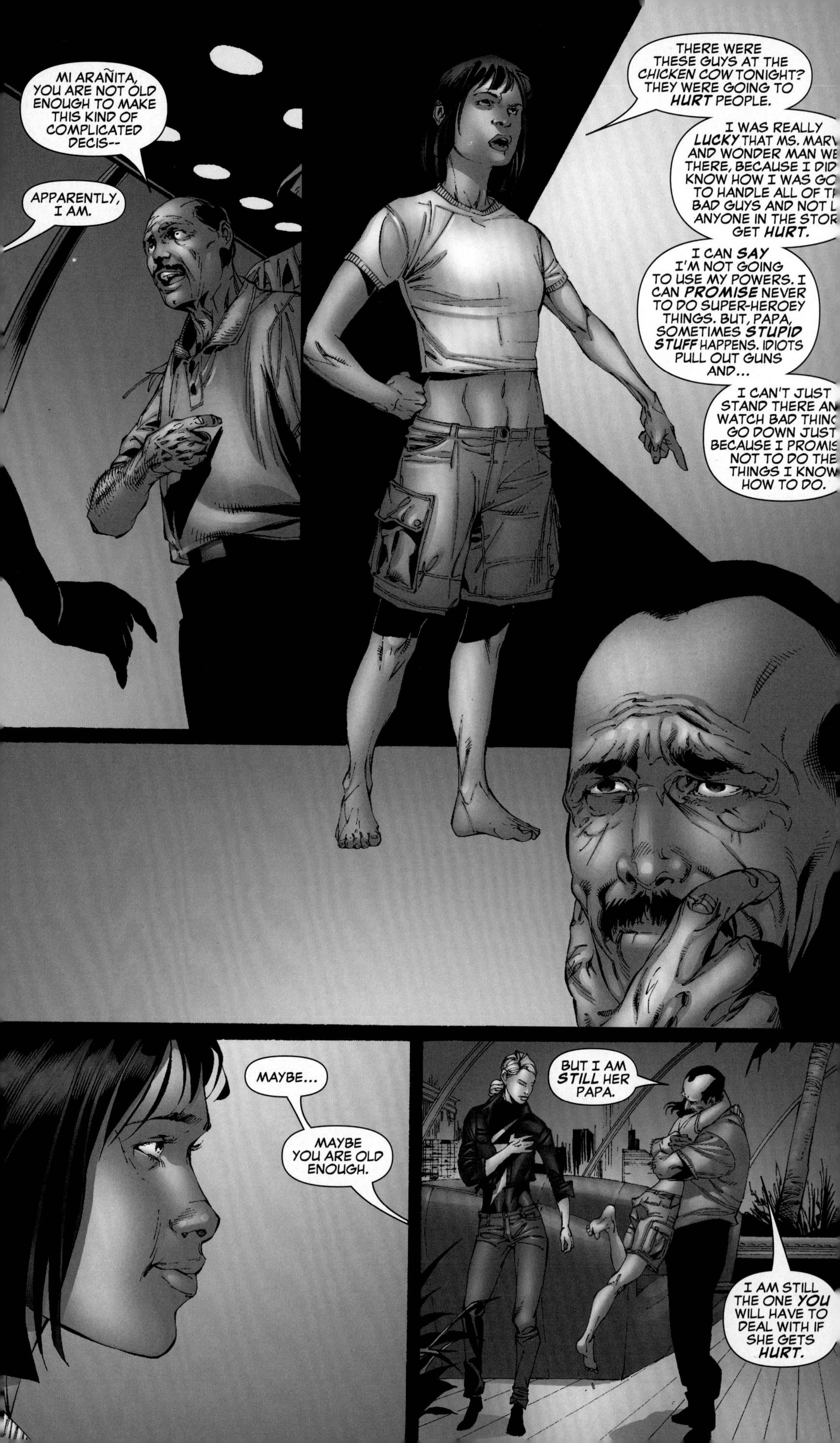
MI ARAÑITA, YOU ARE NOT OLD ENOUGH TO MAKE THIS KIND OF COMPLICATED DECIS--
APPARENTLY, I AM.
THERE WERE THESE GUYS AT THE CHICKEN COW TONIGHT? THEY WERE GOING TO HURT PEOPLE.
I WAS REALLY LUCKY THAT MS. MARV AND WONDER MAN WE THERE, BECAUSE I DID KNOW HOW I WAS GO TO HANDLE ALL OF T BAD GUYS AND NOT L ANYONE IN THE STOR GET HURT.
I CAN SAY I'M NOT GOING TO USE MY POWERS. I CAN PROMISE NEVER TO DO SUPER-HEROEY THINGS. BUT, PAPA, SOMETIMES STUPID STUFF HAPPENS. IDIOTS PULL OUT GUNS AND...
I CAN'T JUST STAND THERE AN WATCH BAD THING GO DOWN JUST BECAUSE I PROMIS NOT TO DO THE THINGS I KNOW HOW TO DO.
MAYBE...
MAYBE YOU ARE OLD ENOUGH.
BUT I AM STILL HER PAPA.
I AM STILL THE ONE YOU WILL HAVE TO DEAL WITH IF SHE GETS HURT.

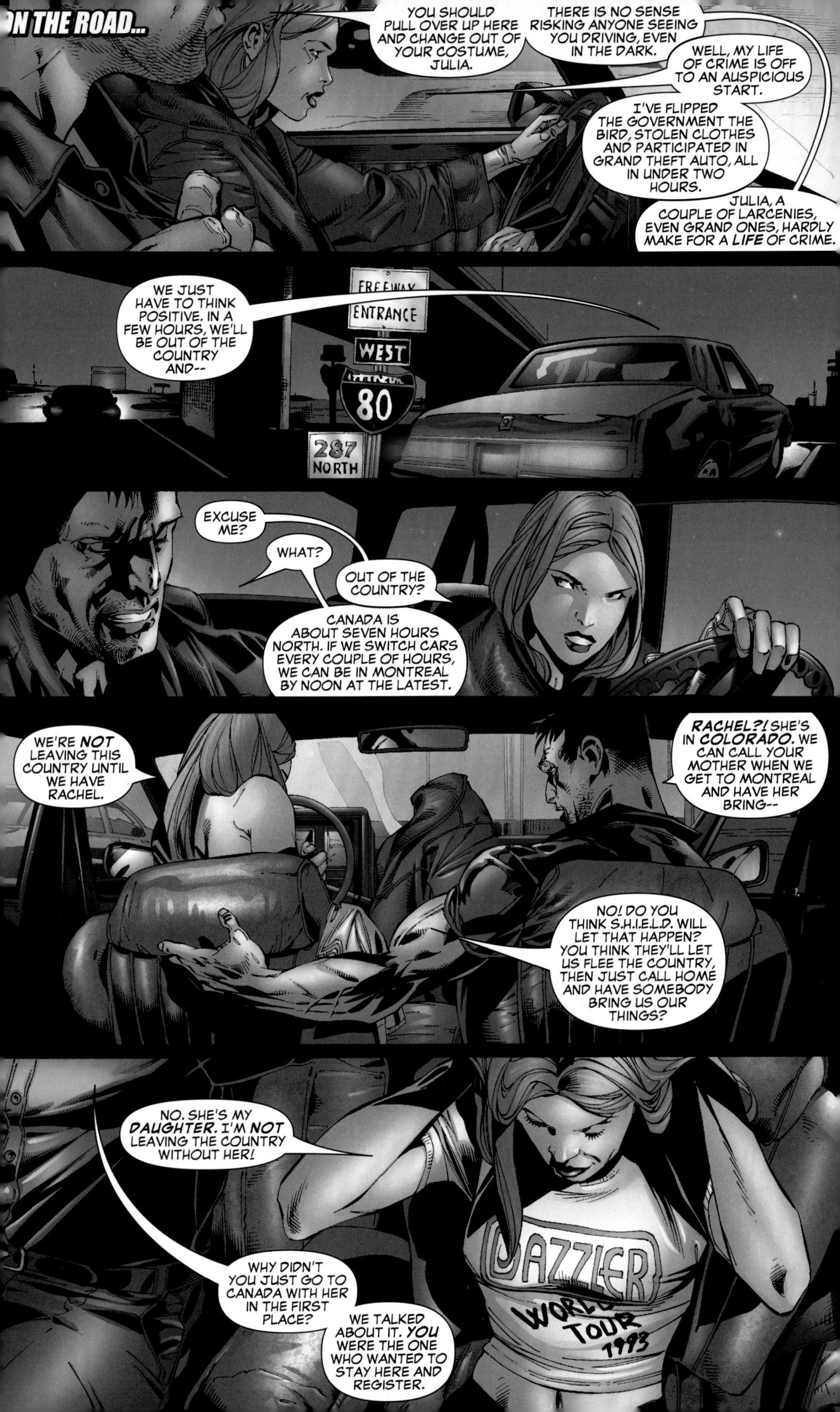
ON THE ROAD...
YOU SHOULD PULL OVER UP HERE AND CHANGE OUT OF YOUR COSTUME, JULIA.
THERE IS NO SENSE RISKING ANYONE SEEING YOU DRIVING, EVEN IN THE DARK.
WELL, MY LIFE OF CRIME IS OFF TO AN AUSPICIOUS START.
I'VE FLIPPED THE GOVERNMENT THE BIRD, STOLEN CLOTHES AND PARTICIPATED IN GRAND THEFT AUTO, ALL IN UNDER TWO HOURS.
JULIA, A COUPLE OF LARCENIES, EVEN GRAND ONES, HARDLY MAKE FOR A *LIFE* OF CRIME.
WE JUST HAVE TO THINK POSITIVE. IN A FEW HOURS, WE'LL BE OUT OF THE COUNTRY AND--
FREEWAY ENTRANCE
WEST
80
287 NORTH
EXCUSE ME?
WHAT?
OUT OF THE COUNTRY?
CANADA IS ABOUT SEVEN HOURS NORTH. IF WE SWITCH CARS EVERY COUPLE OF HOURS, WE CAN BE IN MONTREAL BY NOON AT THE LATEST.
WE'RE *NOT* LEAVING THIS COUNTRY UNTIL WE HAVE RACHEL.
RACHEL?! SHE'S IN *COLORADO.* WE CAN CALL YOUR MOTHER WHEN WE GET TO MONTREAL AND HAVE HER BRING--
NO! DO YOU THINK S.H.I.E.L.D. WILL LET THAT HAPPEN? YOU THINK THEY'LL LET US FLEE THE COUNTRY, THEN JUST CALL HOME AND HAVE SOMEBODY BRING US OUR THINGS?
NO. SHE'S MY *DAUGHTER.* I'M *NOT* LEAVING THE COUNTRY WITHOUT HER!
DAZZLER WORLD TOUR 1993
WHY DIDN'T YOU JUST GO TO CANADA WITH HER IN THE FIRST PLACE?
WE TALKED ABOUT IT. *YOU* WERE THE ONE WHO WANTED TO STAY HERE AND REGISTER.

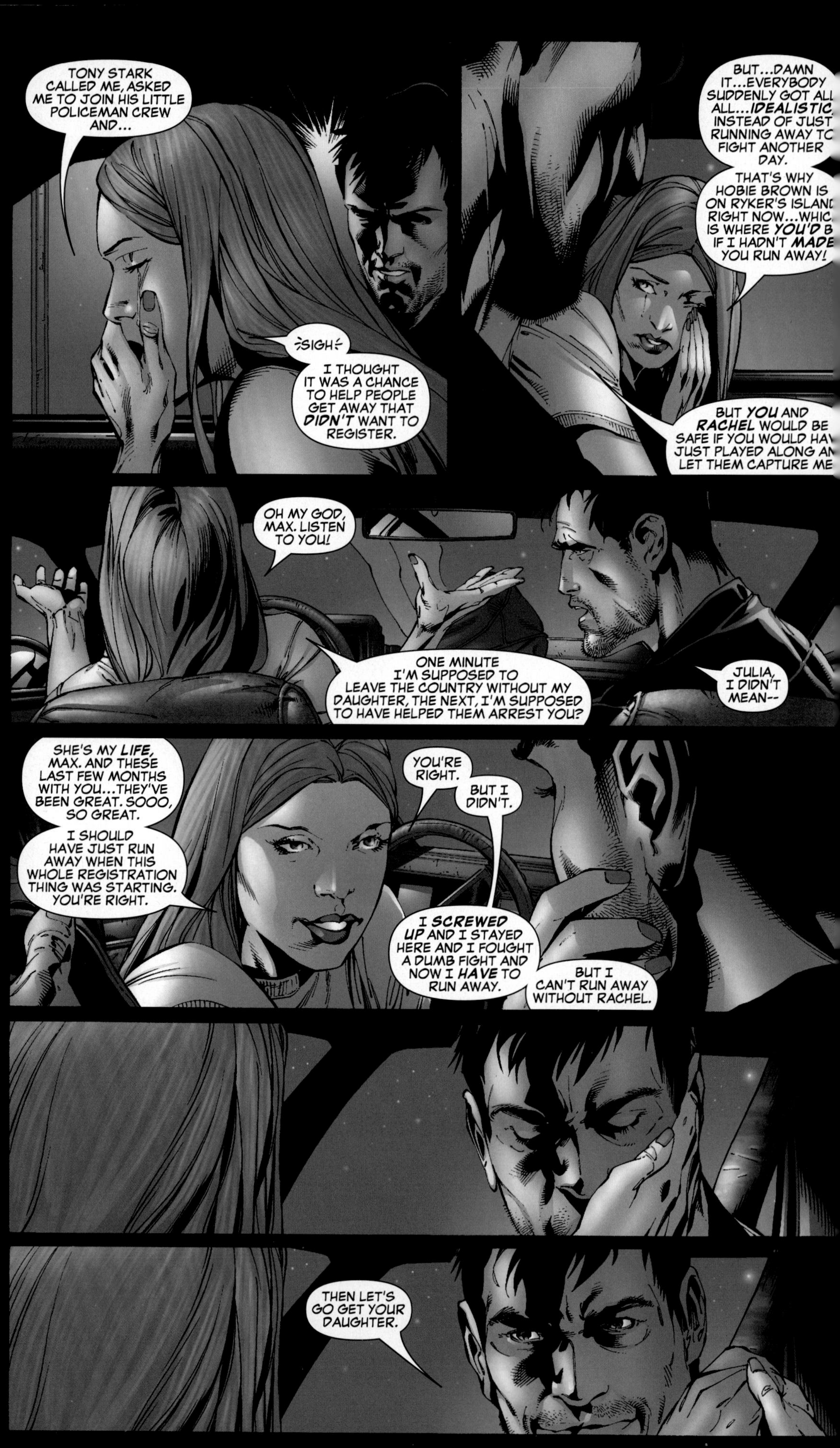
TONY STARK CALLED ME, ASKED ME TO JOIN HIS LITTLE POLICEMAN CREW AND...
-SIGH-
I THOUGHT IT WAS A CHANCE TO HELP PEOPLE GET AWAY THAT DIDN'T WANT TO REGISTER.
BUT...DAMN IT...EVERYBODY SUDDENLY GOT ALL ALL...IDEALISTIC INSTEAD OF JUST RUNNING AWAY TO FIGHT ANOTHER DAY.
THAT'S WHY HOBIE BROWN IS ON RYKER'S ISLAND RIGHT NOW...WHIC IS WHERE YOU'D B IF I HADN'T MADE YOU RUN AWAY!
BUT YOU AND RACHEL WOULD BE SAFE IF YOU WOULD HAV JUST PLAYED ALONG AN LET THEM CAPTURE ME
OH MY GOD, MAX. LISTEN TO YOU!
ONE MINUTE I'M SUPPOSED TO LEAVE THE COUNTRY WITHOUT MY DAUGHTER, THE NEXT, I'M SUPPOSED TO HAVE HELPED THEM ARREST YOU?
JULIA, I DIDN'T MEAN--
SHE'S MY LIFE, MAX. AND THESE LAST FEW MONTHS WITH YOU...THEY'VE BEEN GREAT. SOOO, SO GREAT.
I SHOULD HAVE JUST RUN AWAY WHEN THIS WHOLE REGISTRATION THING WAS STARTING. YOU'RE RIGHT.
YOU'RE RIGHT.
BUT I DIDN'T.
I SCREWED UP AND I STAYED HERE AND I FOUGHT A DUMB FIGHT AND NOW I HAVE TO RUN AWAY.
BUT I CAN'T RUN AWAY WITHOUT RACHEL.
THEN LET'S GO GET YOUR DAUGHTER.

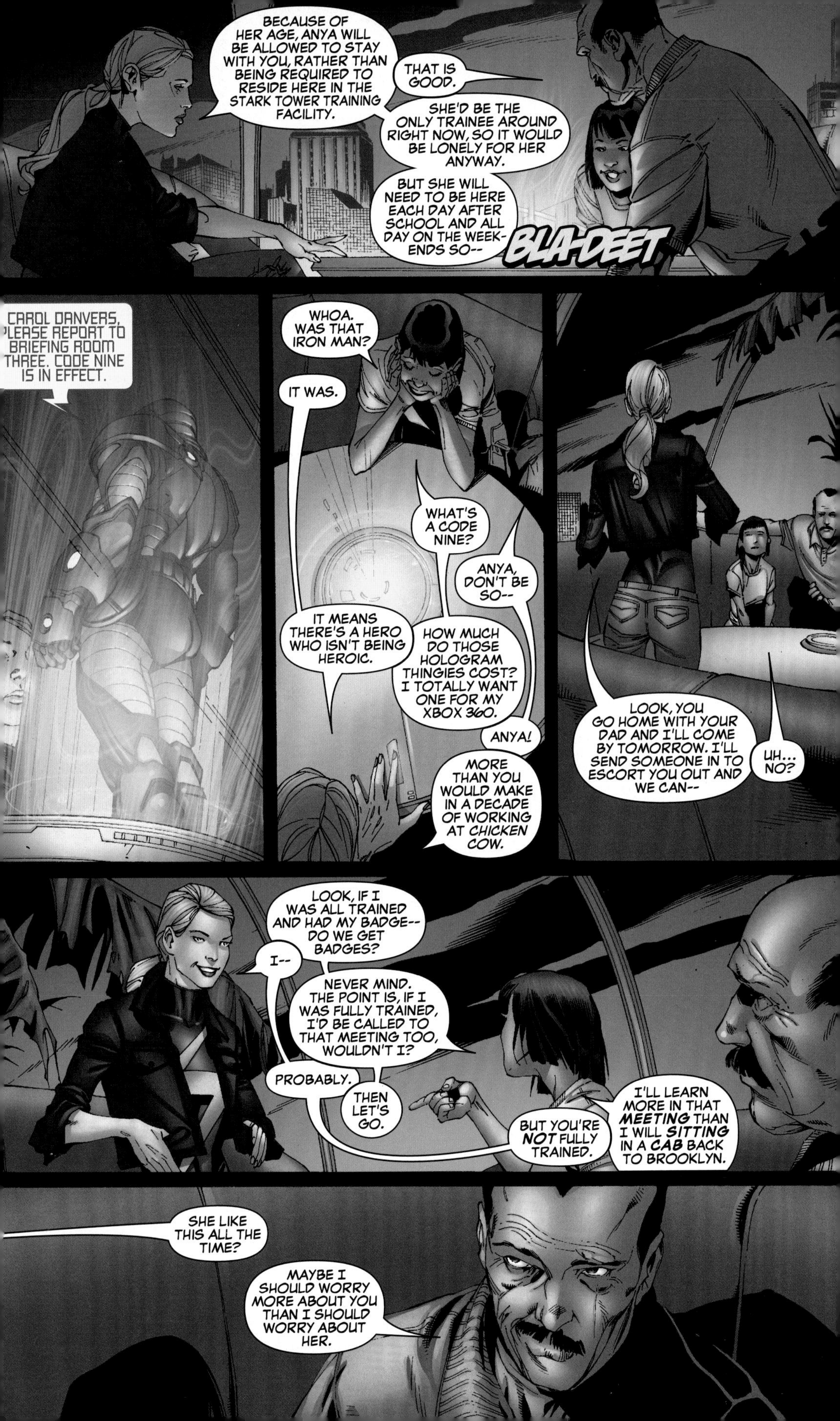
BECAUSE OF HER AGE, ANYA WILL BE ALLOWED TO STAY WITH YOU, RATHER THAN BEING REQUIRED TO RESIDE HERE IN THE STARK TOWER TRAINING FACILITY.
THAT IS GOOD.
SHE'D BE THE ONLY TRAINEE AROUND RIGHT NOW, SO IT WOULD BE LONELY FOR HER ANYWAY.
BUT SHE WILL NEED TO BE HERE EACH DAY AFTER SCHOOL AND ALL DAY ON THE WEEK-ENDS SO--
BLA-DEET
CAROL DANVERS, PLEASE REPORT TO BRIEFING ROOM THREE. CODE NINE IS IN EFFECT.
WHOA. WAS THAT IRON MAN?
IT WAS.
WHAT'S A CODE NINE?
ANYA, DON'T BE SO--
IT MEANS THERE'S A HERO WHO ISN'T BEING HEROIC.
HOW MUCH DO THOSE HOLOGRAM THINGIES COST? I TOTALLY WANT ONE FOR MY XBOX 360.
ANYA!
MORE THAN YOU WOULD MAKE IN A DECADE OF WORKING AT CHICKEN COW.
LOOK, YOU GO HOME WITH YOUR DAD AND I'LL COME BY TOMORROW. I'LL SEND SOMEONE IN TO ESCORT YOU OUT AND WE CAN--
UH... NO?
LOOK, IF I WAS ALL TRAINED AND HAD MY BADGE-- DO WE GET BADGES?
I--
NEVER MIND. THE POINT IS, IF I WAS FULLY TRAINED, I'D BE CALLED TO THAT MEETING TOO, WOULDN'T I?
PROBABLY.
THEN LET'S GO.
BUT YOU'RE NOT FULLY TRAINED.
I'LL LEARN MORE IN THAT MEETING THAN I WILL SITTING IN A CAB BACK TO BROOKLYN.
SHE LIKE THIS ALL THE TIME?
MAYBE I SHOULD WORRY MORE ABOUT YOU THAN I SHOULD WORRY ABOUT HER.

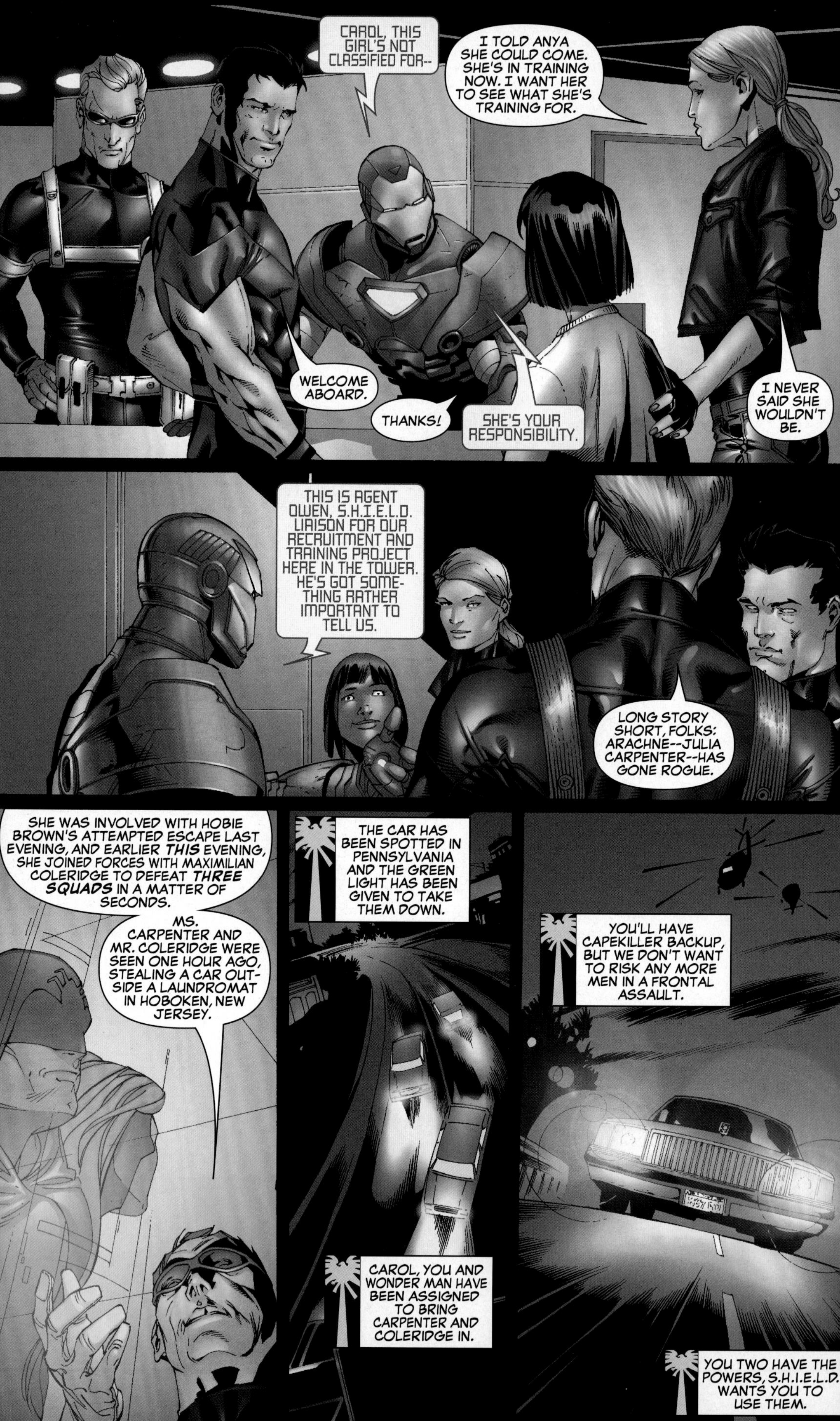
CAROL, THIS GIRL'S NOT CLASSIFIED FOR--
I TOLD ANYA SHE COULD COME. SHE'S IN TRAINING NOW. I WANT HER TO SEE WHAT SHE'S TRAINING FOR.
WELCOME ABOARD.
THANKS!
SHE'S YOUR RESPONSIBILITY.
I NEVER SAID SHE WOULDN'T BE.
THIS IS AGENT OWEN, S.H.I.E.L.D. LIAISON FOR OUR RECRUITMENT AND TRAINING PROJECT HERE IN THE TOWER. HE'S GOT SOME-THING RATHER IMPORTANT TO TELL US.
LONG STORY SHORT, FOLKS: ARACHNE--JULIA CARPENTER--HAS GONE ROGUE.
SHE WAS INVOLVED WITH HOBIE BROWN'S ATTEMPTED ESCAPE LAST EVENING, AND EARLIER THIS EVENING, SHE JOINED FORCES WITH MAXIMILIAN COLERIDGE TO DEFEAT THREE SQUADS IN A MATTER OF SECONDS.
MS. CARPENTER AND MR. COLERIDGE WERE SEEN ONE HOUR AGO, STEALING A CAR OUT-SIDE A LAUNDROMAT IN HOBOKEN, NEW JERSEY.
THE CAR HAS BEEN SPOTTED IN PENNSYLVANIA AND THE GREEN LIGHT HAS BEEN GIVEN TO TAKE THEM DOWN.
CAROL, YOU AND WONDER MAN HAVE BEEN ASSIGNED TO BRING CARPENTER AND COLERIDGE IN.
YOU'LL HAVE CAPEKILLER BACKUP, BUT WE DON'T WANT TO RISK ANY MORE MEN IN A FRONTAL ASSAULT.
YOU TWO HAVE THE POWERS, S.H.I.E.L.D. WANTS YOU TO USE THEM.

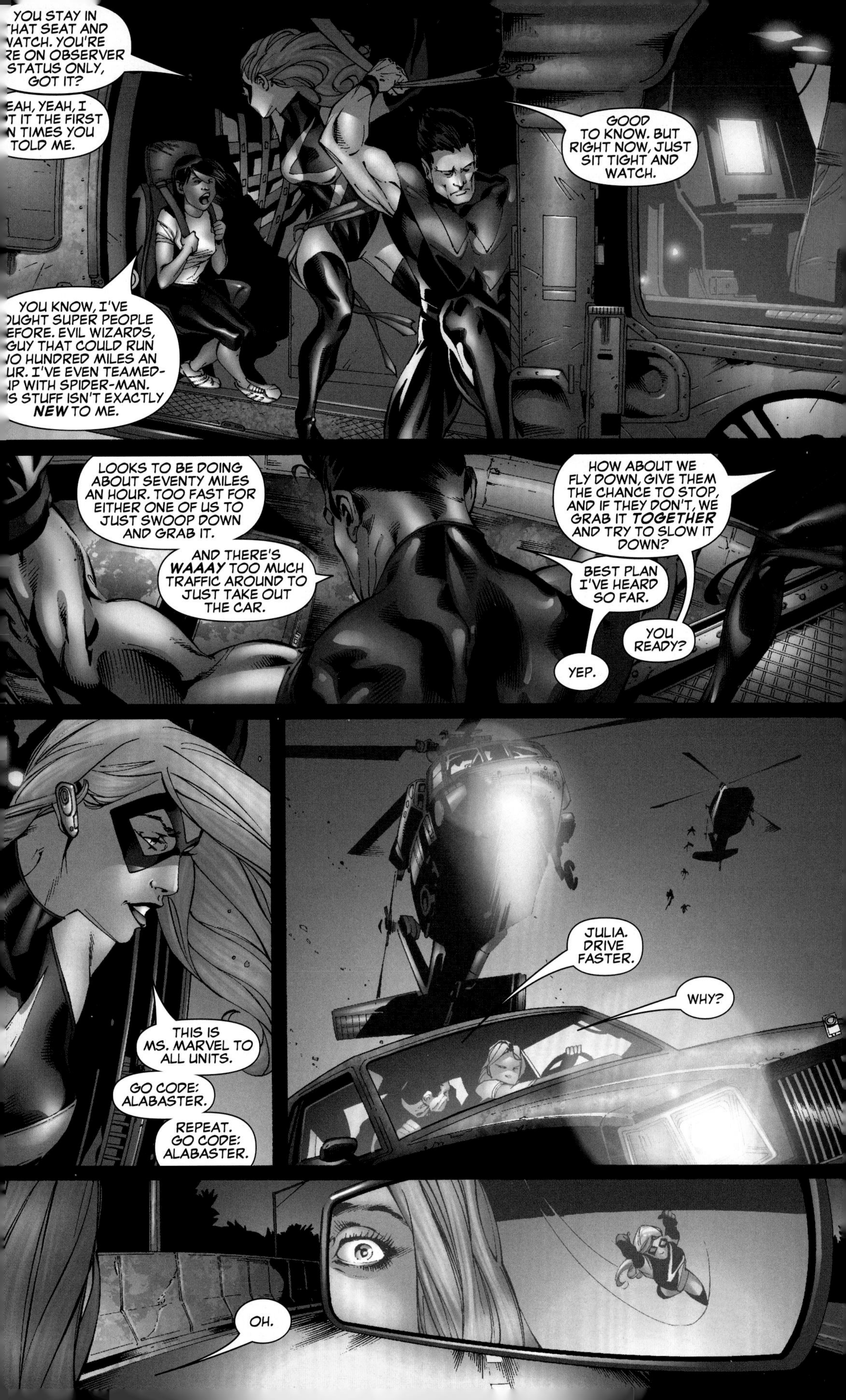
YOU STAY IN HAT SEAT AND VATCH. YOU'RE RE ON OBSERVER STATUS ONLY, GOT IT?
EAH, YEAH, I T IT THE FIRST N TIMES YOU TOLD ME.
GOOD TO KNOW. BUT RIGHT NOW, JUST SIT TIGHT AND WATCH.
YOU KNOW, I'VE OUGHT SUPER PEOPLE EFORE. EVIL WIZARDS, GUY THAT COULD RUN O HUNDRED MILES AN UR. I'VE EVEN TEAMED- P WITH SPIDER-MAN. S STUFF ISN'T EXACTLY NEW TO ME.
LOOKS TO BE DOING ABOUT SEVENTY MILES AN HOUR. TOO FAST FOR EITHER ONE OF US TO JUST SWOOP DOWN AND GRAB IT.
AND THERE'S WAAAY TOO MUCH TRAFFIC AROUND TO JUST TAKE OUT THE CAR.
HOW ABOUT WE FLY DOWN, GIVE THEM THE CHANCE TO STOP, AND IF THEY DON'T, WE GRAB IT TOGETHER AND TRY TO SLOW IT DOWN?
BEST PLAN I'VE HEARD SO FAR.
YOU READY?
YEP.
THIS IS MS. MARVEL TO ALL UNITS.
GO CODE: ALABASTER.
REPEAT. GO CODE: ALABASTER.
JULIA. DRIVE FASTER.
WHY?
OH.

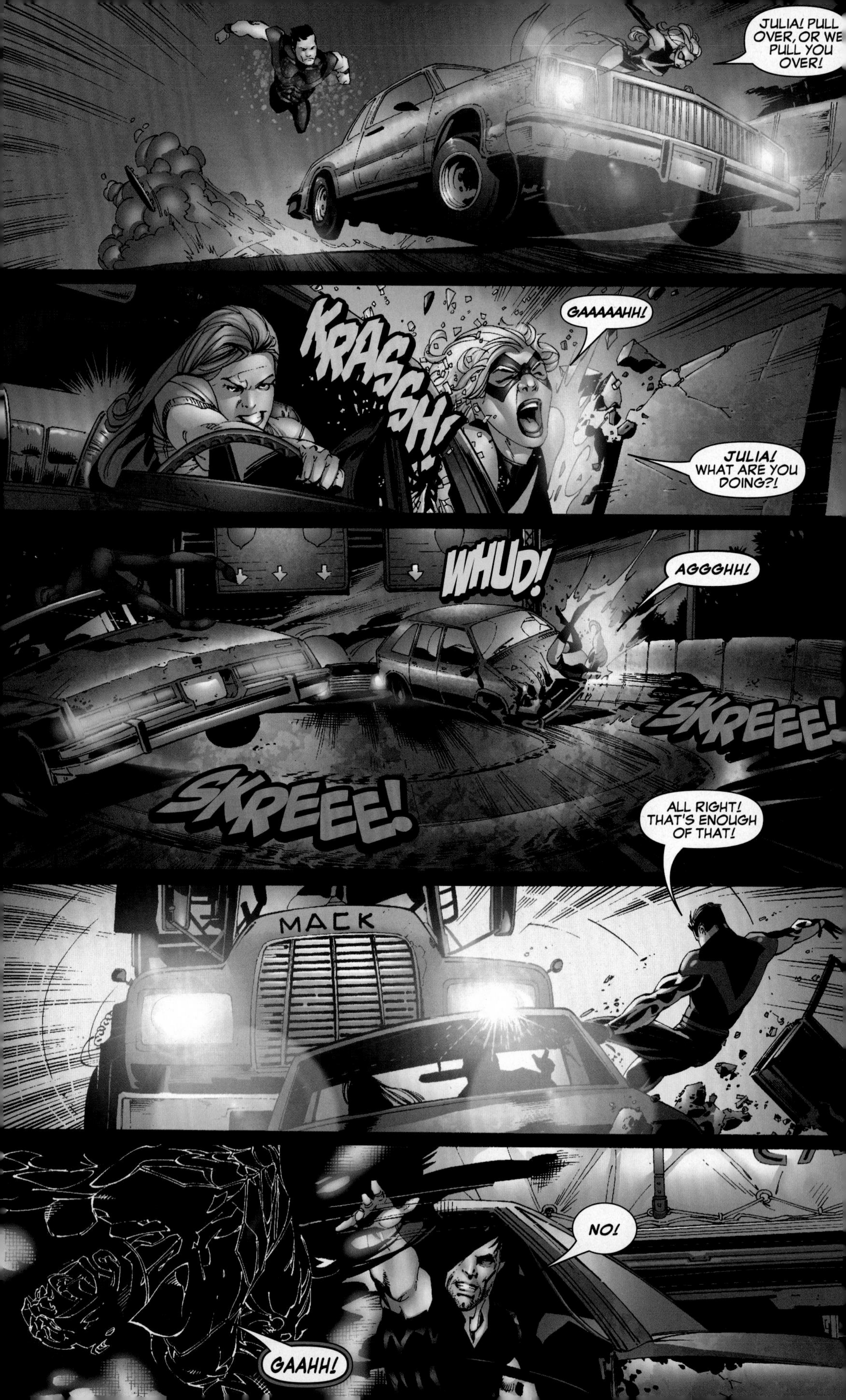
JULIA! PULL OVER, OR WE PULL YOU OVER!
KRASSH!
GAAAAAHH!
JULIA! WHAT ARE YOU DOING?!
WHUD!
AGGGHH!
SKREEE!
SKREEE!
ALL RIGHT! THAT'S ENOUGH OF THAT!
MACK
NO!
GAAHH!

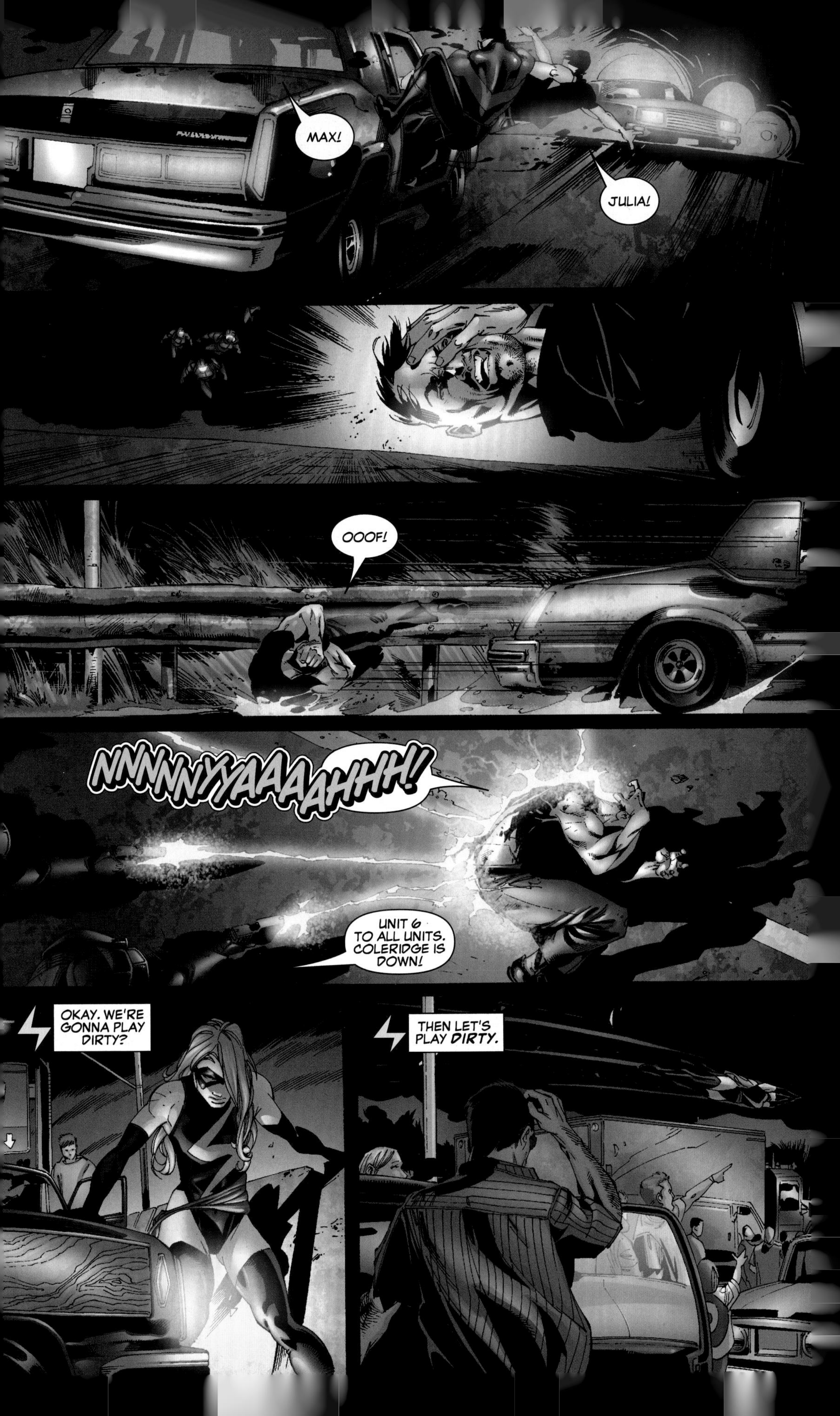
MAX!
JULIA!
OOOF!
NNNNNYYAAAAHHH!
UNIT 6 TO ALL UNITS. COLERIDGE IS DOWN!
OKAY. WE'RE GONNA PLAY DIRTY?
THEN LET'S PLAY DIRTY.

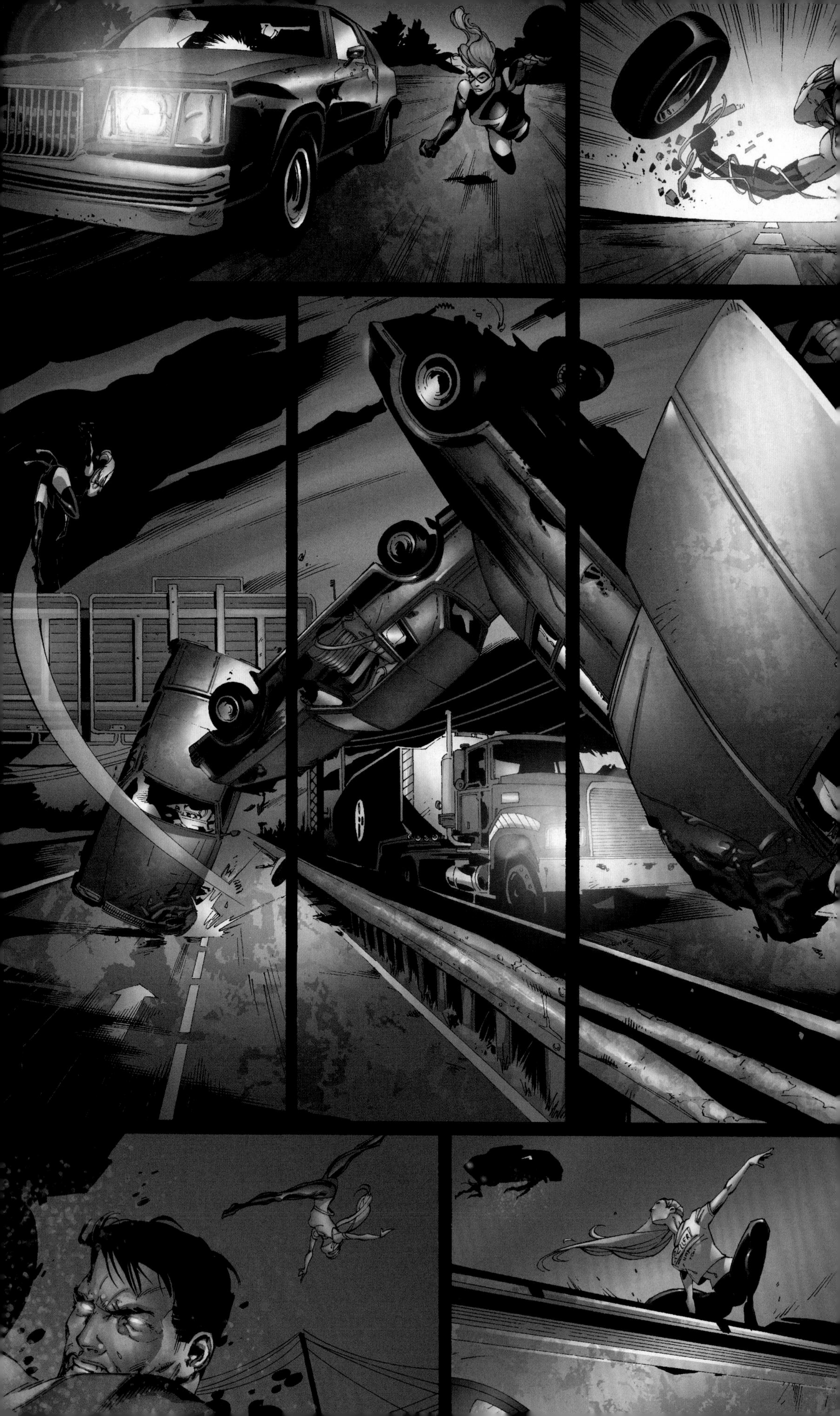

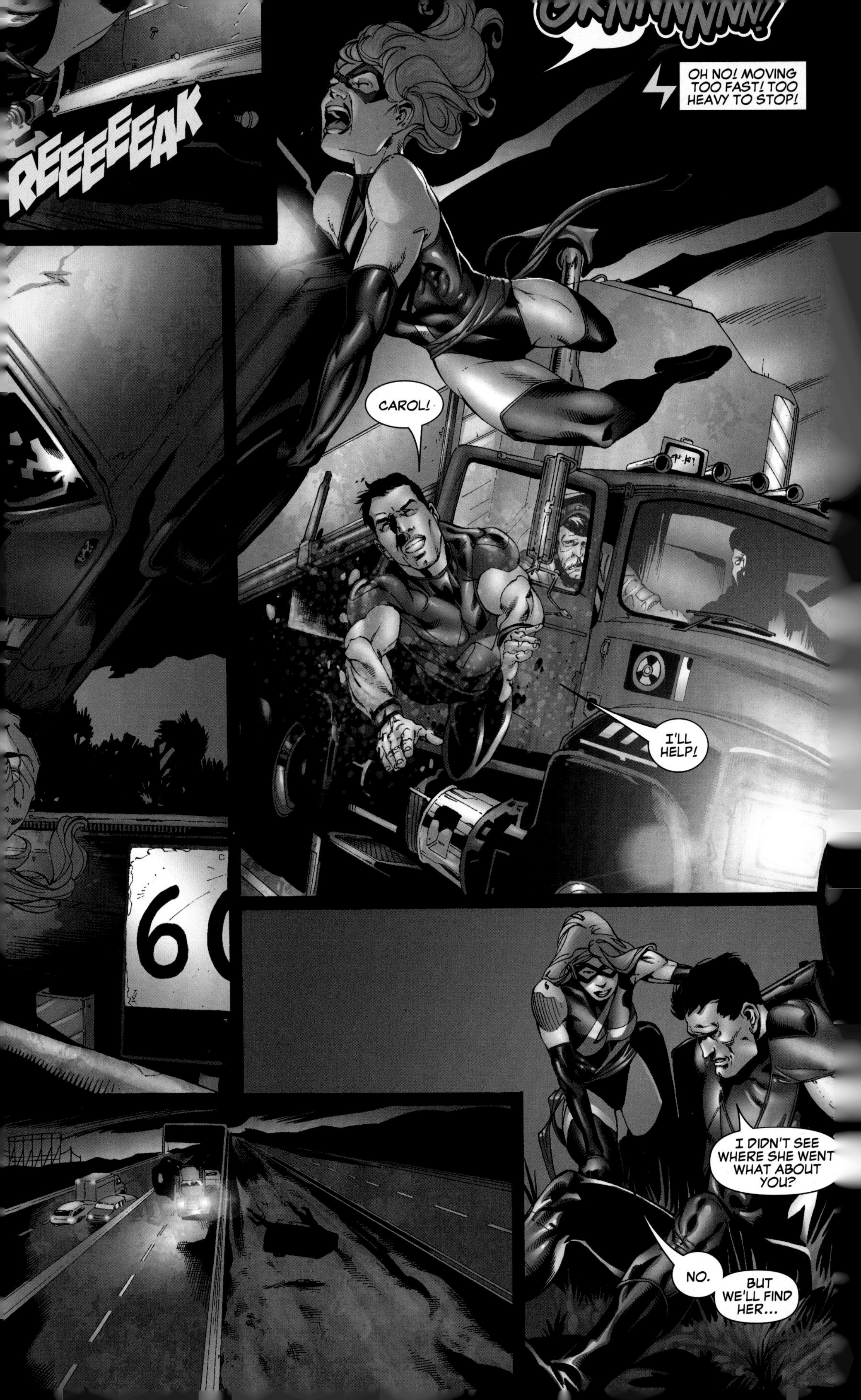
REEEEEAK
OH NO! MOVING TOO FAST! TOO HEAVY TO STOP!
CAROL!
I'LL HELP!
60
I DIDN'T SEE WHERE SHE WENT WHAT ABOUT YOU?
NO.
BUT WE'LL FIND HER...

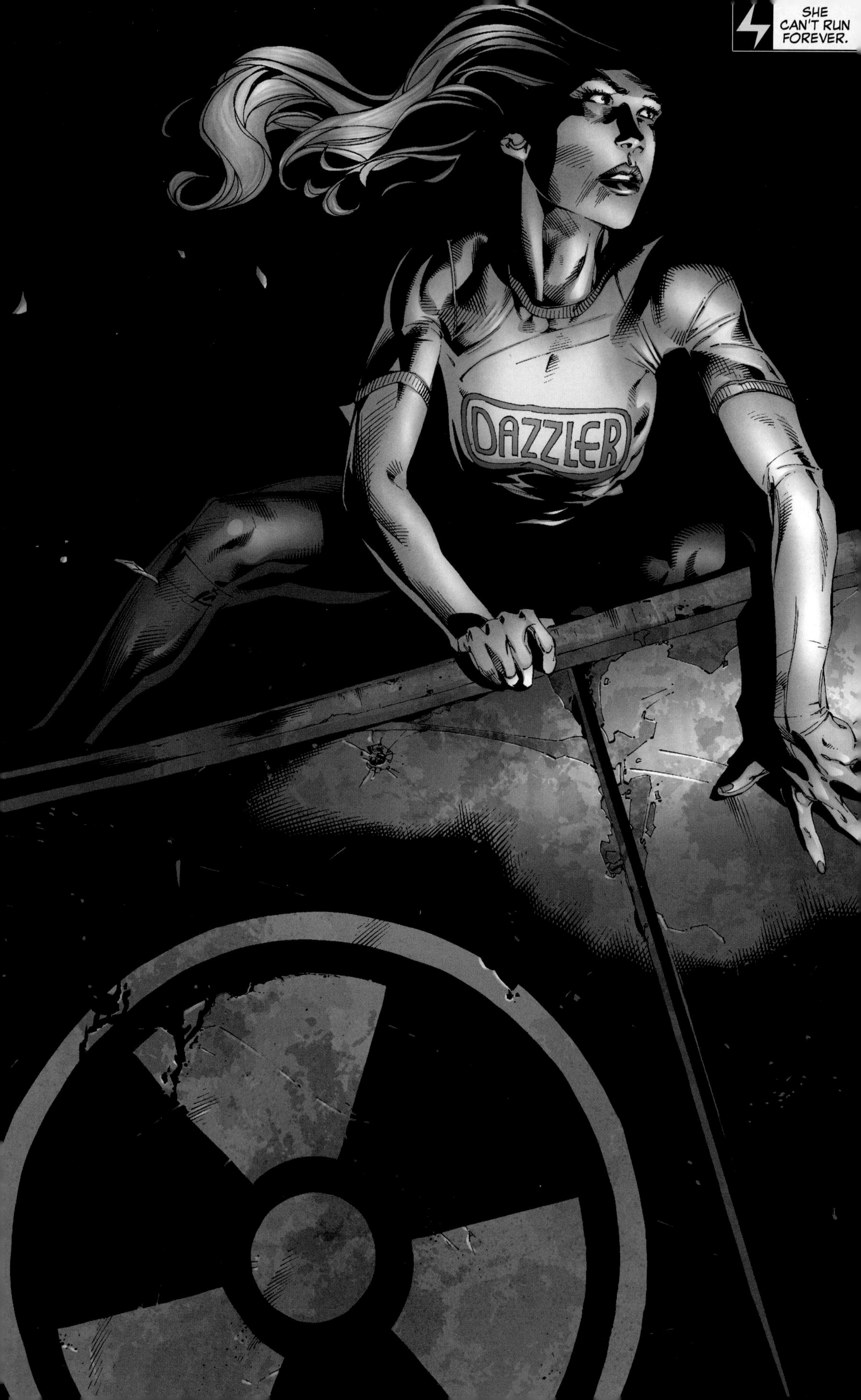
SHE CAN'T RUN FOREVER.
DAZZLER

MS. MARVEL

A MARVEL COMICS EVENT

CIVIL
WAR

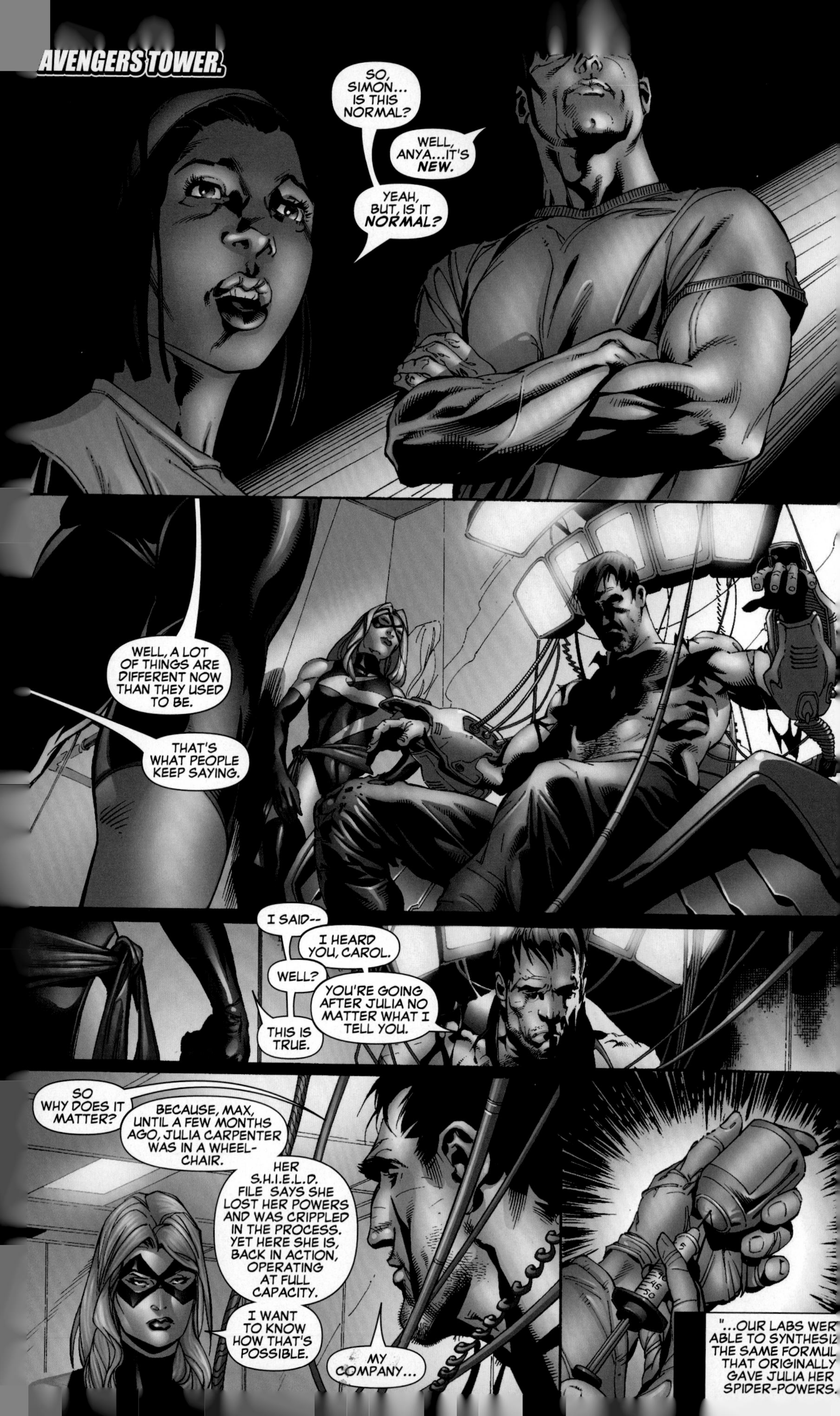
AVENGERS TOWER.
SO, SIMON... IS THIS NORMAL?
WELL, ANYA...IT'S NEW.
YEAH, BUT, IS IT NORMAL?
WELL, A LOT OF THINGS ARE DIFFERENT NOW THAN THEY USED TO BE.
THAT'S WHAT PEOPLE KEEP SAYING.
I SAID--
I HEARD YOU, CAROL.
WELL?
YOU'RE GOING AFTER JULIA NO MATTER WHAT I TELL YOU.
THIS IS TRUE.
SO WHY DOES IT MATTER?
BECAUSE, MAX, UNTIL A FEW MONTHS AGO, JULIA CARPENTER WAS IN A WHEEL-CHAIR.
HER S.H.I.E.L.D. FILE SAYS SHE LOST HER POWERS AND WAS CRIPPLED IN THE PROCESS. YET HERE SHE IS, BACK IN ACTION, OPERATING AT FULL CAPACITY.
I WANT TO KNOW HOW THAT'S POSSIBLE.
MY COMPANY...
"...OUR LABS WER ABLE TO SYNTHESIZ THE SAME FORMUL THAT ORIGINALLY GAVE JULIA HER SPIDER-POWERS.

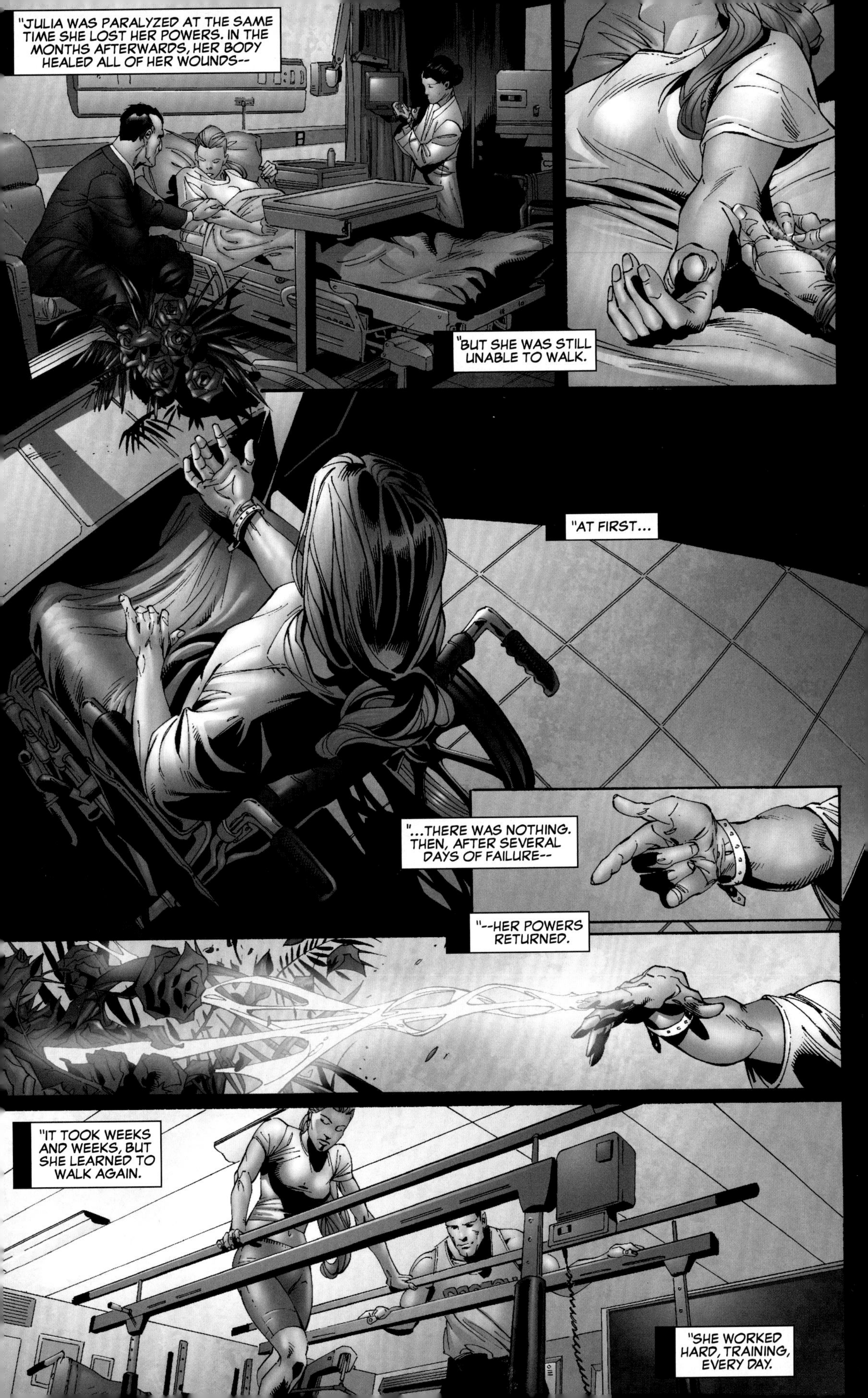
"JULIA WAS PARALYZED AT THE SAME TIME SHE LOST HER POWERS. IN THE MONTHS AFTERWARDS, HER BODY HEALED ALL OF HER WOUNDS--
"BUT SHE WAS STILL UNABLE TO WALK.
"AT FIRST...
"...THERE WAS NOTHING. THEN, AFTER SEVERAL DAYS OF FAILURE--
"--HER POWERS RETURNED.
"IT TOOK WEEKS AND WEEKS, BUT SHE LEARNED TO WALK AGAIN.
"SHE WORKED HARD, TRAINING, EVERY DAY.

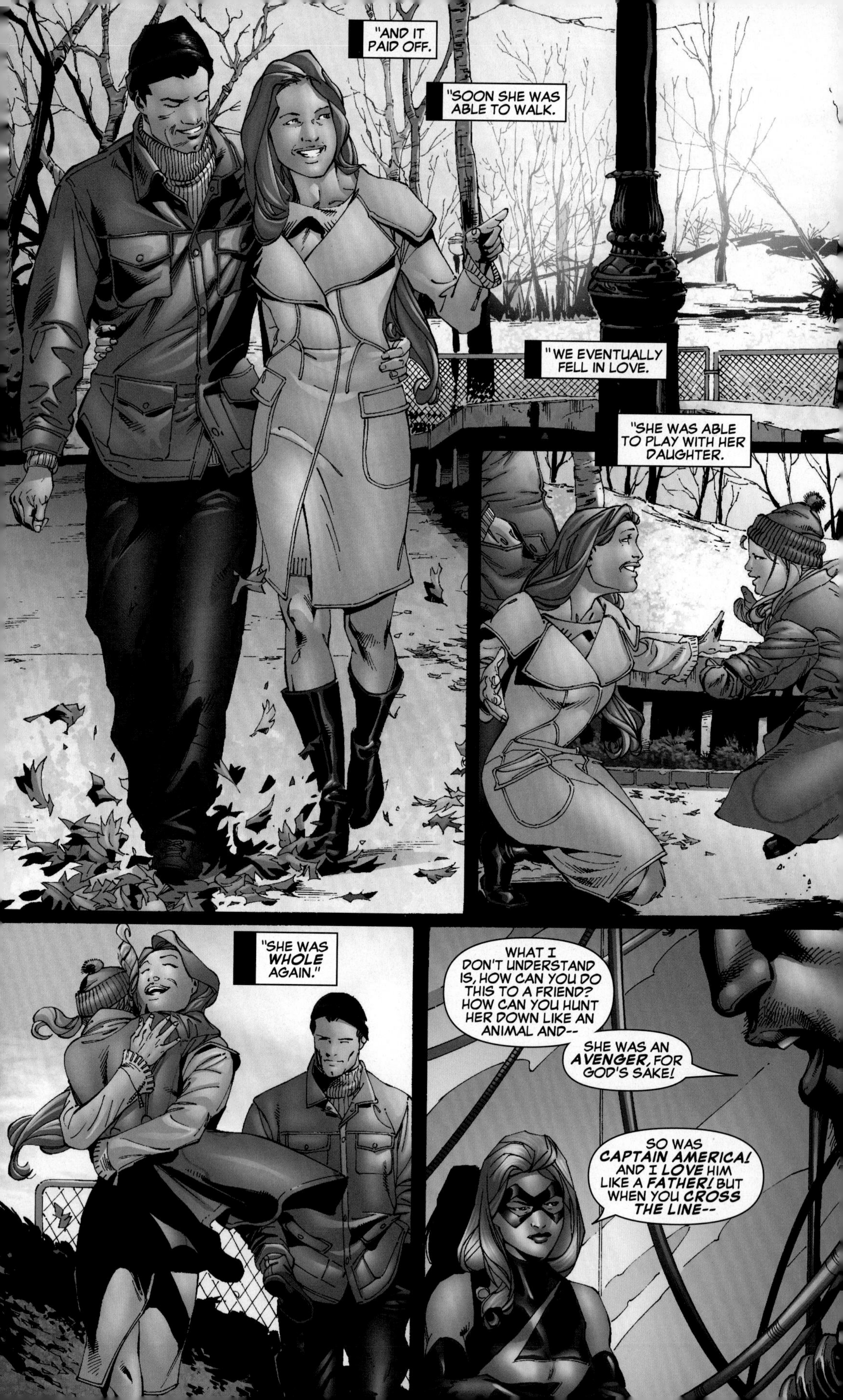
"AND IT PAID OFF.
"SOON SHE WAS ABLE TO WALK.
"WE EVENTUALLY FELL IN LOVE.
"SHE WAS ABLE TO PLAY WITH HER DAUGHTER.
"SHE WAS WHOLE AGAIN."
WHAT I DON'T UNDERSTAND IS, HOW CAN YOU DO THIS TO A FRIEND? HOW CAN YOU HUNT HER DOWN LIKE AN ANIMAL AND--
SHE WAS AN AVENGER, FOR GOD'S SAKE!
SO WAS CAPTAIN AMERICA! AND I LOVE HIM LIKE A FATHER! BUT WHEN YOU CROSS THE LINE--

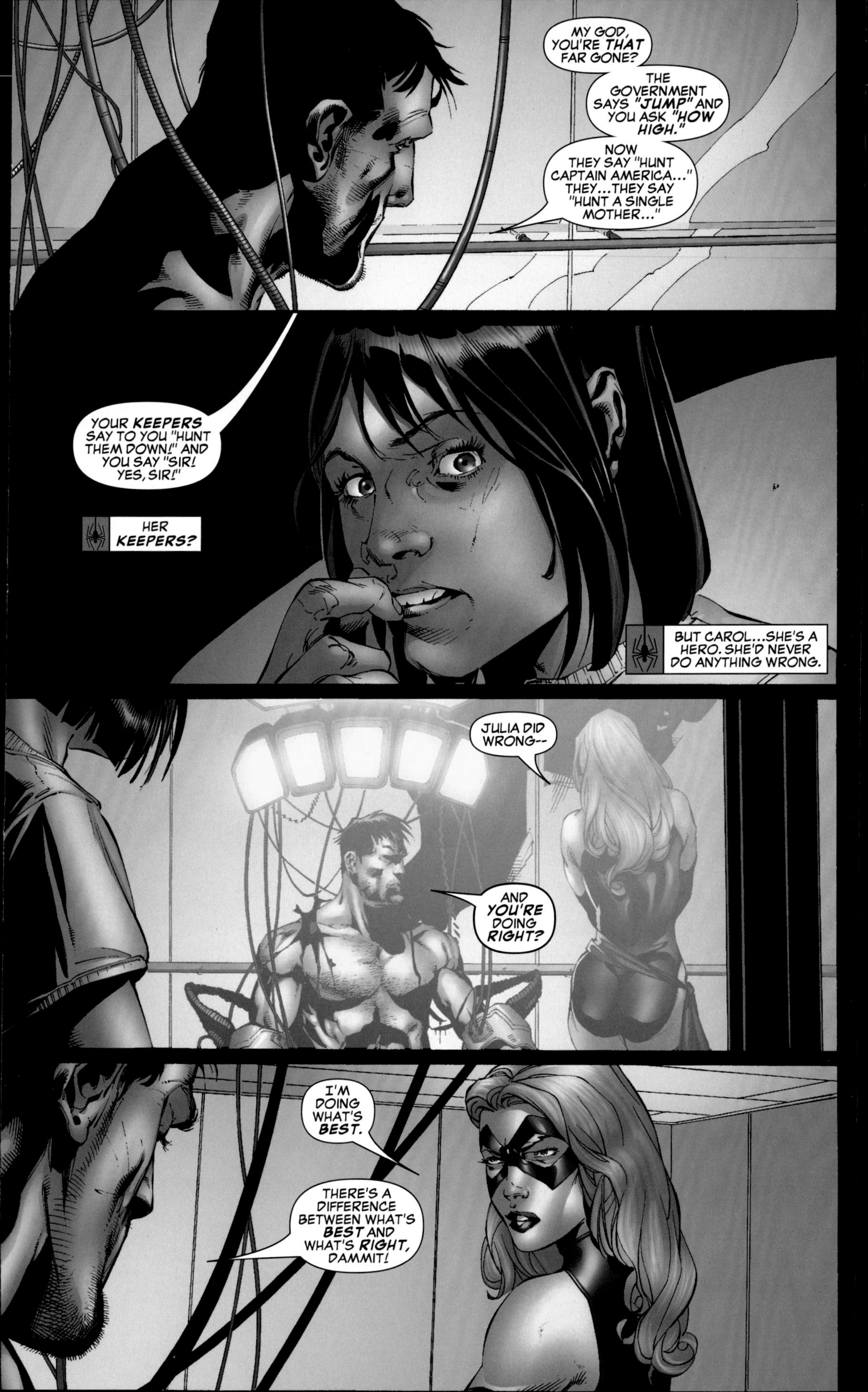
MY GOD, YOU'RE THAT FAR GONE?
THE GOVERNMENT SAYS "JUMP" AND YOU ASK "HOW HIGH."
NOW THEY SAY "HUNT CAPTAIN AMERICA..." THEY...THEY SAY "HUNT A SINGLE MOTHER..."
YOUR KEEPERS SAY TO YOU "HUNT THEM DOWN!" AND YOU SAY "SIR! YES, SIR!"
HER KEEPERS?
BUT CAROL...SHE'S A HERO. SHE'D NEVER DO ANYTHING WRONG.
JULIA DID WRONG--
AND YOU'RE DOING RIGHT?
I'M DOING WHAT'S BEST.
THERE'S A DIFFERENCE BETWEEN WHAT'S BEST AND WHAT'S RIGHT, DAMMIT!

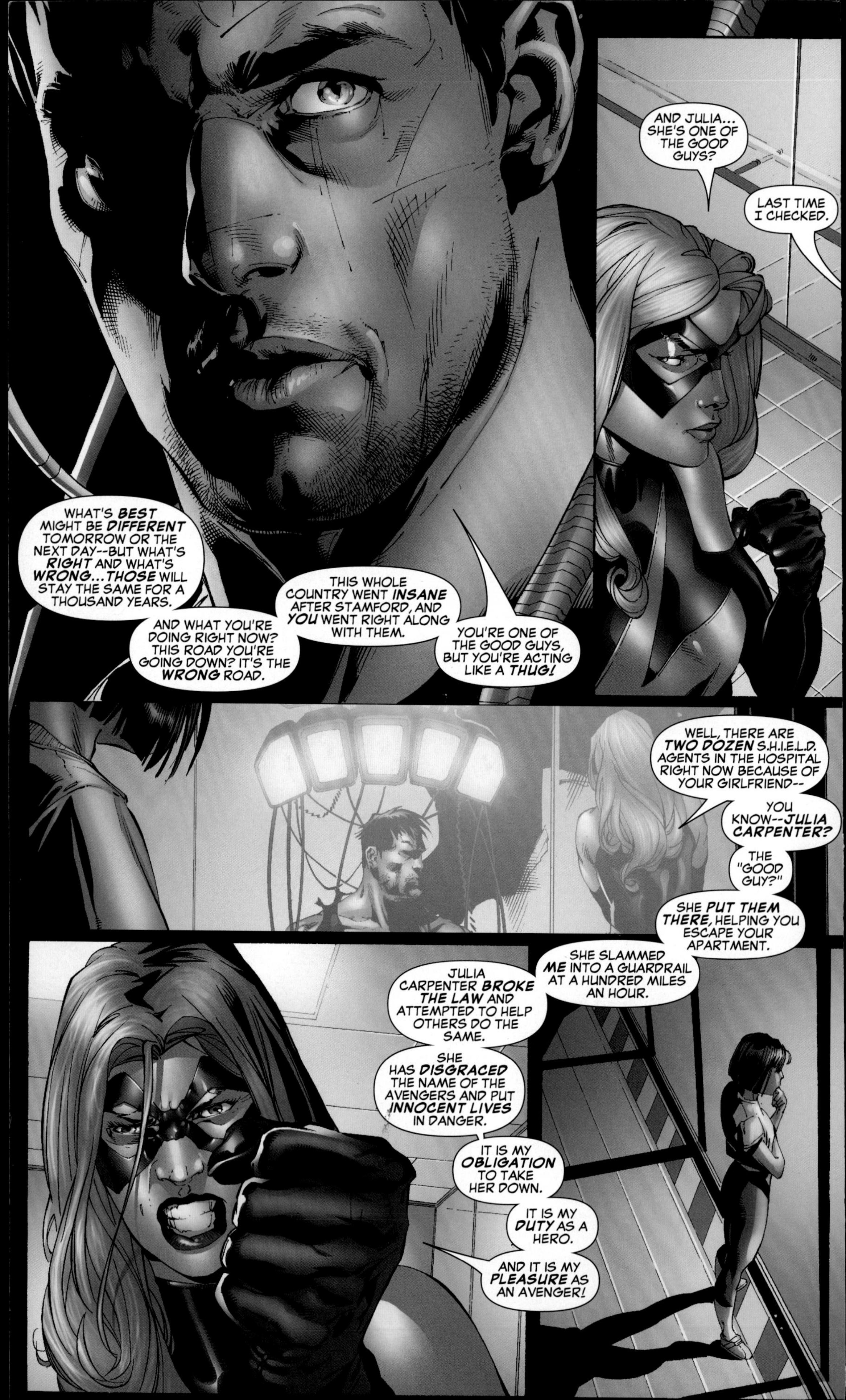
AND JULIA... SHE'S ONE OF THE GOOD GUYS?
LAST TIME I CHECKED.
WHAT'S BEST MIGHT BE DIFFERENT TOMORROW OR THE NEXT DAY--BUT WHAT'S RIGHT AND WHAT'S WRONG...THOSE WILL STAY THE SAME FOR A THOUSAND YEARS.
AND WHAT YOU'RE DOING RIGHT NOW? THIS ROAD YOU'RE GOING DOWN? IT'S THE WRONG ROAD.
THIS WHOLE COUNTRY WENT INSANE AFTER STAMFORD, AND YOU WENT RIGHT ALONG WITH THEM.
YOU'RE ONE OF THE GOOD GUYS, BUT YOU'RE ACTING LIKE A THUG!
WELL, THERE ARE TWO DOZEN S.H.I.E.L.D. AGENTS IN THE HOSPITAL RIGHT NOW BECAUSE OF YOUR GIRLFRIEND--
YOU KNOW--JULIA CARPENTER?
THE "GOOD GUY?"
SHE PUT THEM THERE, HELPING YOU ESCAPE YOUR APARTMENT.
SHE SLAMMED ME INTO A GUARDRAIL AT A HUNDRED MILES AN HOUR.
JULIA CARPENTER BROKE THE LAW AND ATTEMPTED TO HELP OTHERS DO THE SAME.
SHE HAS DISGRACED THE NAME OF THE AVENGERS AND PUT INNOCENT LIVES IN DANGER.
IT IS MY OBLIGATION TO TAKE HER DOWN.
IT IS MY DUTY AS A HERO.
AND IT IS MY PLEASURE AS AN AVENGER!

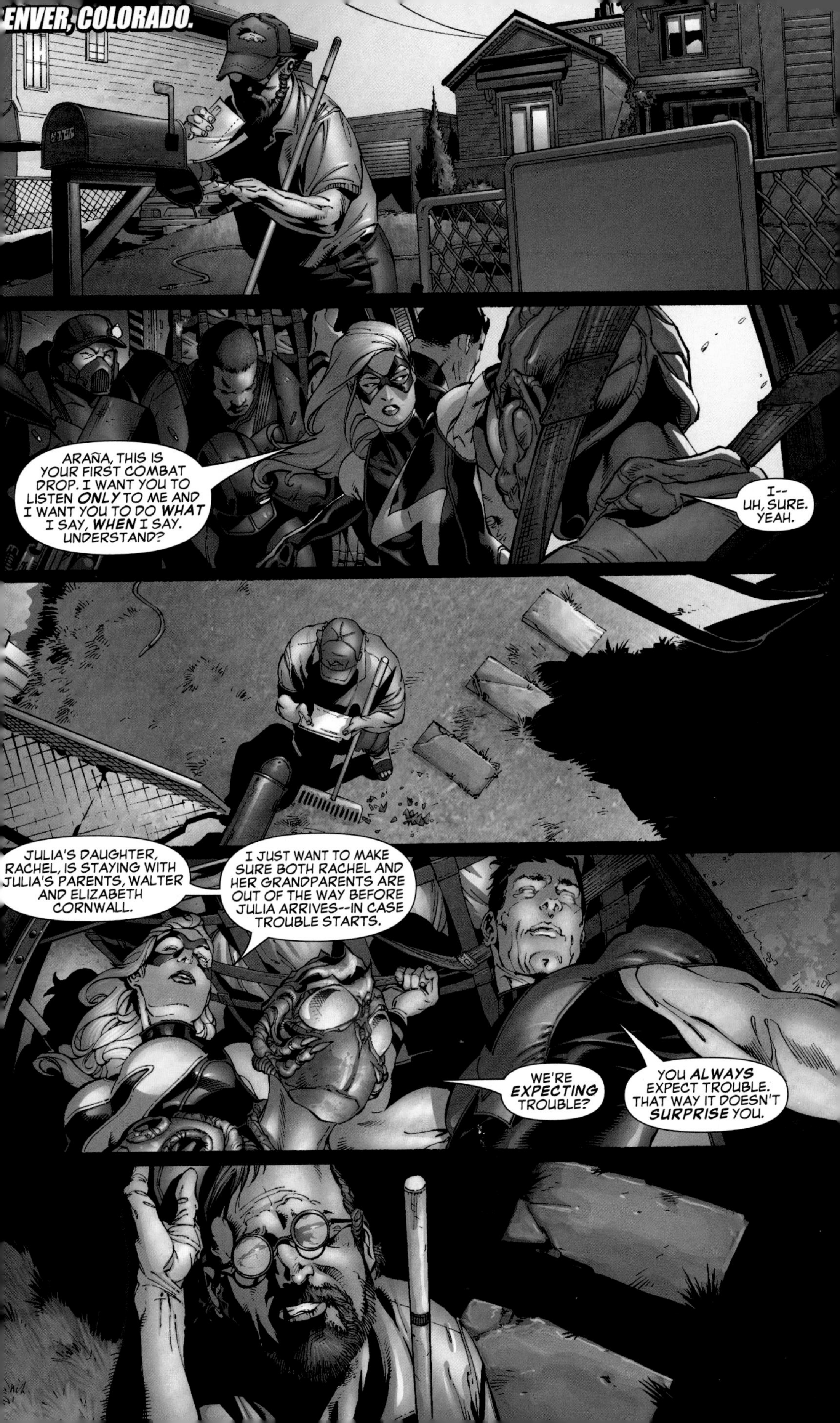
ENVER, COLORADO.
ARAÑA, THIS IS YOUR FIRST COMBAT DROP. I WANT YOU TO LISTEN ONLY TO ME AND I WANT YOU TO DO WHAT I SAY, WHEN I SAY. UNDERSTAND?
I-- UH, SURE. YEAH.
JULIA'S DAUGHTER, RACHEL, IS STAYING WITH JULIA'S PARENTS, WALTER AND ELIZABETH CORNWALL.
I JUST WANT TO MAKE SURE BOTH RACHEL AND HER GRANDPARENTS ARE OUT OF THE WAY BEFORE JULIA ARRIVES--IN CASE TROUBLE STARTS.
WE'RE EXPECTING TROUBLE?
YOU ALWAYS EXPECT TROUBLE. THAT WAY IT DOESN'T SURPRISE YOU.

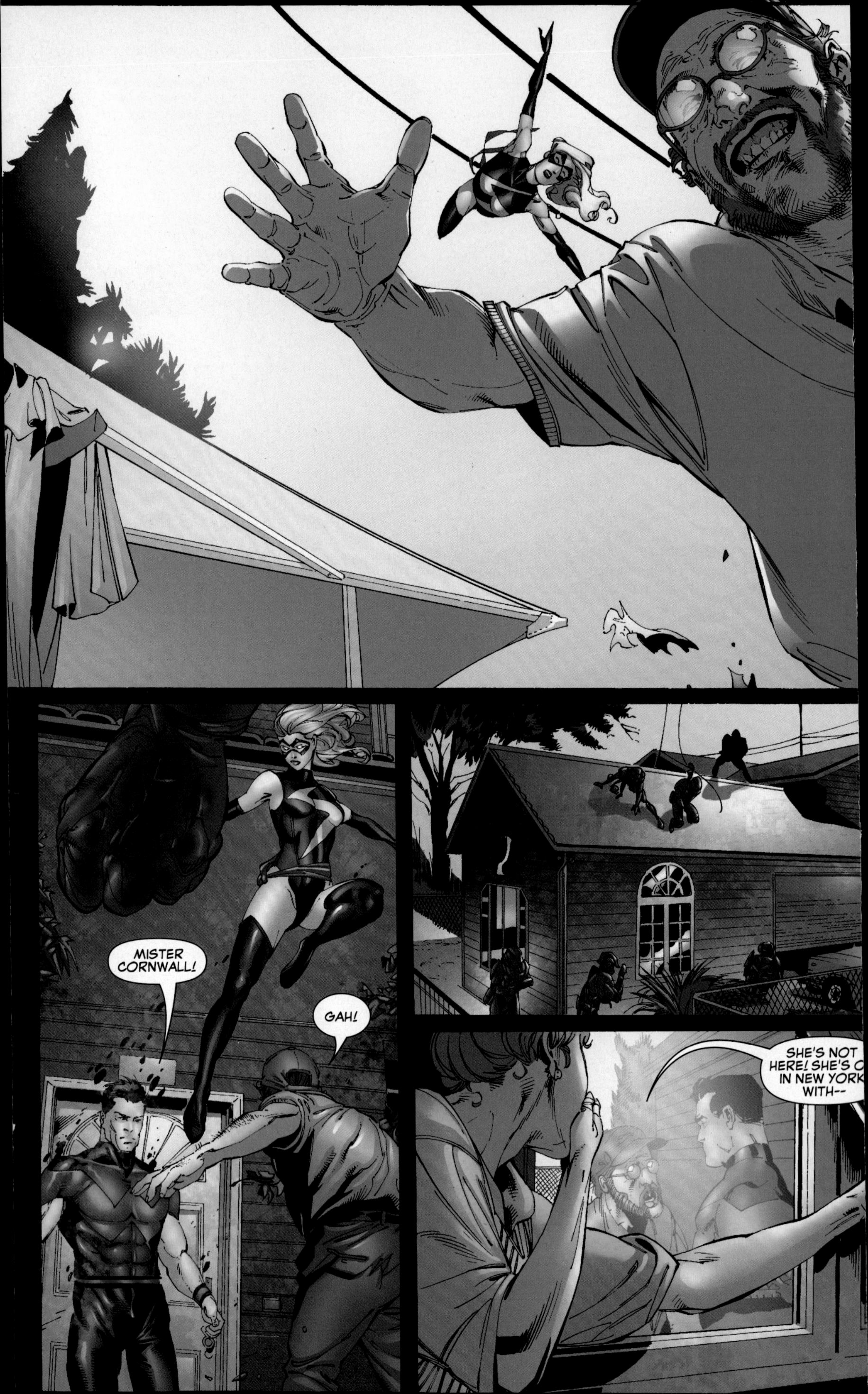
MISTER CORNWALL!
GAH!
SHE'S NOT HERE! SHE'S O
IN NEW YORK
WITH--

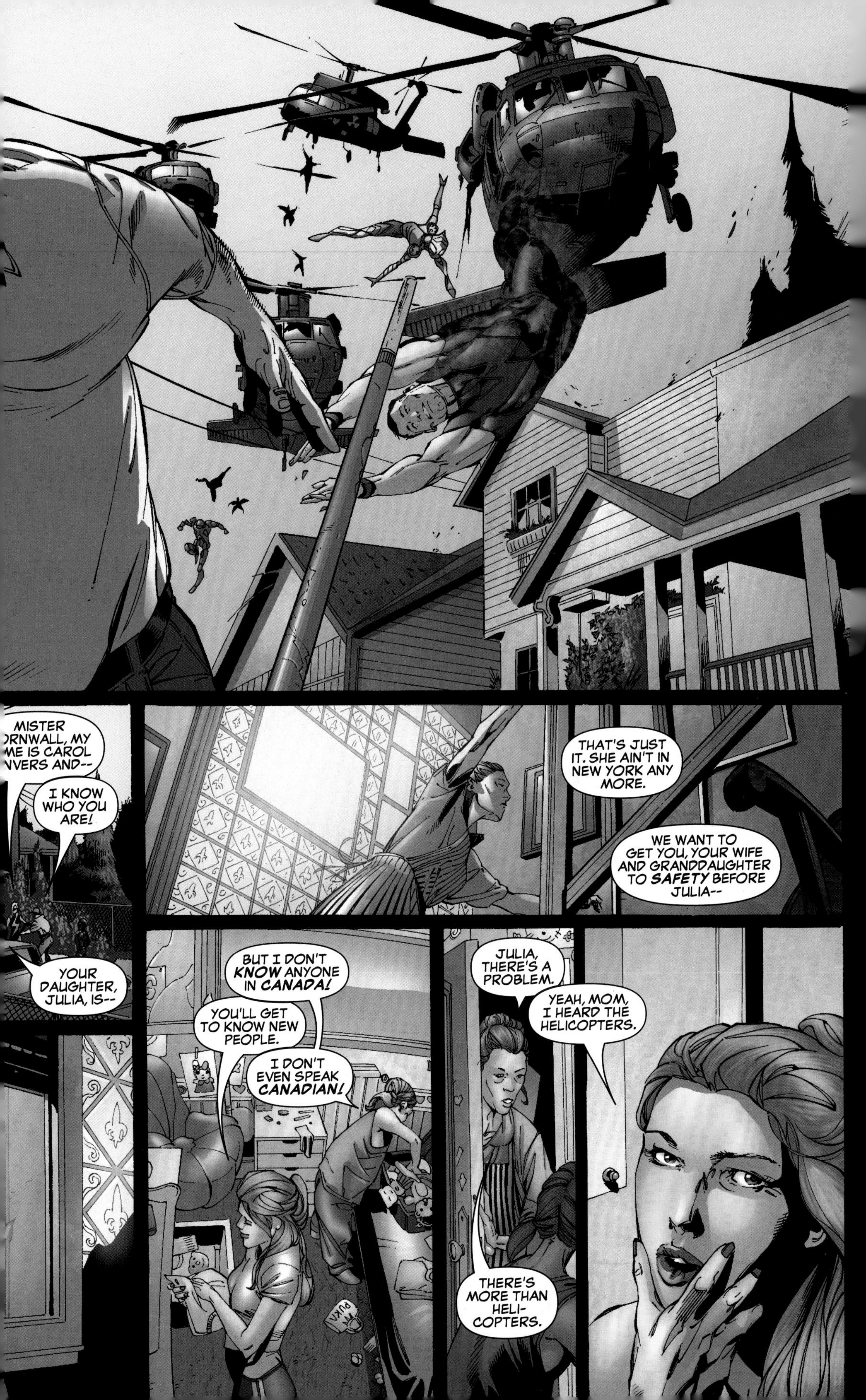
MISTER
RNWALL, MY
ME IS CAROL
NVERS AND--
I KNOW WHO YOU ARE!
YOUR DAUGHTER, JULIA, IS--
THAT'S JUST IT. SHE AIN'T IN NEW YORK ANY MORE.
WE WANT TO GET YOU, YOUR WIFE AND GRANDDAUGHTER TO SAFETY BEFORE JULIA--
BUT I DON'T KNOW ANYONE IN CANADA!
YOU'LL GET TO KNOW NEW PEOPLE.
I DON'T EVEN SPEAK CANADIAN!
JULIA, THERE'S A PROBLEM.
YEAH, MOM, I HEARD THE HELICOPTERS.
THERE'S MORE THAN HELI-COPTERS.

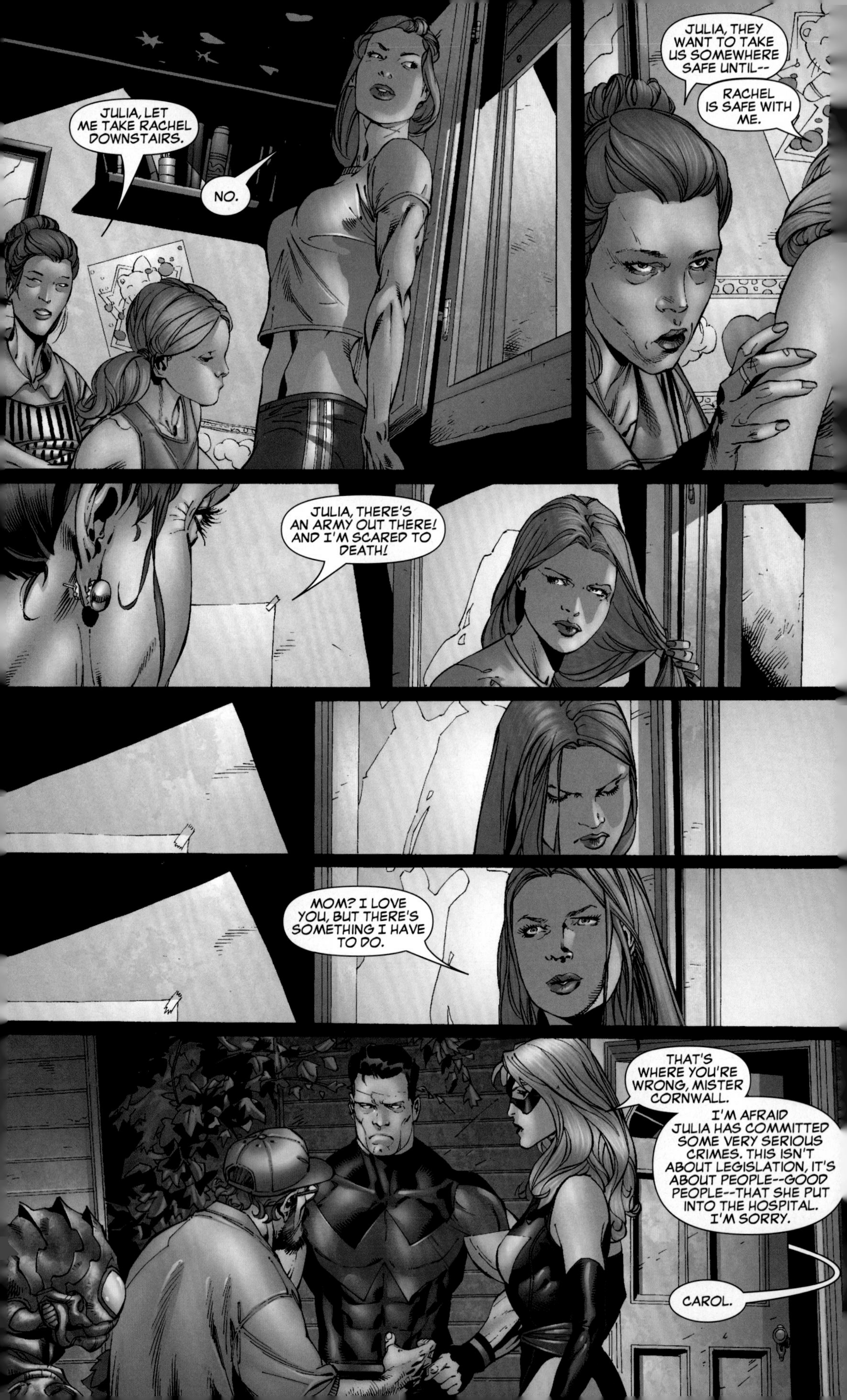
JULIA, LET ME TAKE RACHEL DOWNSTAIRS.
NO.
JULIA, THEY WANT TO TAKE US SOMEWHERE SAFE UNTIL--
RACHEL IS SAFE WITH ME.
JULIA, THERE'S AN ARMY OUT THERE! AND I'M SCARED TO DEATH!
MOM? I LOVE YOU, BUT THERE'S SOMETHING I HAVE TO DO.
THAT'S WHERE YOU'RE WRONG, MISTER CORNWALL.
I'M AFRAID JULIA HAS COMMITTED SOME VERY SERIOUS CRIMES. THIS ISN'T ABOUT LEGISLATION, IT'S ABOUT PEOPLE--GOOD PEOPLE--THAT SHE PUT INTO THE HOSPITAL. I'M SORRY.
CAROL.

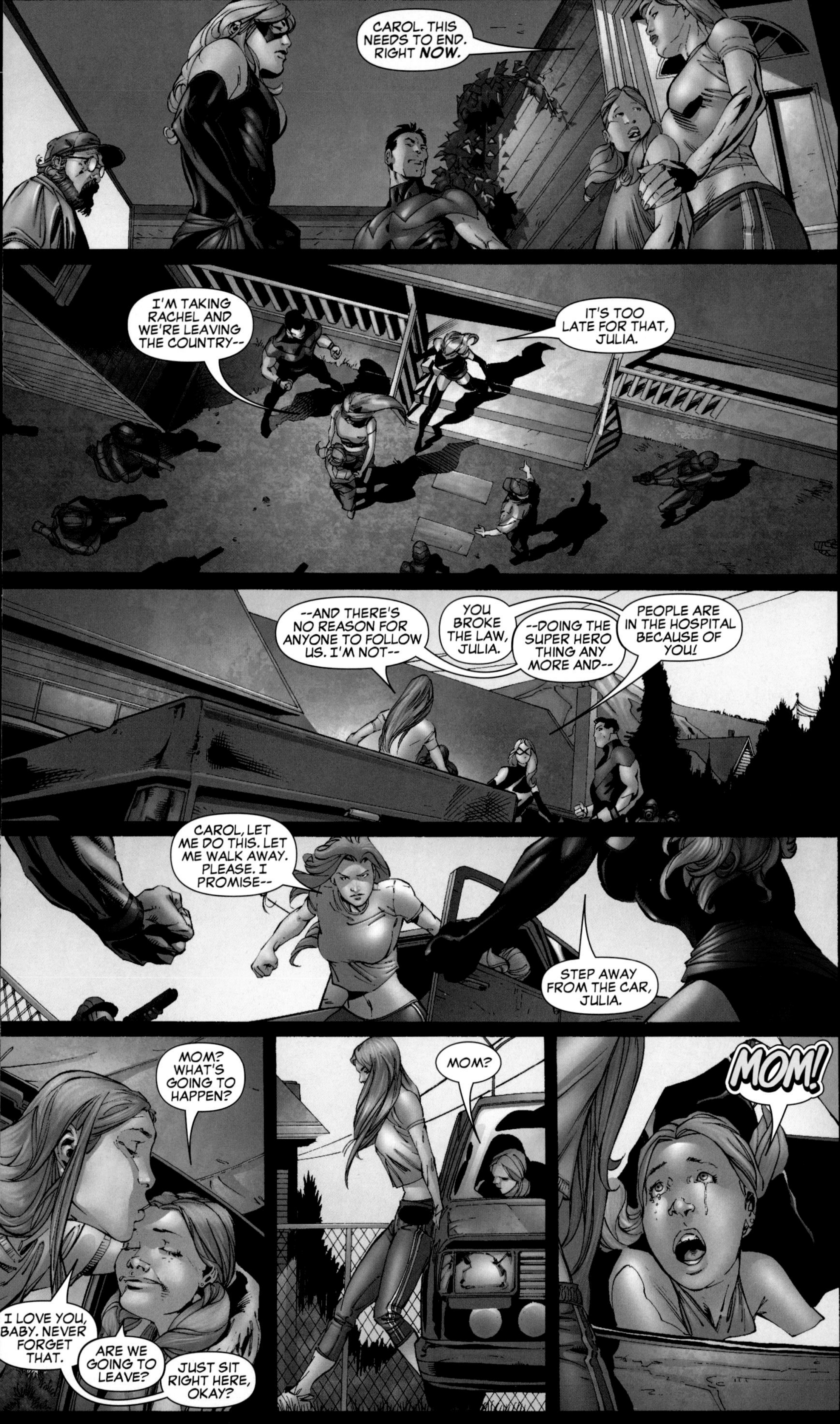
CAROL. THIS NEEDS TO END. RIGHT **NOW**.
I'M TAKING RACHEL AND WE'RE LEAVING THE COUNTRY--
IT'S TOO LATE FOR THAT, JULIA.
--AND THERE'S NO REASON FOR ANYONE TO FOLLOW US. I'M NOT--
YOU BROKE THE LAW, JULIA.
--DOING THE SUPER HERO THING ANY MORE AND--
PEOPLE ARE IN THE HOSPITAL BECAUSE OF YOU!
CAROL, LET ME DO THIS. LET ME WALK AWAY. PLEASE. I PROMISE--
STEP AWAY FROM THE CAR, JULIA.
MOM? WHAT'S GOING TO HAPPEN?
I LOVE YOU, BABY. NEVER FORGET THAT.
ARE WE GOING TO LEAVE?
JUST SIT RIGHT HERE, OKAY?
MOM?
MOM!

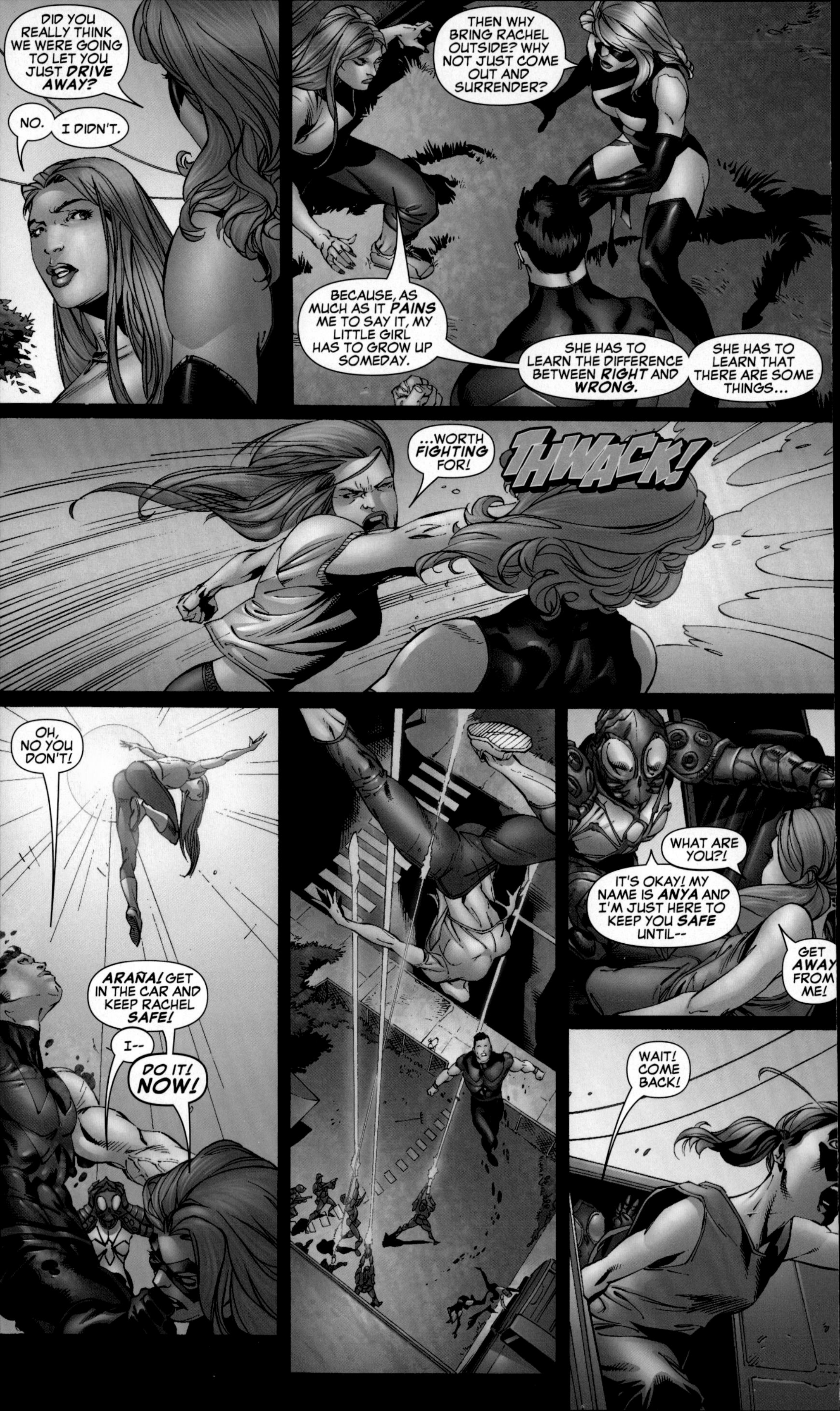
DID YOU REALLY THINK WE WERE GOING TO LET YOU JUST DRIVE AWAY?
NO.
I DIDN'T.
THEN WHY BRING RACHEL OUTSIDE? WHY NOT JUST COME OUT AND SURRENDER?
BECAUSE, AS MUCH AS IT PAINS ME TO SAY IT, MY LITTLE GIRL HAS TO GROW UP SOMEDAY.
SHE HAS TO LEARN THE DIFFERENCE BETWEEN RIGHT AND WRONG.
SHE HAS TO LEARN THAT THERE ARE SOME THINGS...
...WORTH FIGHTING FOR!
THWACK!
OH, NO YOU DON'T!
ARAÑA! GET IN THE CAR AND KEEP RACHEL SAFE!
I--
DO IT! NOW!
WHAT ARE YOU?!
IT'S OKAY! MY NAME IS ANYA AND I'M JUST HERE TO KEEP YOU SAFE UNTIL--
GET AWAY FROM ME!
WAIT! COME BACK!

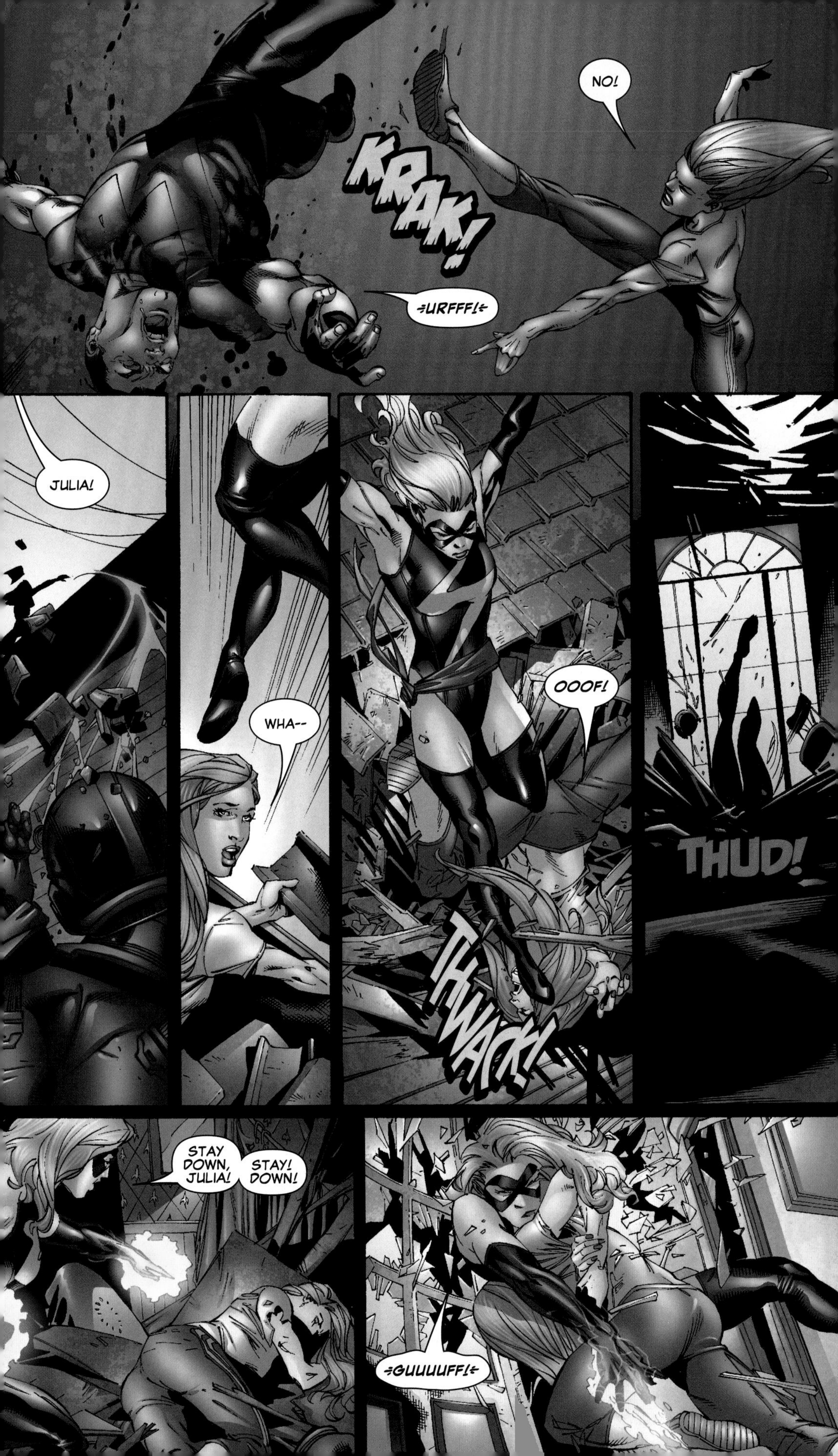
NO!
KRAK!
=URFFF!=
JULIA!
WHA--
OOOF!
THWACK!
THUD!
STAY DOWN, JULIA!
STAY! DOWN!
=GUUUUFF!=

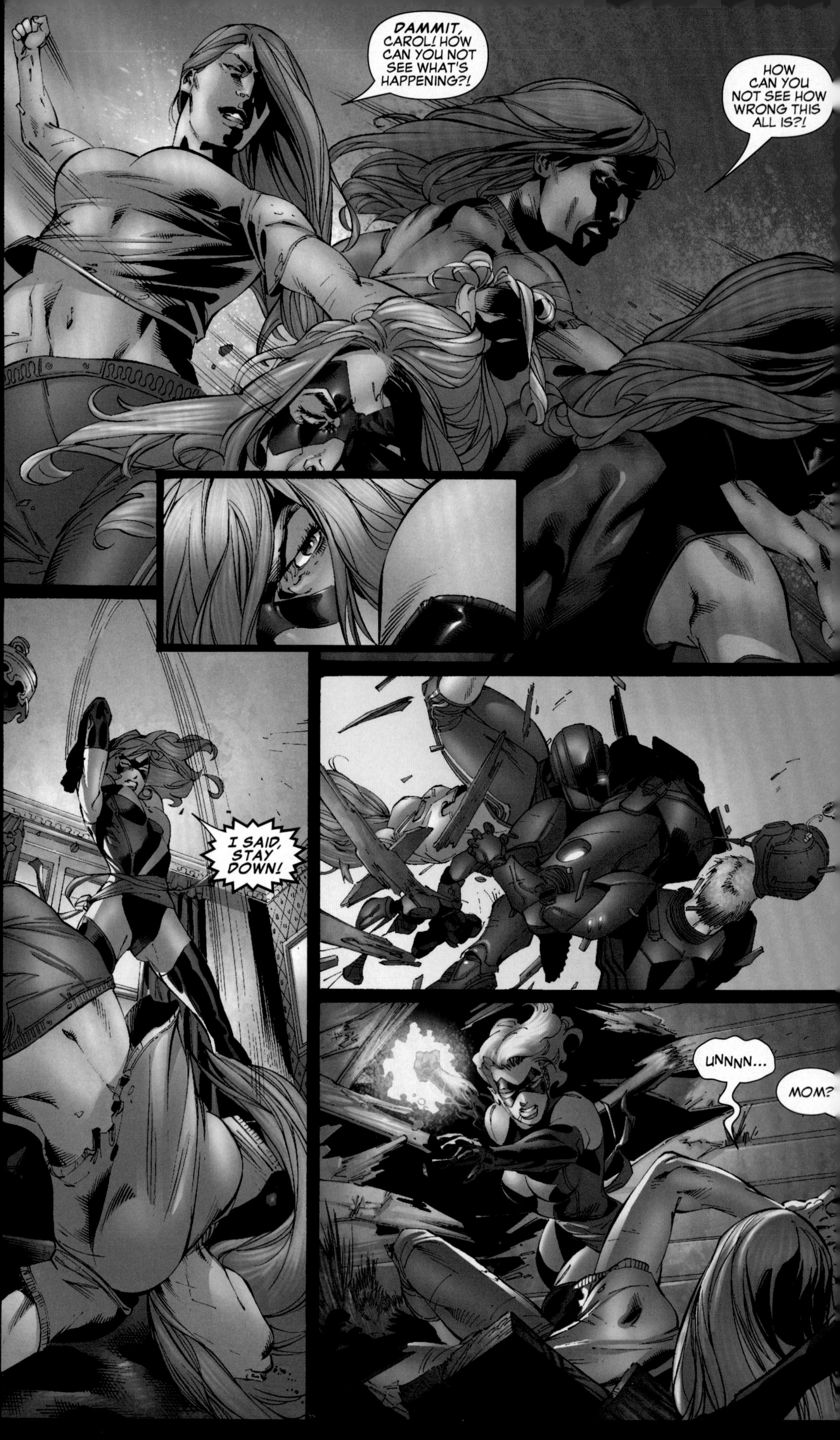
DAMMIT, CAROL! HOW CAN YOU NOT SEE WHAT'S HAPPENING?!
HOW CAN YOU NOT SEE HOW WRONG THIS ALL IS?!
I SAID, STAY DOWN!
UNNNN...
MOM?

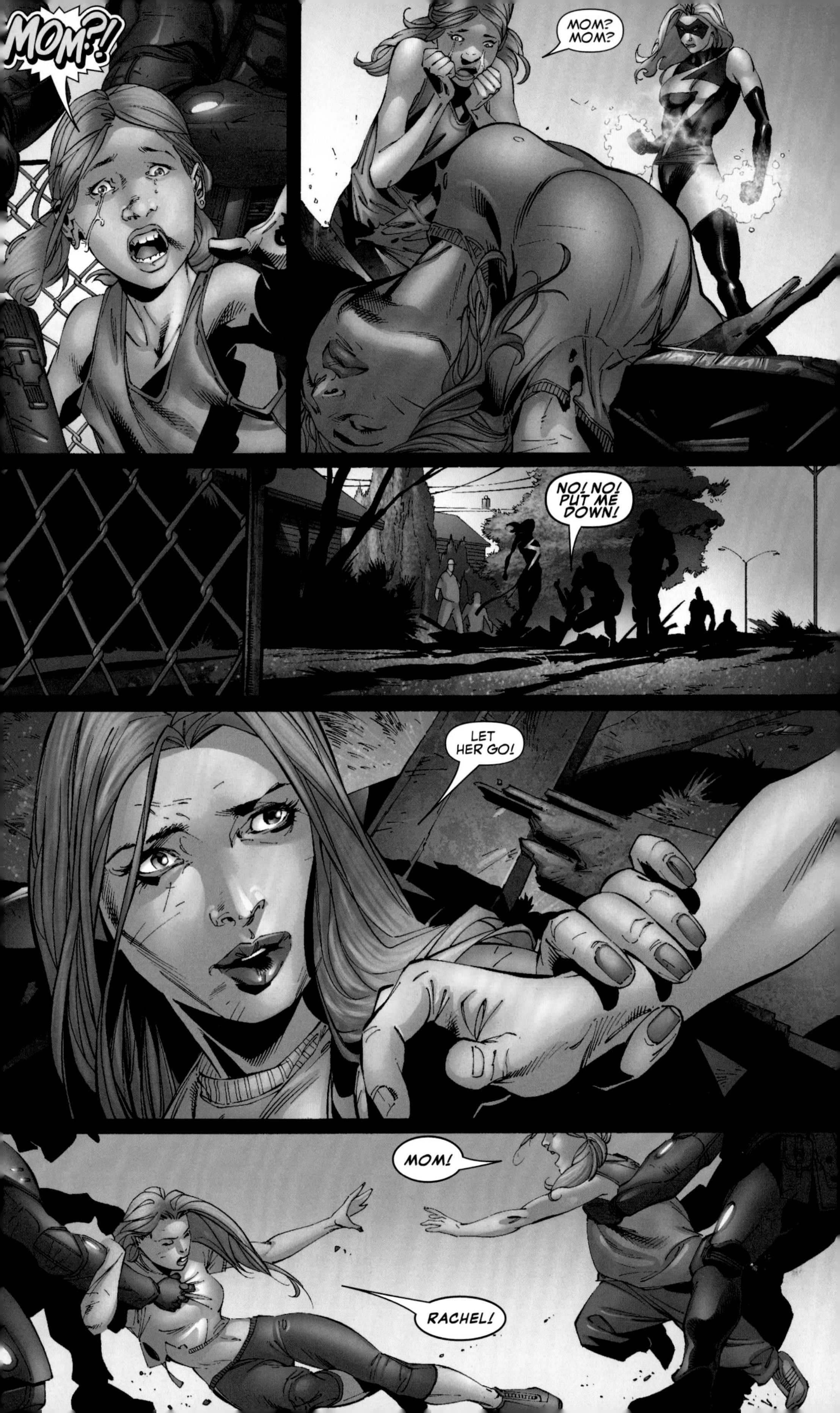
MOM?!
MOM? MOM?
NO! NO! PUT ME DOWN!
LET HER GO!
MOM!
RACHEL!

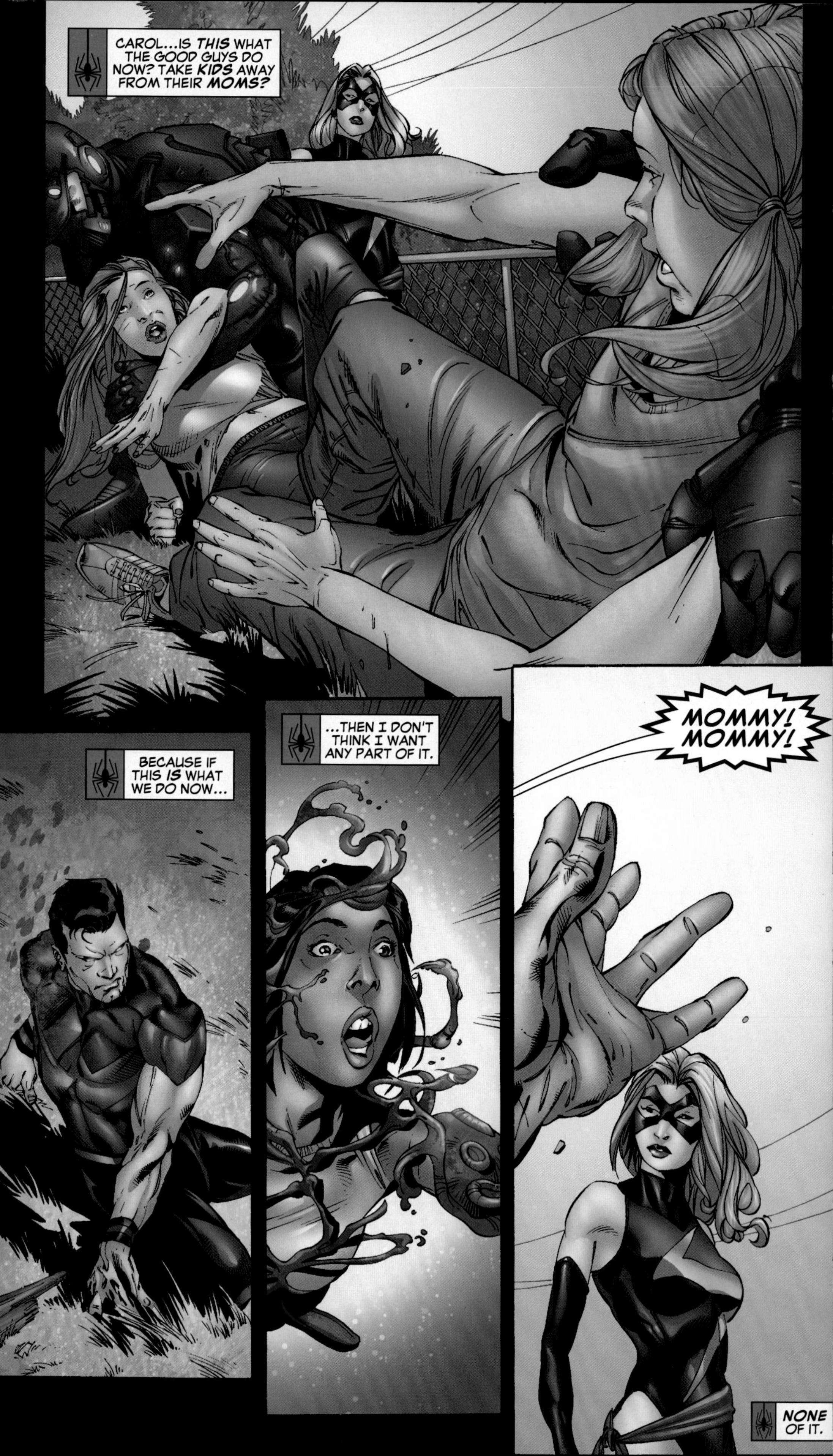
CAROL...IS THIS WHAT THE GOOD GUYS DO NOW? TAKE KIDS AWAY FROM THEIR MOMS?
BECAUSE IF THIS IS WHAT WE DO NOW...
...THEN I DON'T THINK I WANT ANY PART OF IT.
MOMMY! MOMMY!
NONE OF IT.

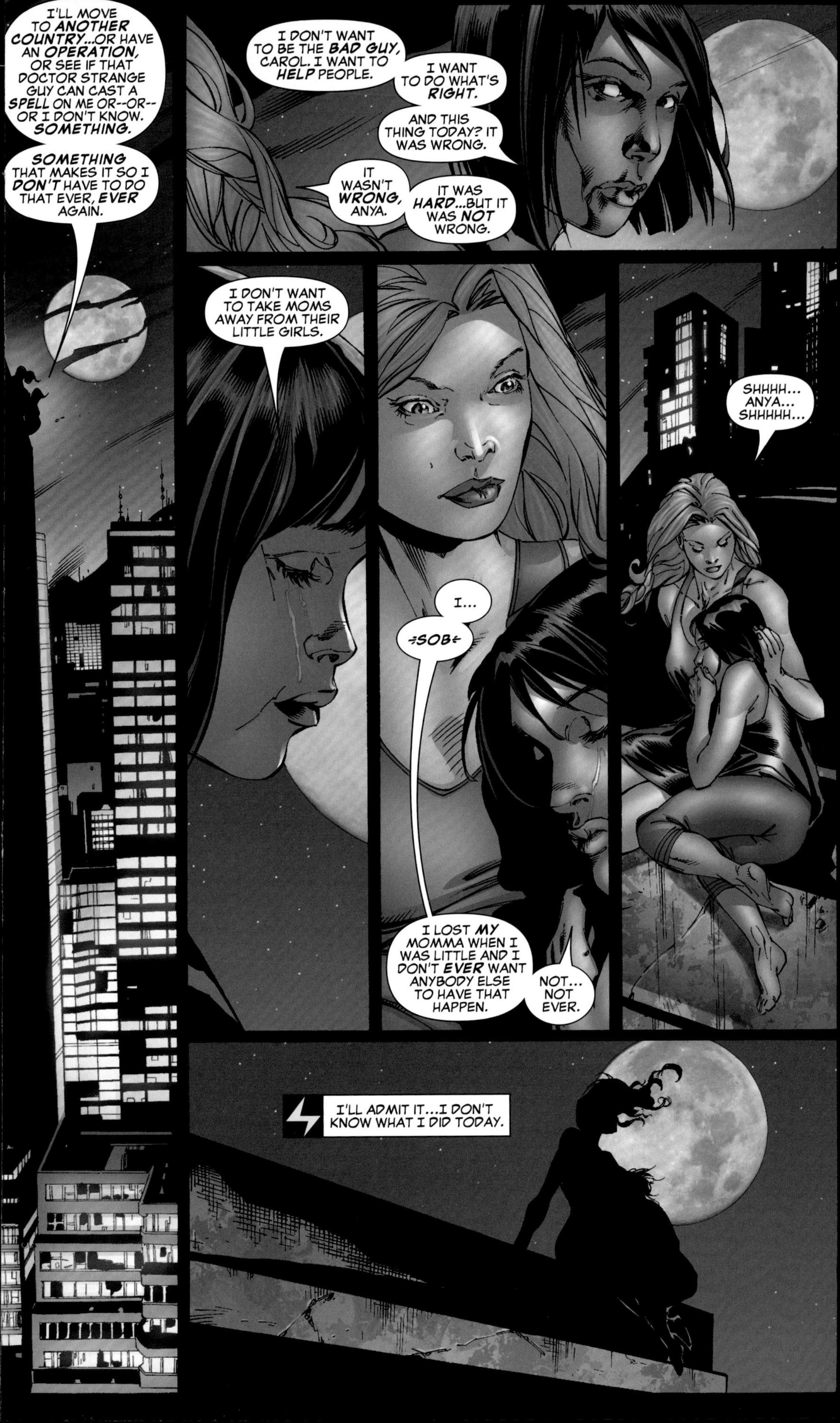
I'LL MOVE TO ANOTHER COUNTRY...OR HAVE AN OPERATION, OR SEE IF THAT DOCTOR STRANGE GUY CAN CAST A SPELL ON ME OR--OR--OR I DON'T KNOW. SOMETHING.
SOMETHING THAT MAKES IT SO I DON'T HAVE TO DO THAT EVER, EVER AGAIN.
I DON'T WANT TO BE THE BAD GUY, CAROL. I WANT TO HELP PEOPLE.
I WANT TO DO WHAT'S RIGHT.
AND THIS THING TODAY? IT WAS WRONG.
IT WASN'T WRONG, ANYA.
IT WAS HARD...BUT IT WAS NOT WRONG.
I DON'T WANT TO TAKE MOMS AWAY FROM THEIR LITTLE GIRLS.
I...
SOB
I LOST MY MOMMA WHEN I WAS LITTLE AND I DON'T EVER WANT ANYBODY ELSE TO HAVE THAT HAPPEN.
NOT... NOT EVER.
SHHHH... ANYA... SHHHHH...
I'LL ADMIT IT...I DON'T KNOW WHAT I DID TODAY.

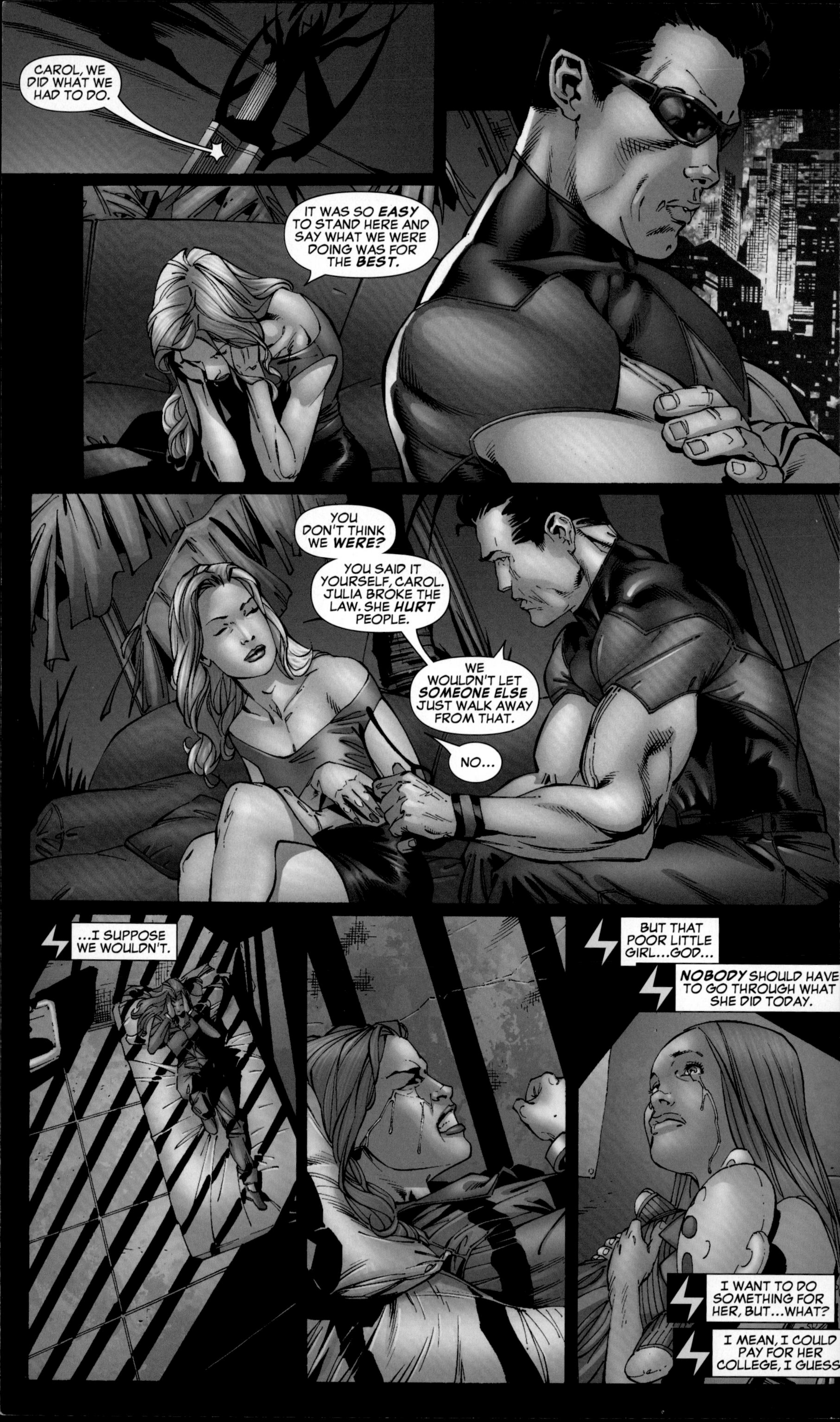

CAROL, WE DID WHAT WE HAD TO DO.
IT WAS SO EASY TO STAND HERE AND SAY WHAT WE WERE DOING WAS FOR THE BEST.
YOU DON'T THINK WE WERE?
YOU SAID IT YOURSELF, CAROL. JULIA BROKE THE LAW. SHE HURT PEOPLE.
WE WOULDN'T LET SOMEONE ELSE JUST WALK AWAY FROM THAT.
NO...
...I SUPPOSE WE WOULDN'T.
BUT THAT POOR LITTLE GIRL...GOD...
NOBODY SHOULD HAVE TO GO THROUGH WHAT SHE DID TODAY.
I WANT TO DO SOMETHING FOR HER, BUT...WHAT?
I MEAN, I COULD PAY FOR HER COLLEGE, I GUESS

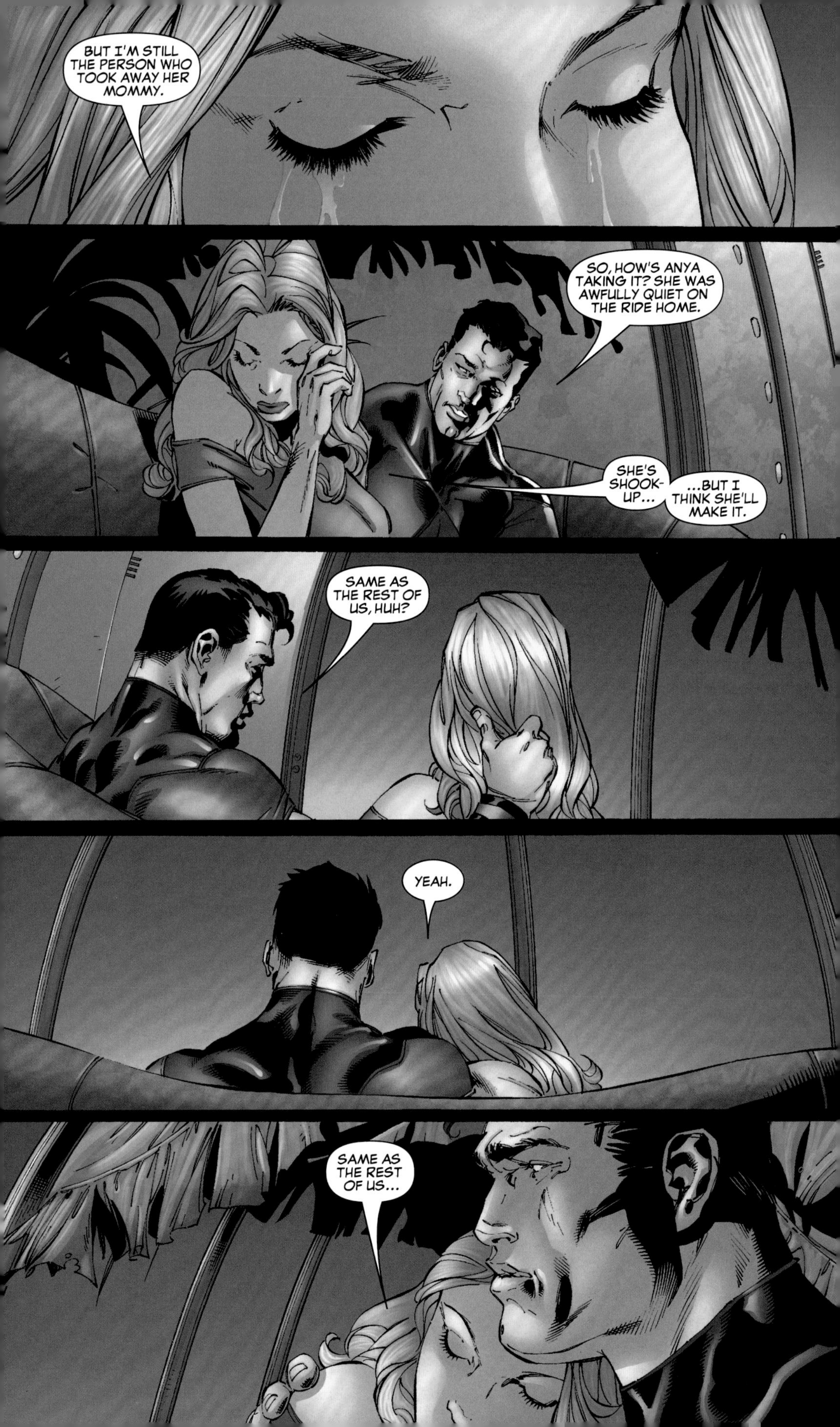
BUT I'M STILL THE PERSON WHO TOOK AWAY HER MOMMY.
SO, HOW'S ANYA TAKING IT? SHE WAS AWFULLY QUIET ON THE RIDE HOME.
SHE'S SHOOK-UP...
...BUT I THINK SHE'LL MAKE IT.
SAME AS THE REST OF US, HUH?
YEAH.
SAME AS THE REST OF US...

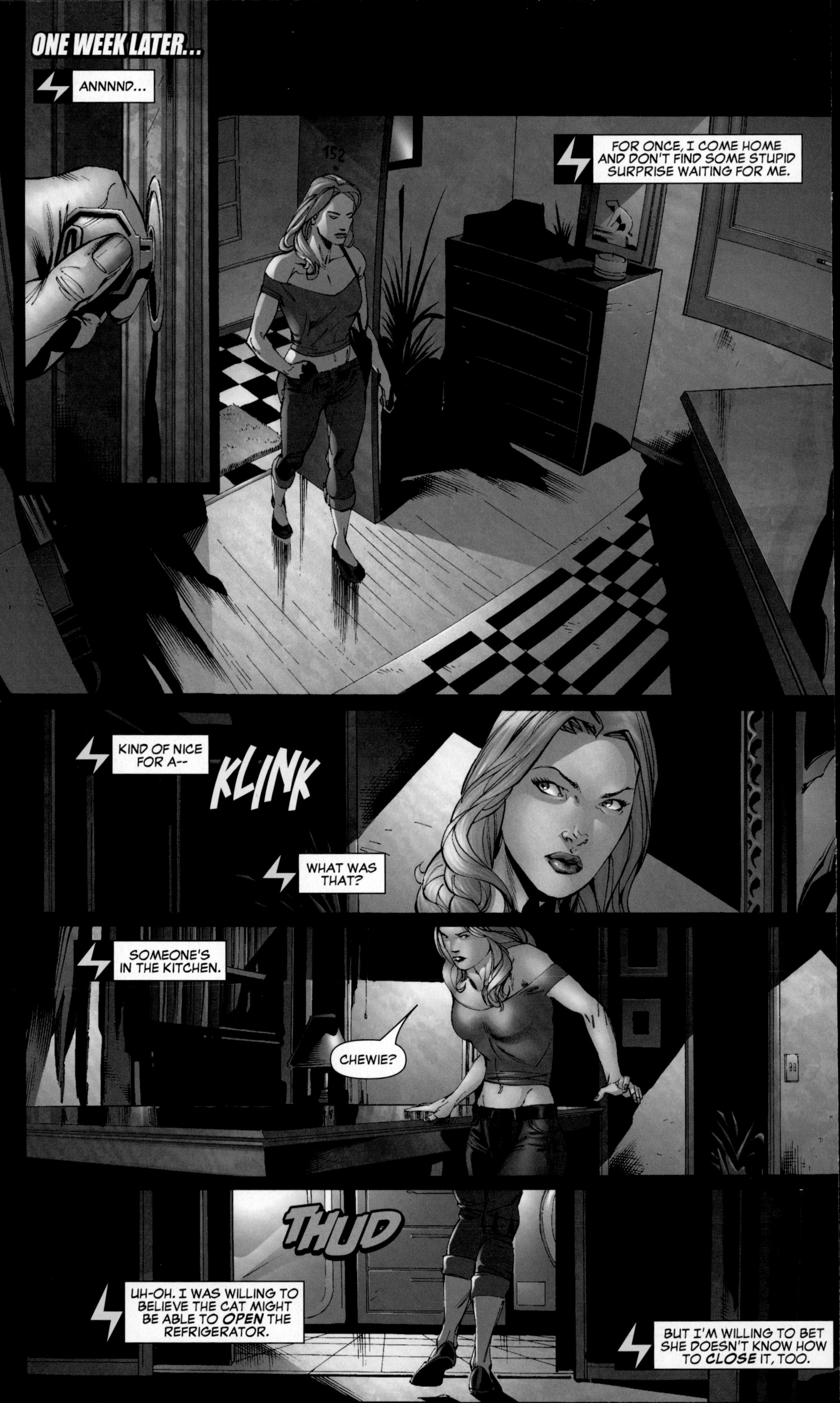
ONE WEEK LATER...
ANNNND...
FOR ONCE, I COME HOME AND DON'T FIND SOME STUPID SURPRISE WAITING FOR ME.
KIND OF NICE FOR A--
KLINK
WHAT WAS THAT?
SOMEONE'S IN THE KITCHEN.
CHEWIE?
THUD
UH-OH. I WAS WILLING TO BELIEVE THE CAT MIGHT BE ABLE TO OPEN THE REFRIGERATOR.
BUT I'M WILLING TO BET SHE DOESN'T KNOW HOW TO CLOSE IT, TOO.

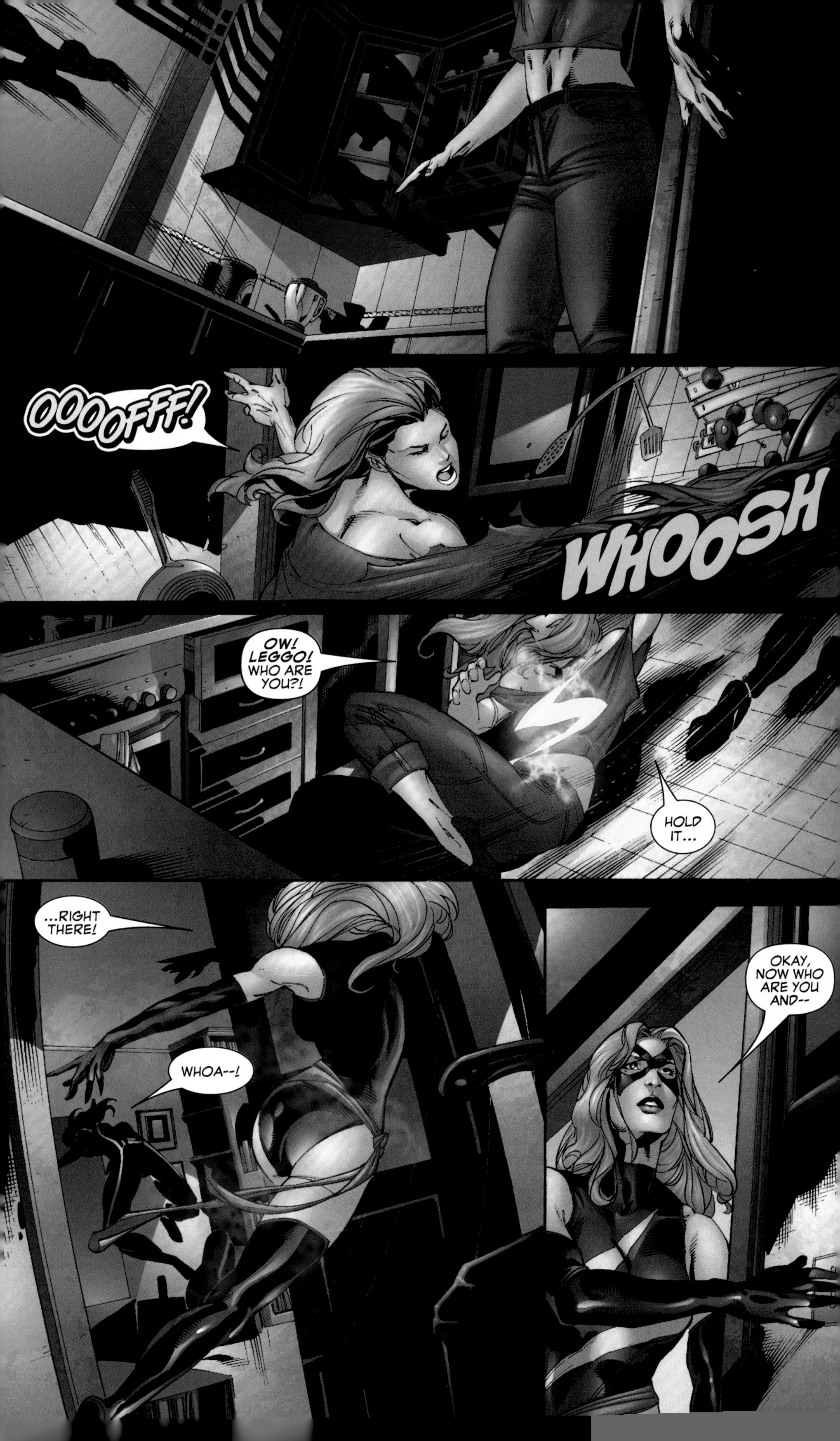

OOOOFFF!
WHOOSH
OW! LEGGO! WHO ARE YOU?!
HOLD IT...
...RIGHT THERE!
WHOA--!
OKAY, NOW WHO ARE YOU AND--

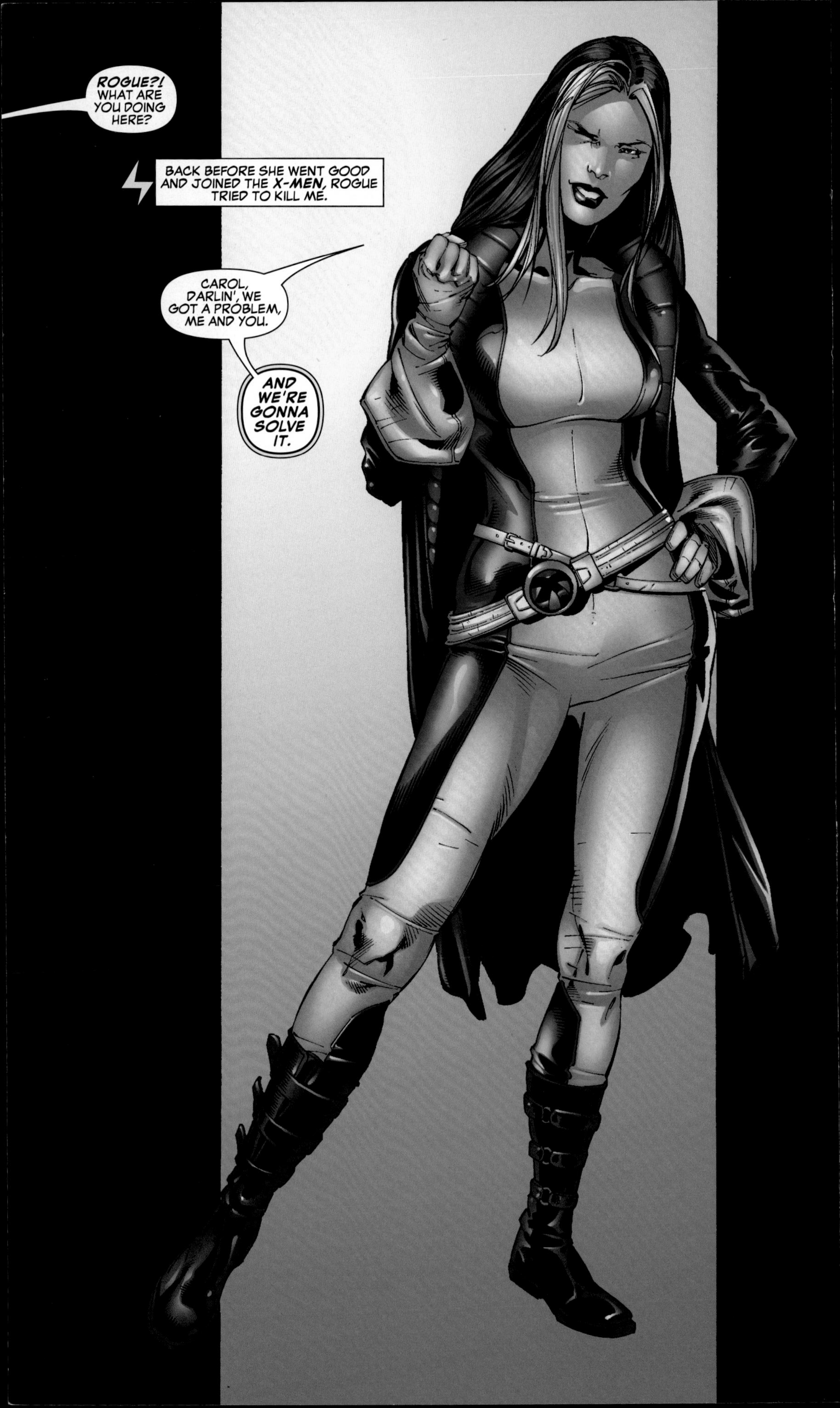
ROGUE?! WHAT ARE YOU DOING HERE?
BACK BEFORE SHE WENT GOOD AND JOINED THE X-MEN, ROGUE TRIED TO KILL ME.
CAROL, DARLIN', WE GOT A PROBLEM, ME AND YOU.
AND WE'RE GONNA SOLVE IT.

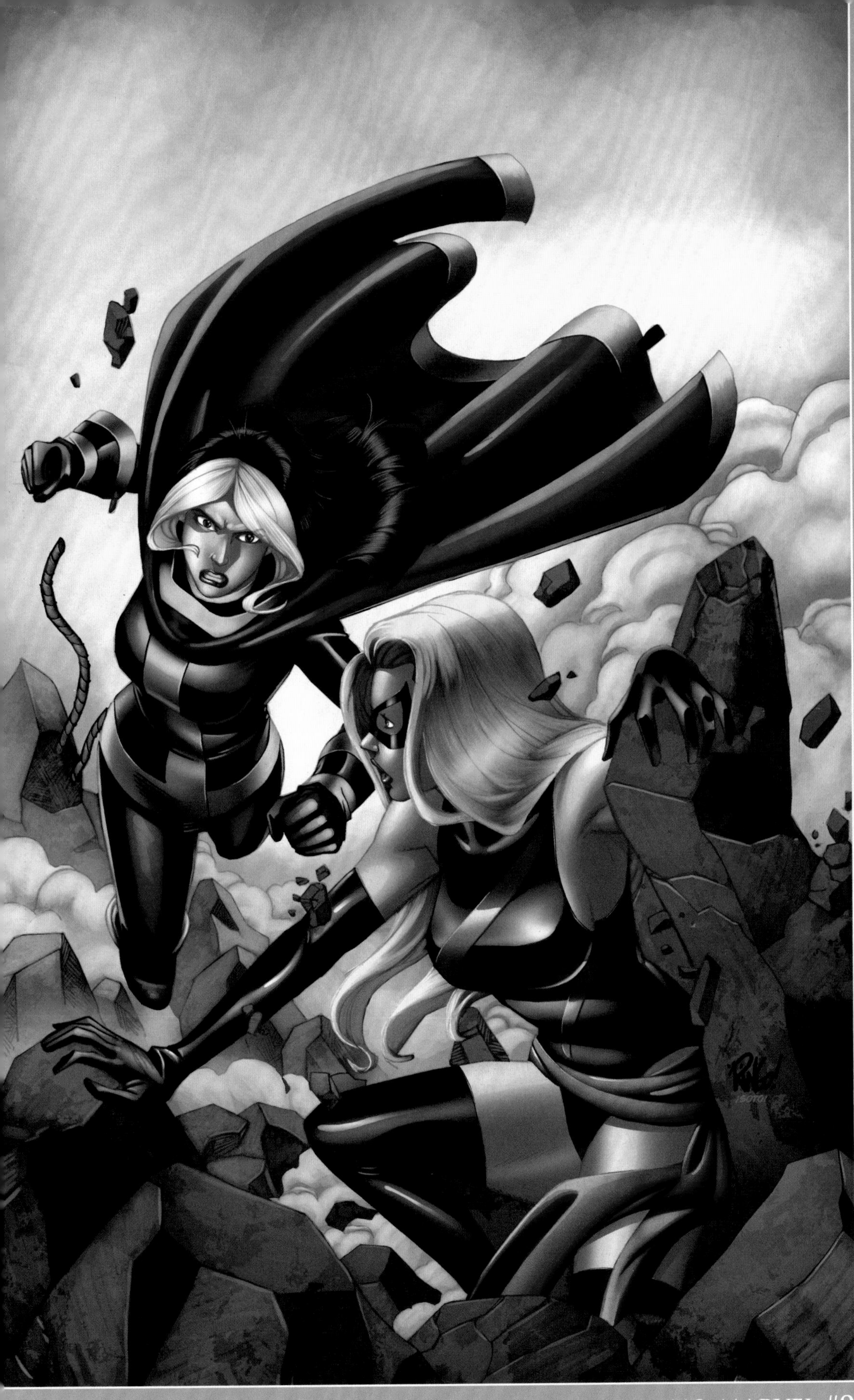

MS. MARVEL #9

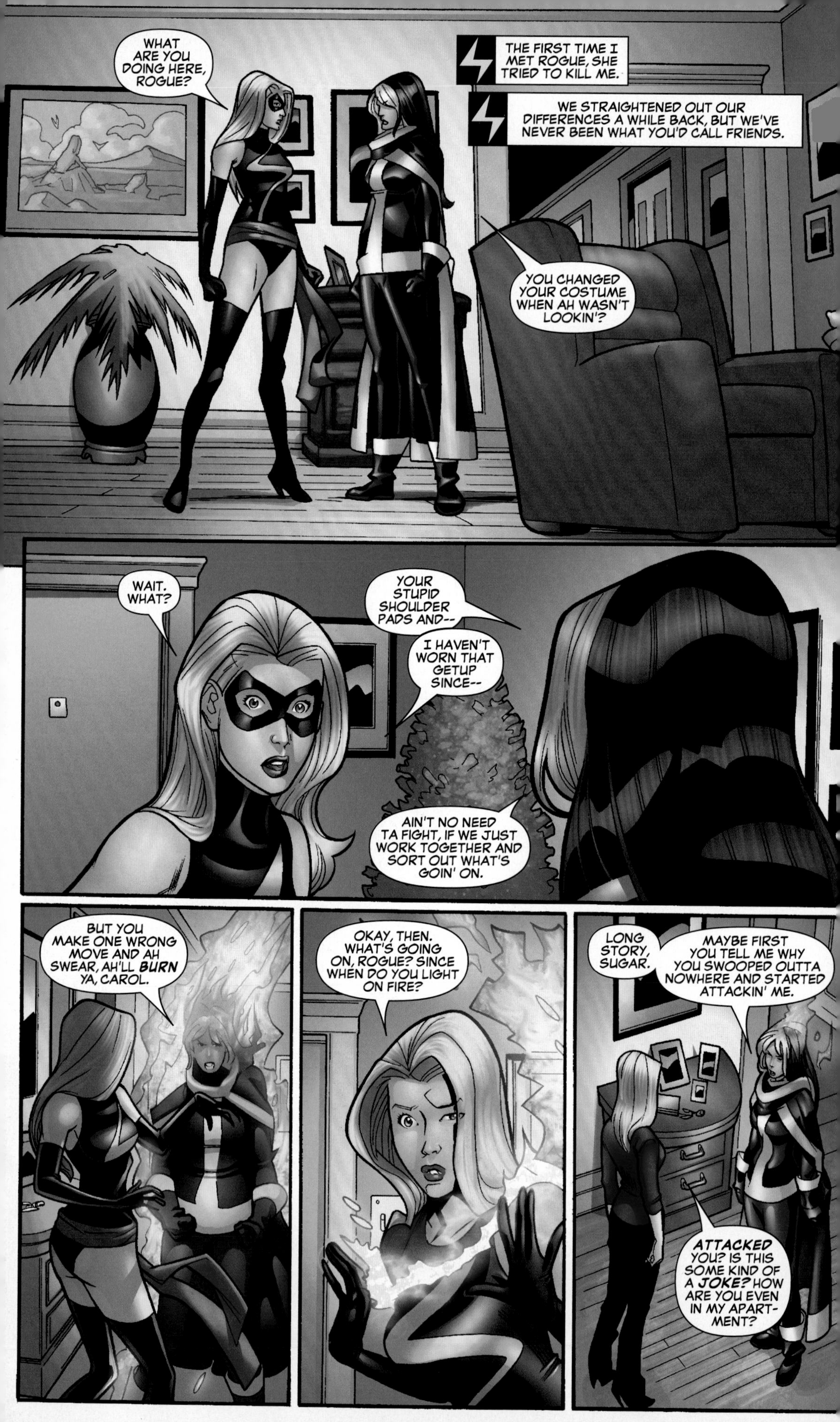
WHAT ARE YOU DOING HERE, ROGUE?
THE FIRST TIME I MET ROGUE, SHE TRIED TO KILL ME.
WE STRAIGHTENED OUT OUR DIFFERENCES A WHILE BACK, BUT WE'VE NEVER BEEN WHAT YOU'D CALL FRIENDS.
YOU CHANGED YOUR COSTUME WHEN AH WASN'T LOOKIN'?
WAIT. WHAT?
YOUR STUPID SHOULDER PADS AND--
I HAVEN'T WORN THAT GETUP SINCE--
AIN'T NO NEED TA FIGHT, IF WE JUST WORK TOGETHER AND SORT OUT WHAT'S GOIN' ON.
BUT YOU MAKE ONE WRONG MOVE AND AH SWEAR, AH'LL **BURN** YA, CAROL.
OKAY, THEN. WHAT'S GOING ON, ROGUE? SINCE WHEN DO YOU LIGHT ON FIRE?
LONG STORY, SUGAR.
MAYBE FIRST YOU TELL ME WHY YOU SWOOPED OUTTA NOWHERE AND STARTED ATTACKIN' ME.
ATTACKED YOU? IS THIS SOME KIND OF A **JOKE?** HOW ARE YOU EVEN IN MY APART-MENT?

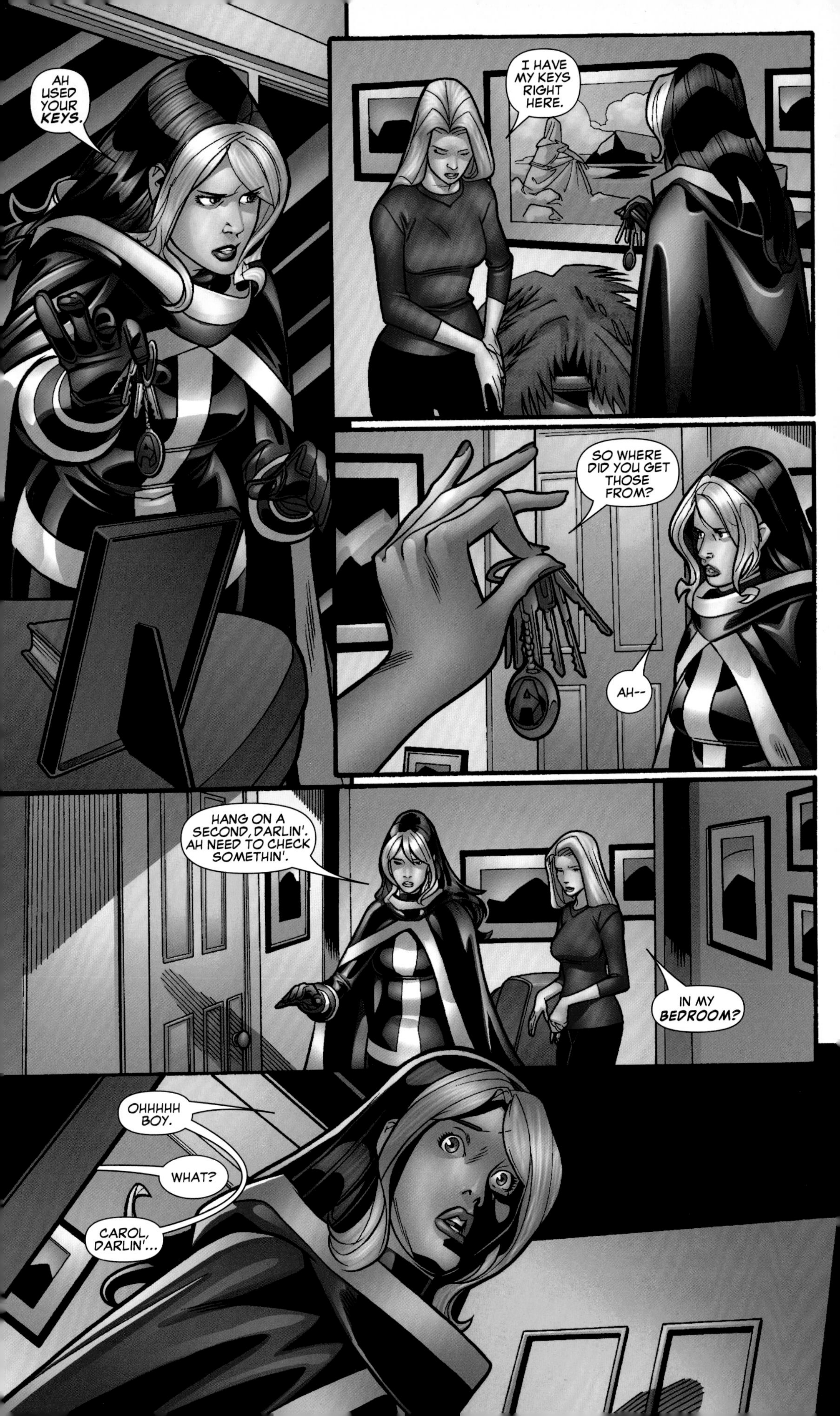
AH USED YOUR KEYS.
I HAVE MY KEYS RIGHT HERE.
SO WHERE DID YOU GET THOSE FROM?
AH--
HANG ON A SECOND, DARLIN'. AH NEED TO CHECK SOMETHIN'.
IN MY BEDROOM?
OHHHHH BOY.
WHAT?
CAROL, DARLIN'...

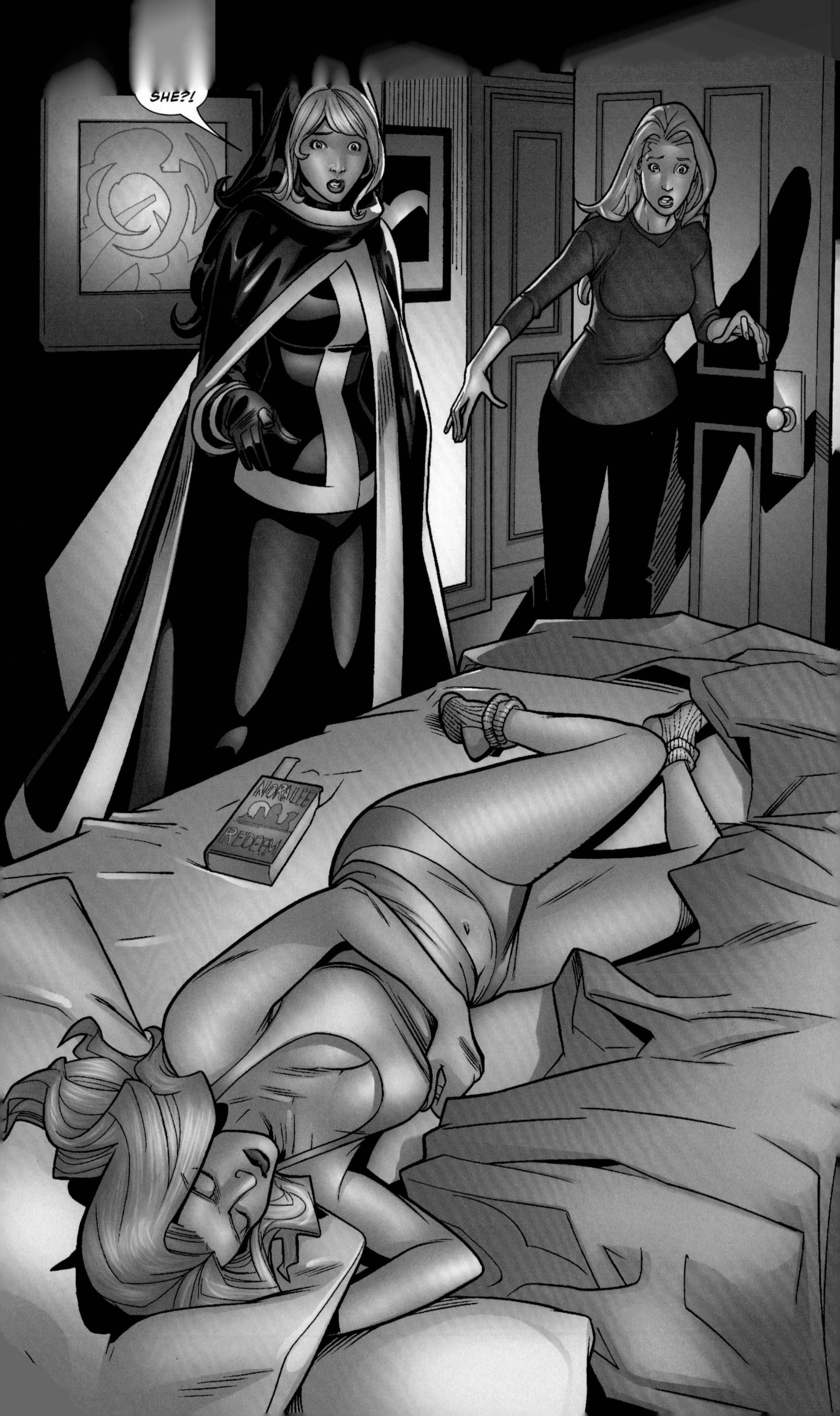
SHE?!
NORA LEE
REDEEM

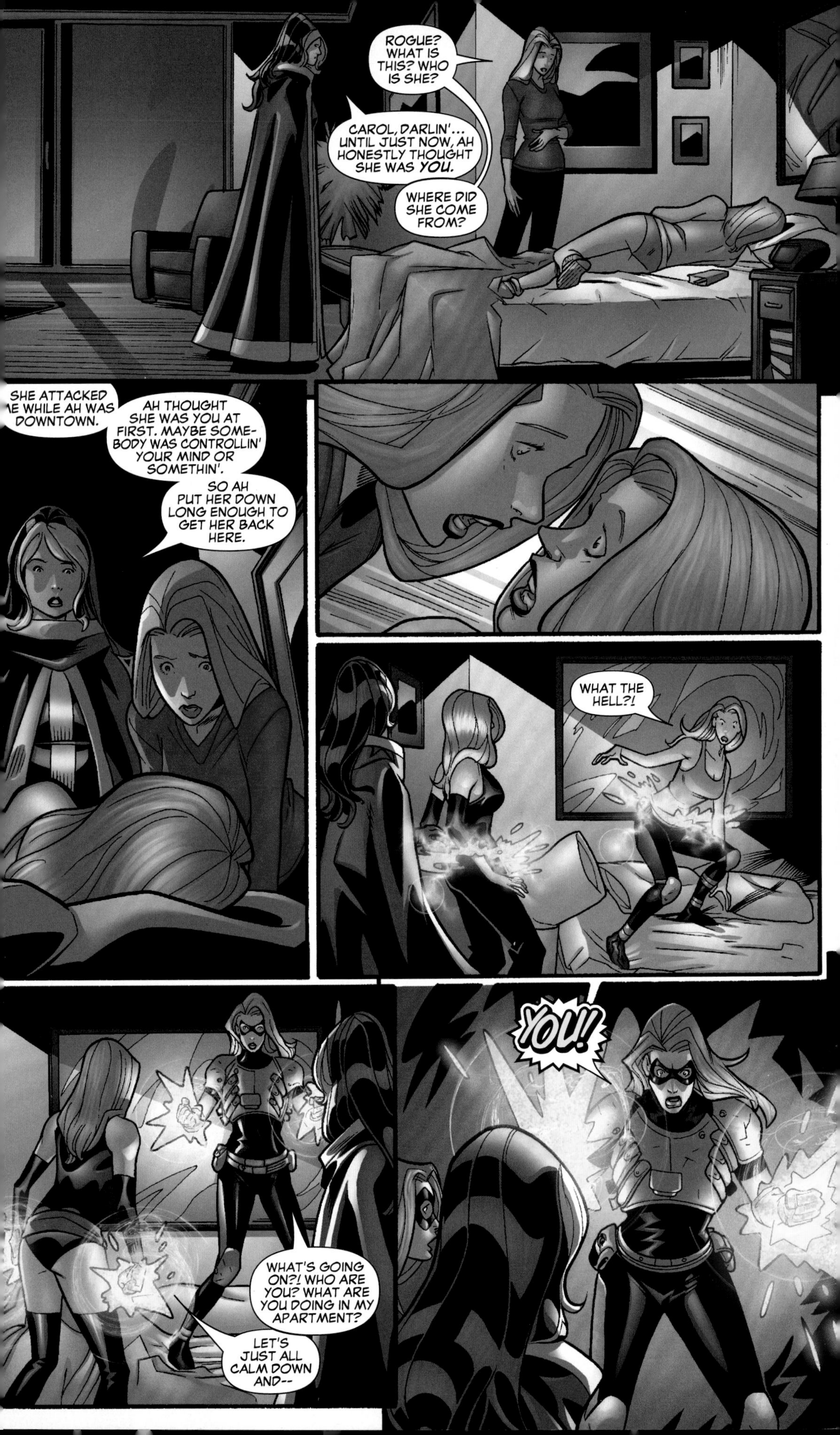

ROGUE? WHAT IS THIS? WHO IS SHE?
CAROL, DARLIN'... UNTIL JUST NOW, AH HONESTLY THOUGHT SHE WAS *YOU.*
WHERE DID SHE COME FROM?
SHE ATTACKED ME WHILE AH WAS DOWNTOWN.
AH THOUGHT SHE WAS YOU AT FIRST. MAYBE SOME-BODY WAS CONTROLLIN' YOUR MIND OR SOMETHIN'.
SO AH PUT HER DOWN LONG ENOUGH TO GET HER BACK HERE.
WHAT THE HELL?!
WHAT'S GOING ON?! WHO ARE YOU? WHAT ARE YOU DOING IN MY APARTMENT?
LET'S JUST ALL CALM DOWN AND--
YOU!!

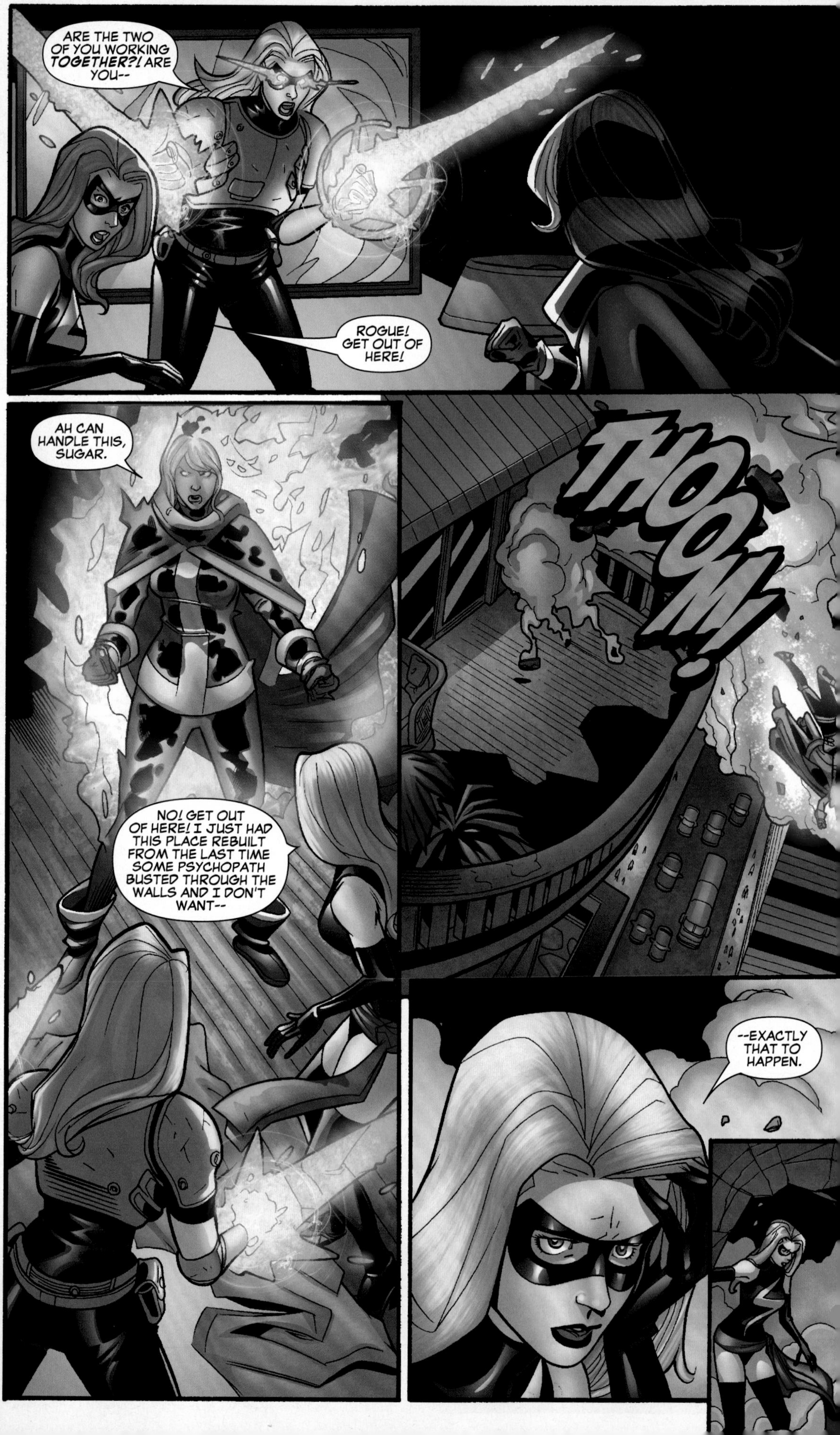
ARE THE TWO OF YOU WORKING *TOGETHER?!* ARE YOU--
ROGUE! GET OUT OF HERE!
AH CAN HANDLE THIS, SUGAR.
NO! GET OUT OF HERE! I JUST HAD THIS PLACE REBUILT FROM THE LAST TIME SOME PSYCHOPATH BUSTED THROUGH THE WALLS AND I DON'T WANT--
THOOM!
--EXACTLY THAT TO HAPPEN.

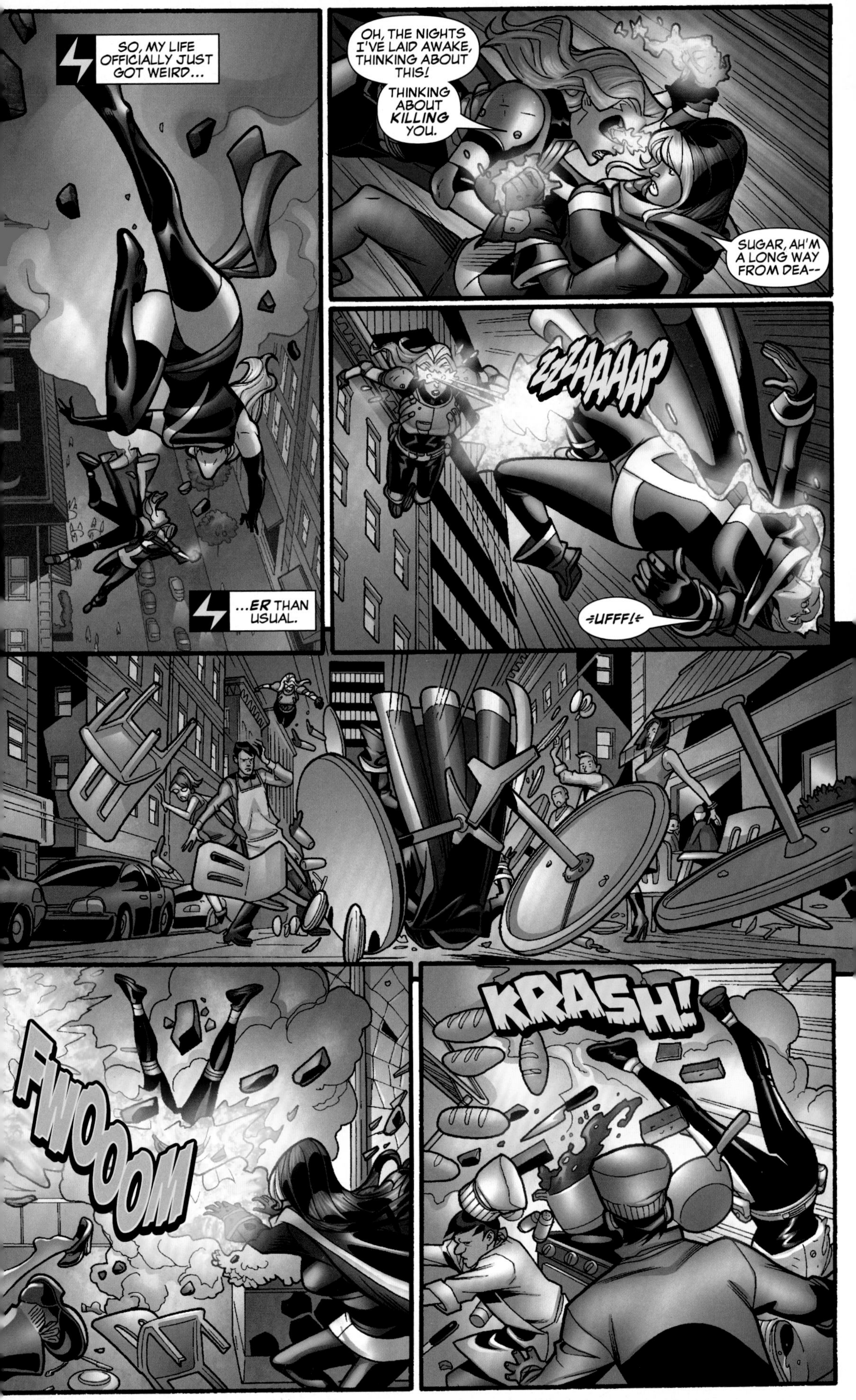

SO, MY LIFE OFFICIALLY JUST GOT WEIRD...
...ER THAN USUAL.
OH, THE NIGHTS I'VE LAID AWAKE, THINKING ABOUT THIS!
THINKING ABOUT KILLING YOU.
SUGAR, AH'M A LONG WAY FROM DEA--
ZZZAAAAP
UFFF!
FWOOOOM
KRASH!

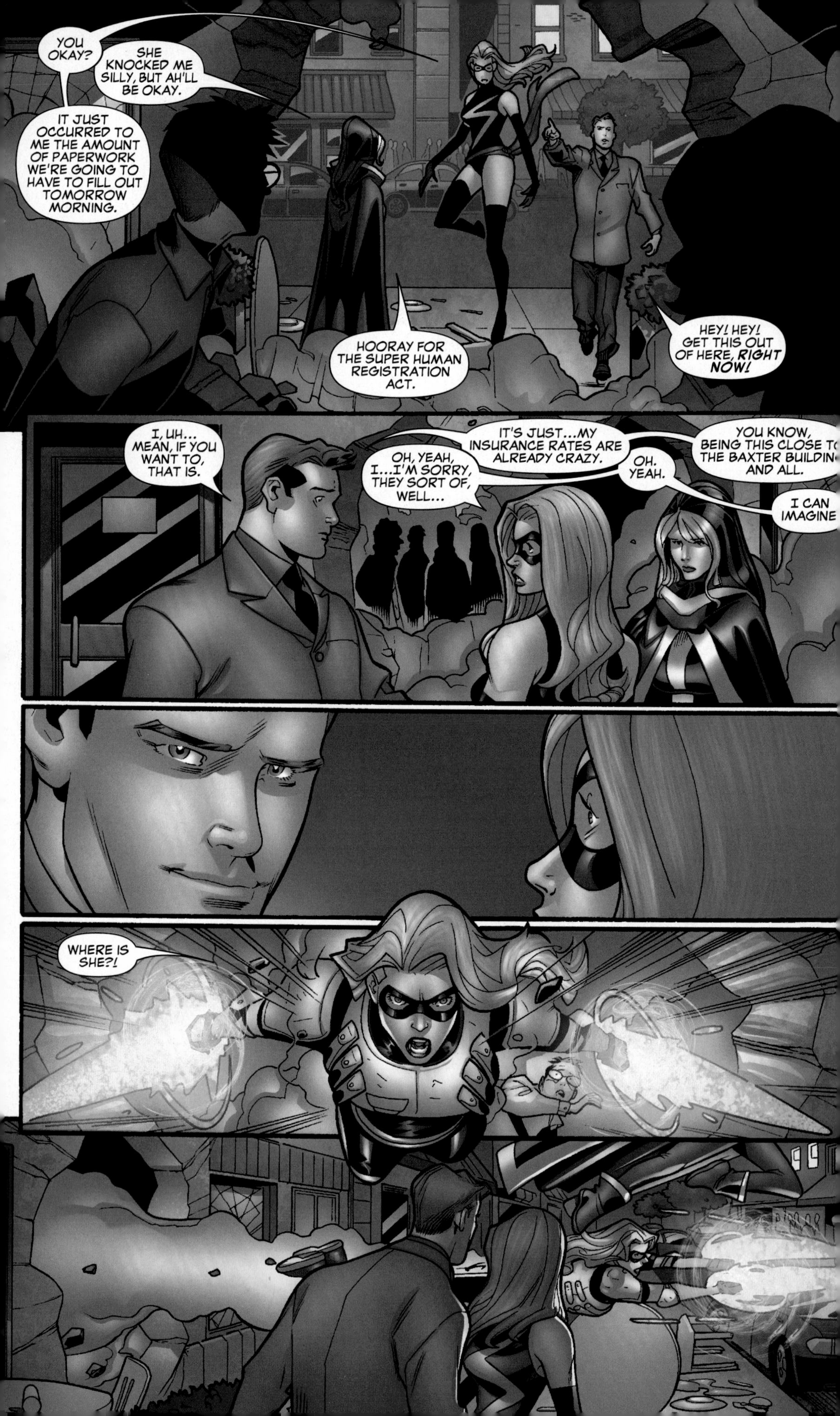
YOU OKAY?
SHE KNOCKED ME SILLY, BUT AH'LL BE OKAY.
IT JUST OCCURRED TO ME THE AMOUNT OF PAPERWORK WE'RE GOING TO HAVE TO FILL OUT TOMORROW MORNING.
HOORAY FOR THE SUPER HUMAN REGISTRATION ACT.
HEY! HEY! GET THIS OUT OF HERE, **RIGHT NOW!**
I, UH... MEAN, IF YOU WANT TO, THAT IS.
OH, YEAH, I...I'M SORRY, THEY SORT OF, WELL...
IT'S JUST...MY INSURANCE RATES ARE ALREADY CRAZY.
OH. YEAH.
YOU KNOW, BEING THIS CLOSE T THE BAXTER BUILDIN AND ALL.
I CAN IMAGINE
WHERE IS SHE?!

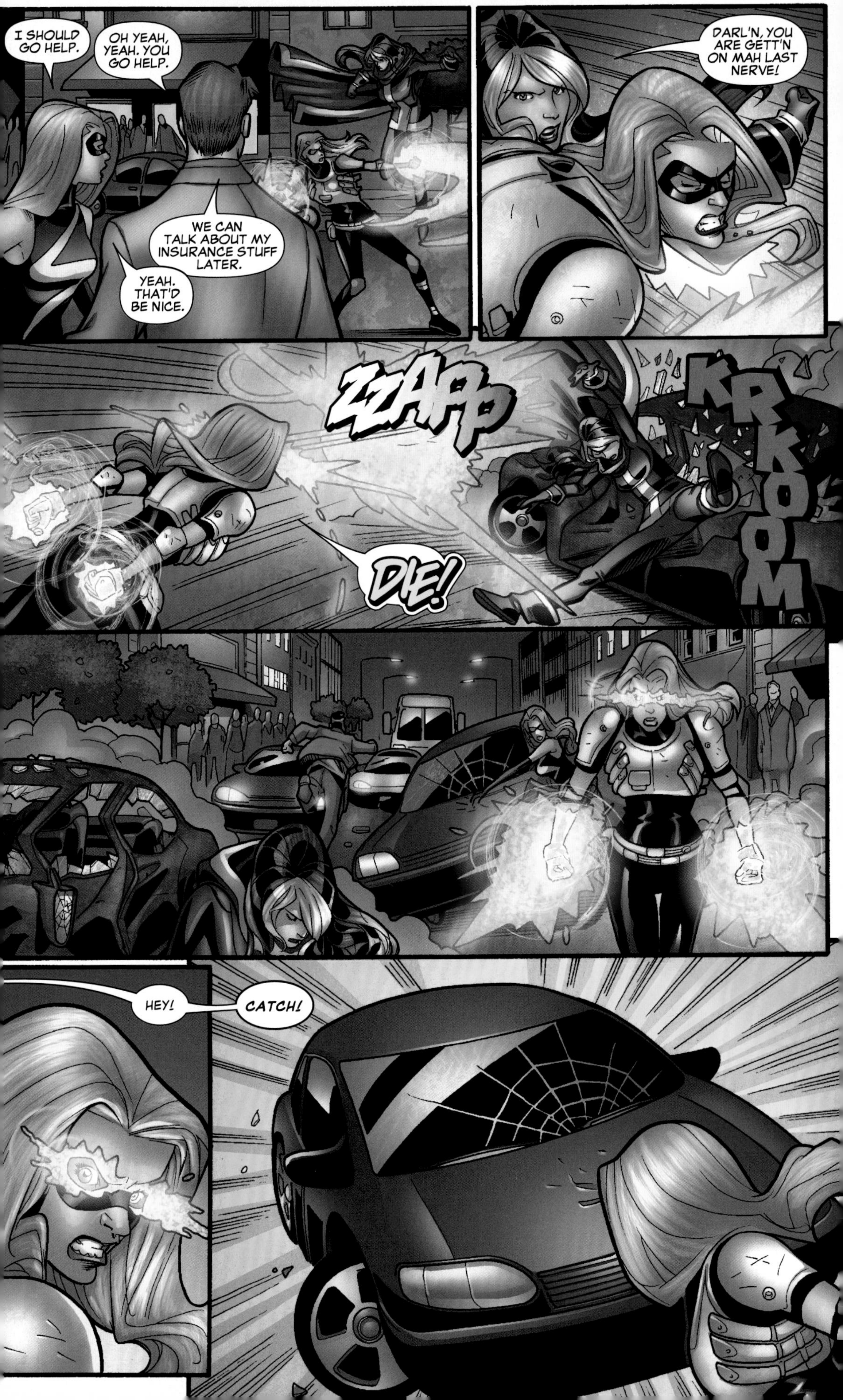
I SHOULD GO HELP.
OH YEAH, YEAH. YOU GO HELP.
WE CAN TALK ABOUT MY INSURANCE STUFF LATER.
YEAH. THAT'D BE NICE.
DARL'N, YOU ARE GETT'N ON MAH LAST NERVE!
ZZARP
KRKOOM
DIE!
HEY!
CATCH!

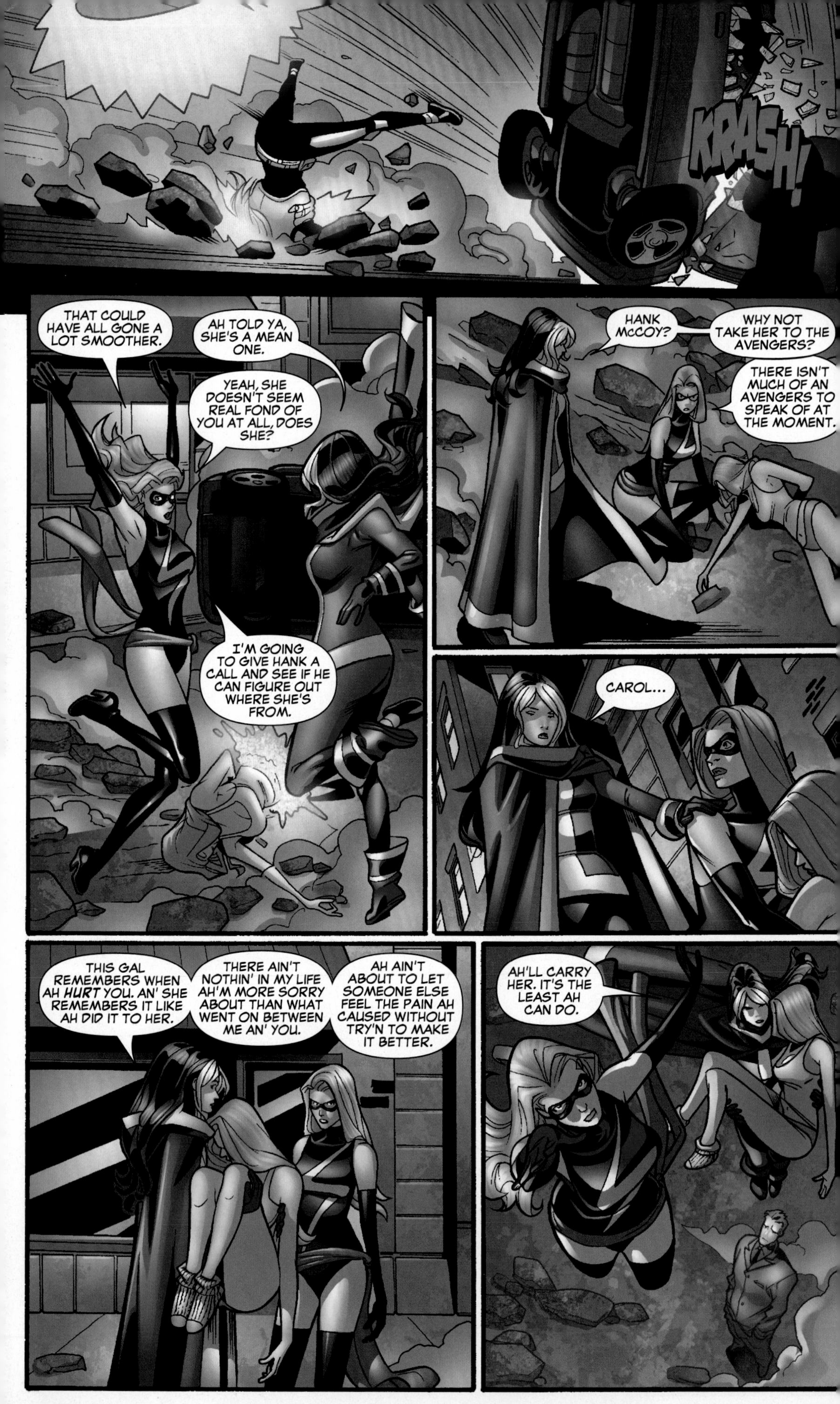
KRASH!
THAT COULD HAVE ALL GONE A LOT SMOOTHER.
AH TOLD YA, SHE'S A MEAN ONE.
YEAH, SHE DOESN'T SEEM REAL FOND OF YOU AT ALL, DOES SHE?
I'M GOING TO GIVE HANK A CALL AND SEE IF HE CAN FIGURE OUT WHERE SHE'S FROM.
HANK McCOY?
WHY NOT TAKE HER TO THE AVENGERS?
THERE ISN'T MUCH OF AN AVENGERS TO SPEAK OF AT THE MOMENT.
CAROL...
THIS GAL REMEMBERS WHEN AH *HURT* YOU. AN' SHE REMEMBERS IT LIKE AH DID IT TO HER.
THERE AIN'T NOTHIN' IN MY LIFE AH'M MORE SORRY ABOUT THAN WHAT WENT ON BETWEEN ME AN' YOU.
AH AIN'T ABOUT TO LET SOMEONE ELSE FEEL THE PAIN AH CAUSED WITHOUT TRY'N TO MAKE IT BETTER.
AH'LL CARRY HER. IT'S THE LEAST AH CAN DO.

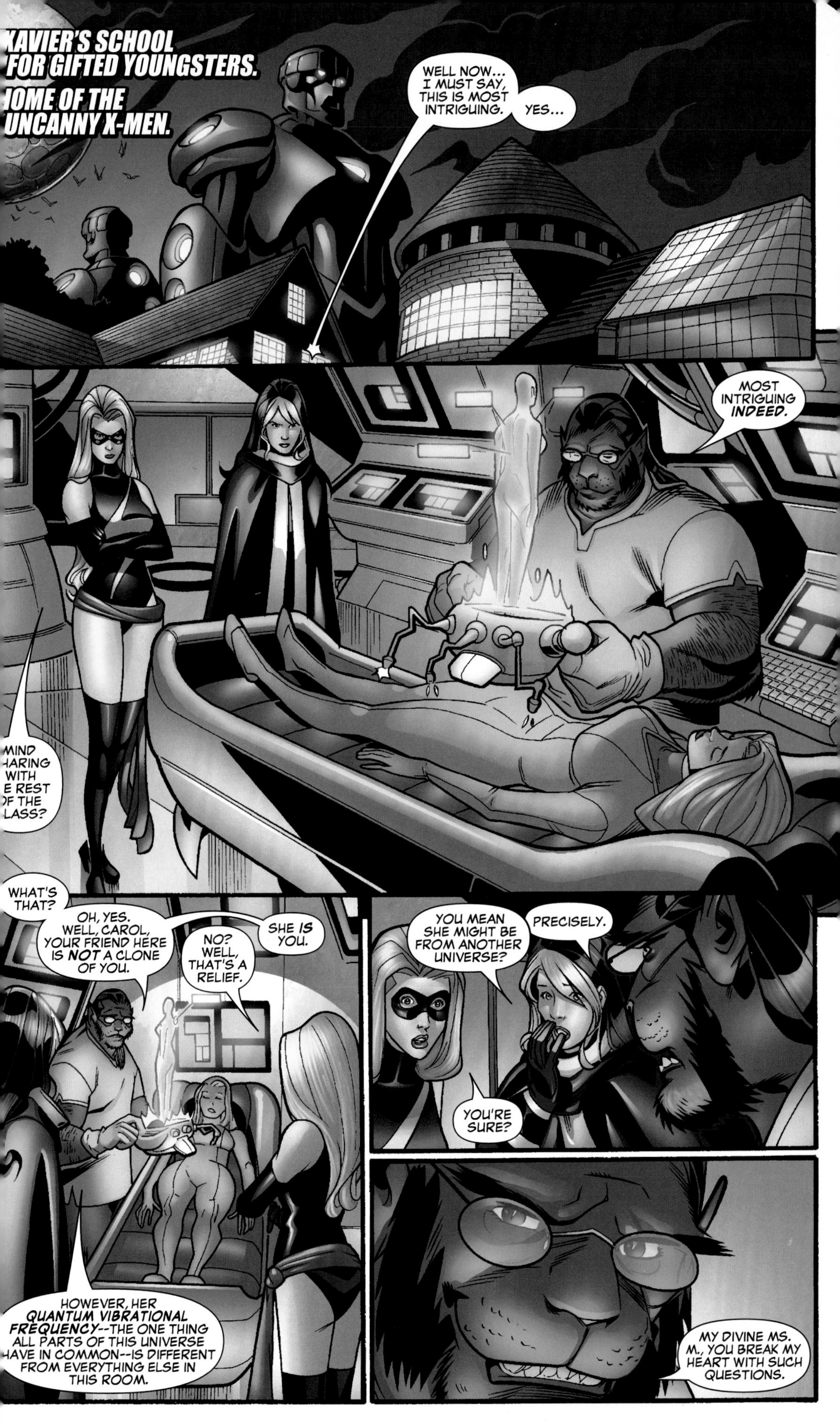

XAVIER'S SCHOOL FOR GIFTED YOUNGSTERS.
HOME OF THE UNCANNY X-MEN.
WELL NOW... I MUST SAY, THIS IS MOST INTRIGUING.
YES...
MOST INTRIGUING INDEED.
MIND SHARING WITH THE REST OF THE CLASS?
WHAT'S THAT?
OH, YES. WELL, CAROL, YOUR FRIEND HERE IS NOT A CLONE OF YOU.
NO? WELL, THAT'S A RELIEF.
SHE IS YOU.
HOWEVER, HER QUANTUM VIBRATIONAL FREQUENCY--THE ONE THING ALL PARTS OF THIS UNIVERSE HAVE IN COMMON--IS DIFFERENT FROM EVERYTHING ELSE IN THIS ROOM.
YOU MEAN SHE MIGHT BE FROM ANOTHER UNIVERSE?
PRECISELY.
YOU'RE SURE?
MY DIVINE MS. M., YOU BREAK MY HEART WITH SUCH QUESTIONS.

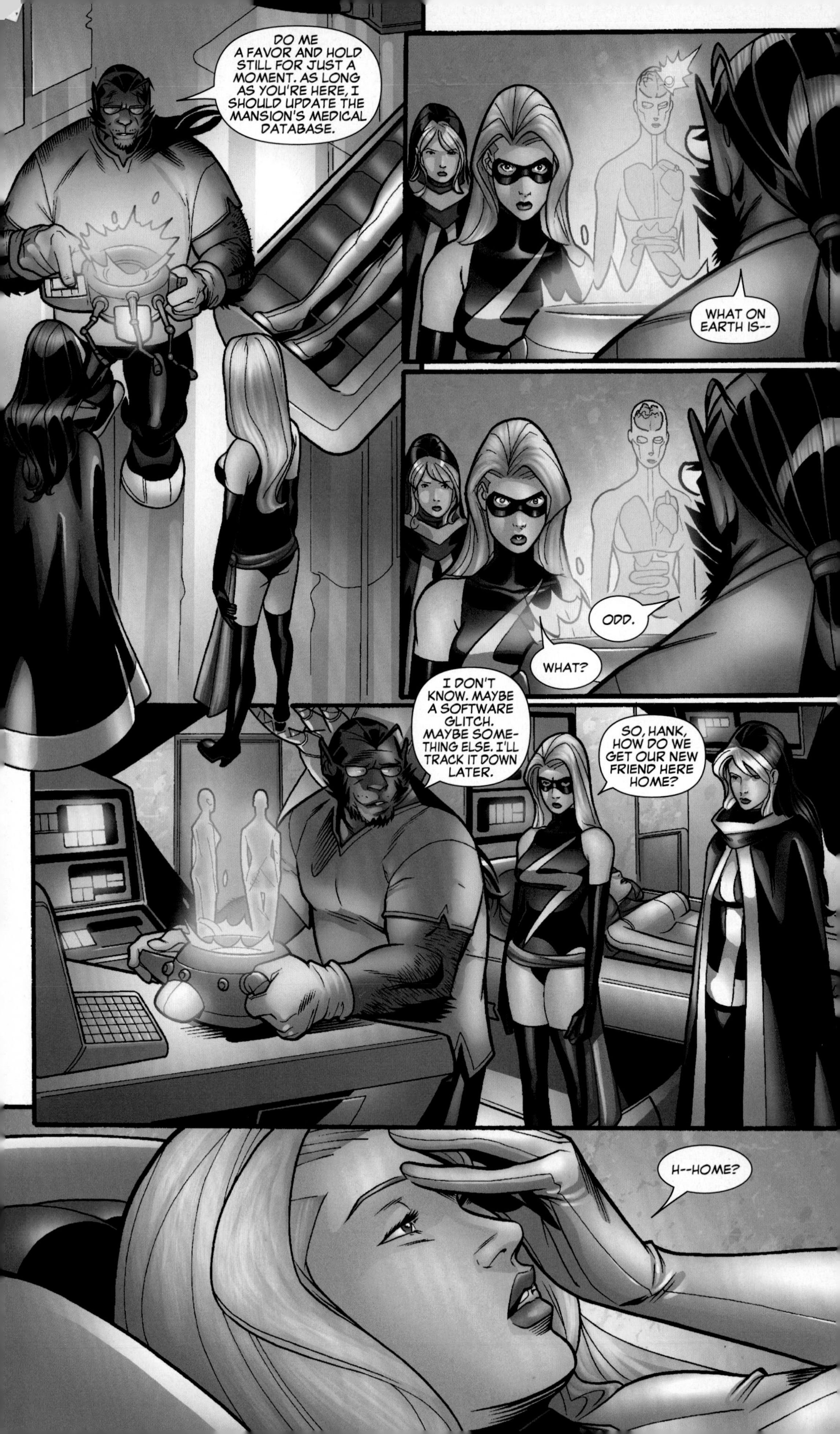
DO ME A FAVOR AND HOLD STILL FOR JUST A MOMENT. AS LONG AS YOU'RE HERE, I SHOULD UPDATE THE MANSION'S MEDICAL DATABASE.
WHAT ON EARTH IS--
ODD.
WHAT?
I DON'T KNOW. MAYBE A SOFTWARE GLITCH. MAYBE SOMETHING ELSE. I'LL TRACK IT DOWN LATER.
SO, HANK, HOW DO WE GET OUR NEW FRIEND HERE HOME?
H--HOME?

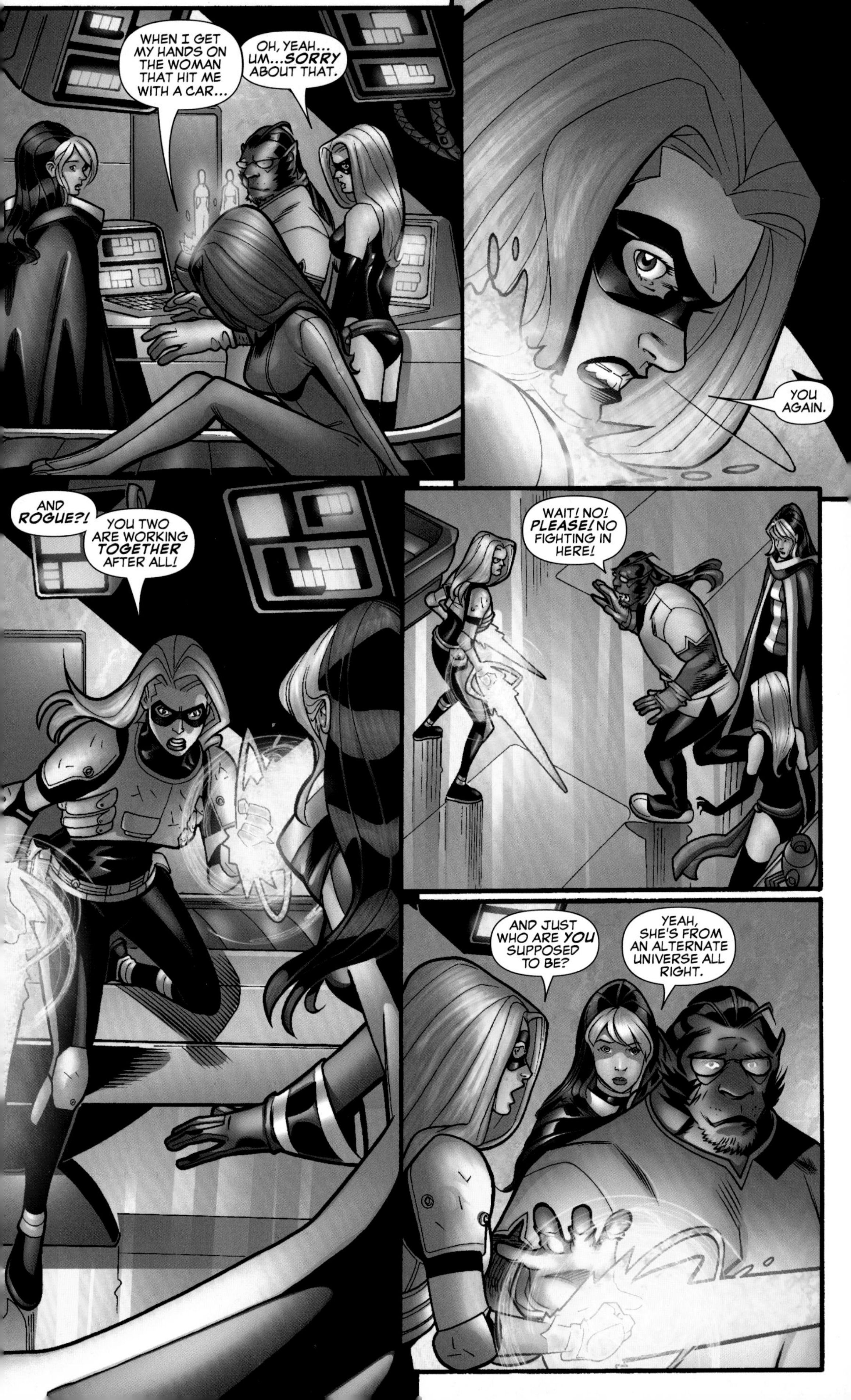
WHEN I GET MY HANDS ON THE WOMAN THAT HIT ME WITH A CAR...
OH, YEAH... UM...SORRY ABOUT THAT.
YOU AGAIN.
AND ROGUE?!
YOU TWO ARE WORKING TOGETHER AFTER ALL!
WAIT! NO! PLEASE! NO FIGHTING IN HERE!
AND JUST WHO ARE YOU SUPPOSED TO BE?
YEAH, SHE'S FROM AN ALTERNATE UNIVERSE ALL RIGHT.

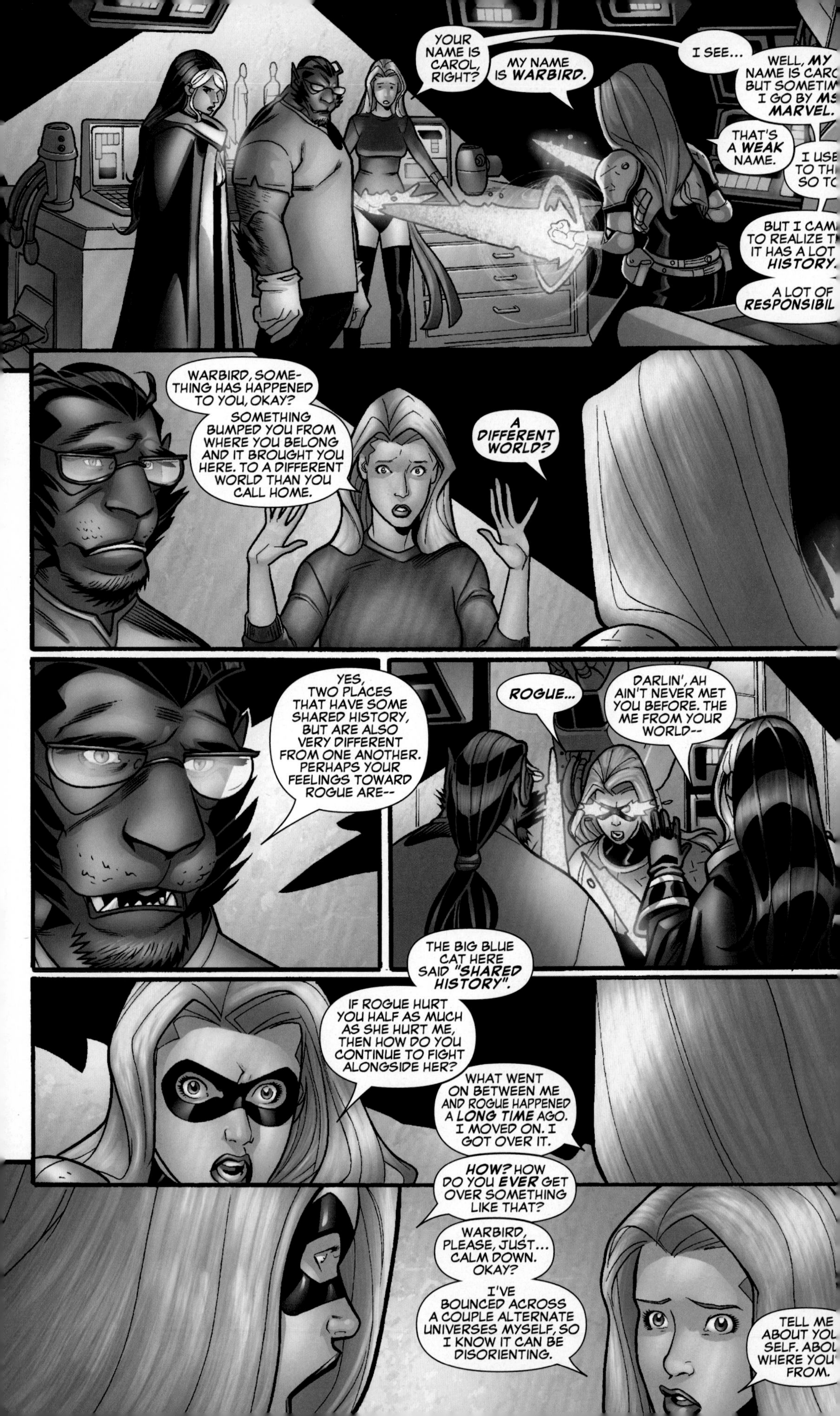

YOUR NAME IS CAROL, RIGHT?
MY NAME IS WARBIRD.
I SEE...
WELL, MY NAME IS CARC BUT SOMETIM I GO BY MS MARVEL.
THAT'S A WEAK NAME.
I USE TO TH SO TO
BUT I CAM TO REALIZE T IT HAS A LOT HISTORY.
A LOT OF RESPONSIBIL
WARBIRD, SOMETHING HAS HAPPENED TO YOU, OKAY?
SOMETHING BUMPED YOU FROM WHERE YOU BELONG AND IT BROUGHT YOU HERE. TO A DIFFERENT WORLD THAN YOU CALL HOME.
A DIFFERENT WORLD?
YES, TWO PLACES THAT HAVE SOME SHARED HISTORY, BUT ARE ALSO VERY DIFFERENT FROM ONE ANOTHER. PERHAPS YOUR FEELINGS TOWARD ROGUE ARE--
ROGUE...
DARLIN', AH AIN'T NEVER MET YOU BEFORE. THE ME FROM YOUR WORLD--
THE BIG BLUE CAT HERE SAID "SHARED HISTORY".
IF ROGUE HURT YOU HALF AS MUCH AS SHE HURT ME, THEN HOW DO YOU CONTINUE TO FIGHT ALONGSIDE HER?
WHAT WENT ON BETWEEN ME AND ROGUE HAPPENED A LONG TIME AGO. I MOVED ON. I GOT OVER IT.
HOW? HOW DO YOU EVER GET OVER SOMETHING LIKE THAT?
WARBIRD, PLEASE, JUST... CALM DOWN. OKAY?
I'VE BOUNCED ACROSS A COUPLE ALTERNATE UNIVERSES MYSELF, SO I KNOW IT CAN BE DISORIENTING.
TELL ME ABOUT YOU SELF. ABOU WHERE YOU FROM.

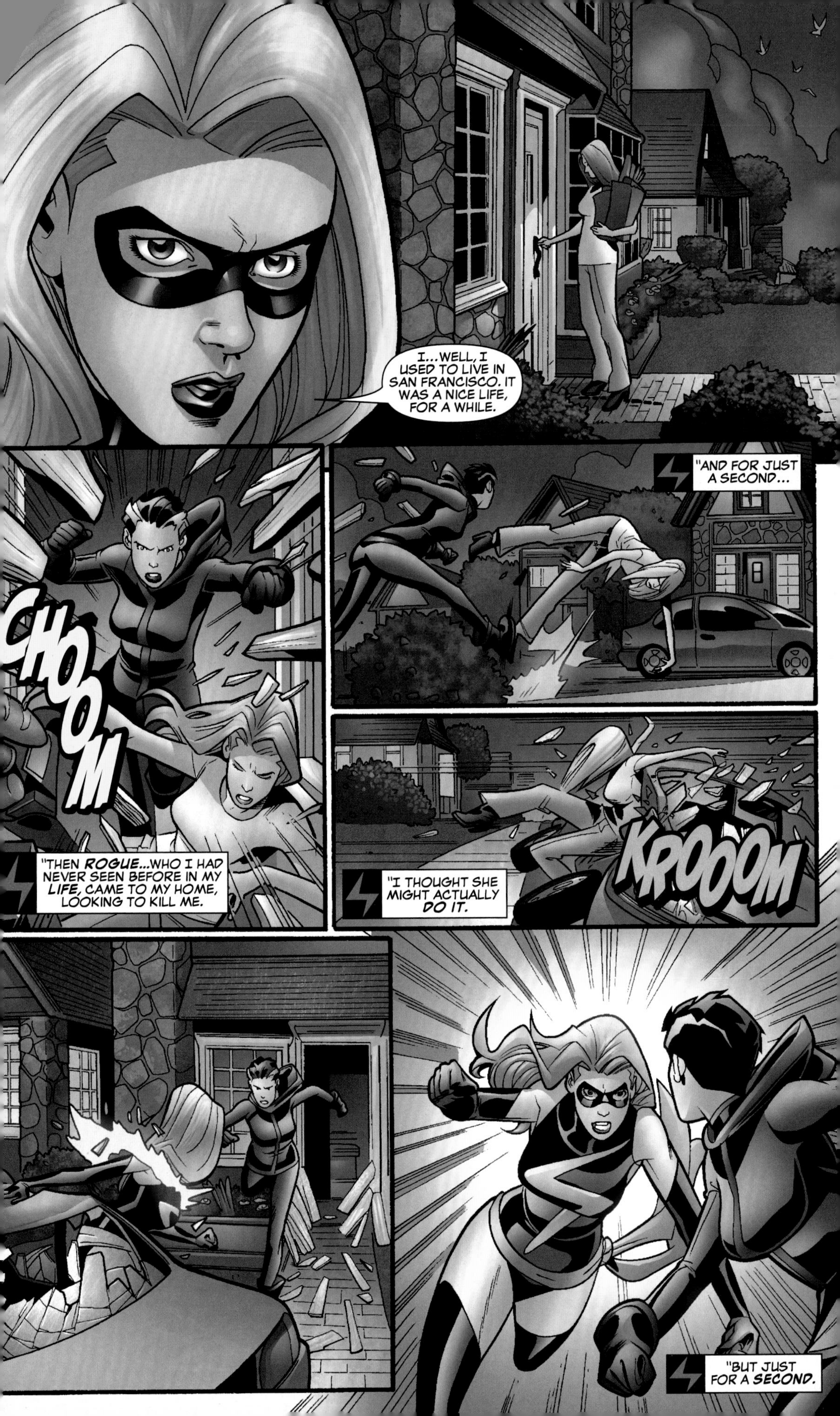
I...WELL, I USED TO LIVE IN SAN FRANCISCO. IT WAS A NICE LIFE, FOR A WHILE.
"THEN ROGUE...WHO I HAD NEVER SEEN BEFORE IN MY LIFE, CAME TO MY HOME, LOOKING TO KILL ME.
CHOOM
"AND FOR JUST A SECOND...
"I THOUGHT SHE MIGHT ACTUALLY DO IT.
KROOOM
"BUT JUST FOR A SECOND.

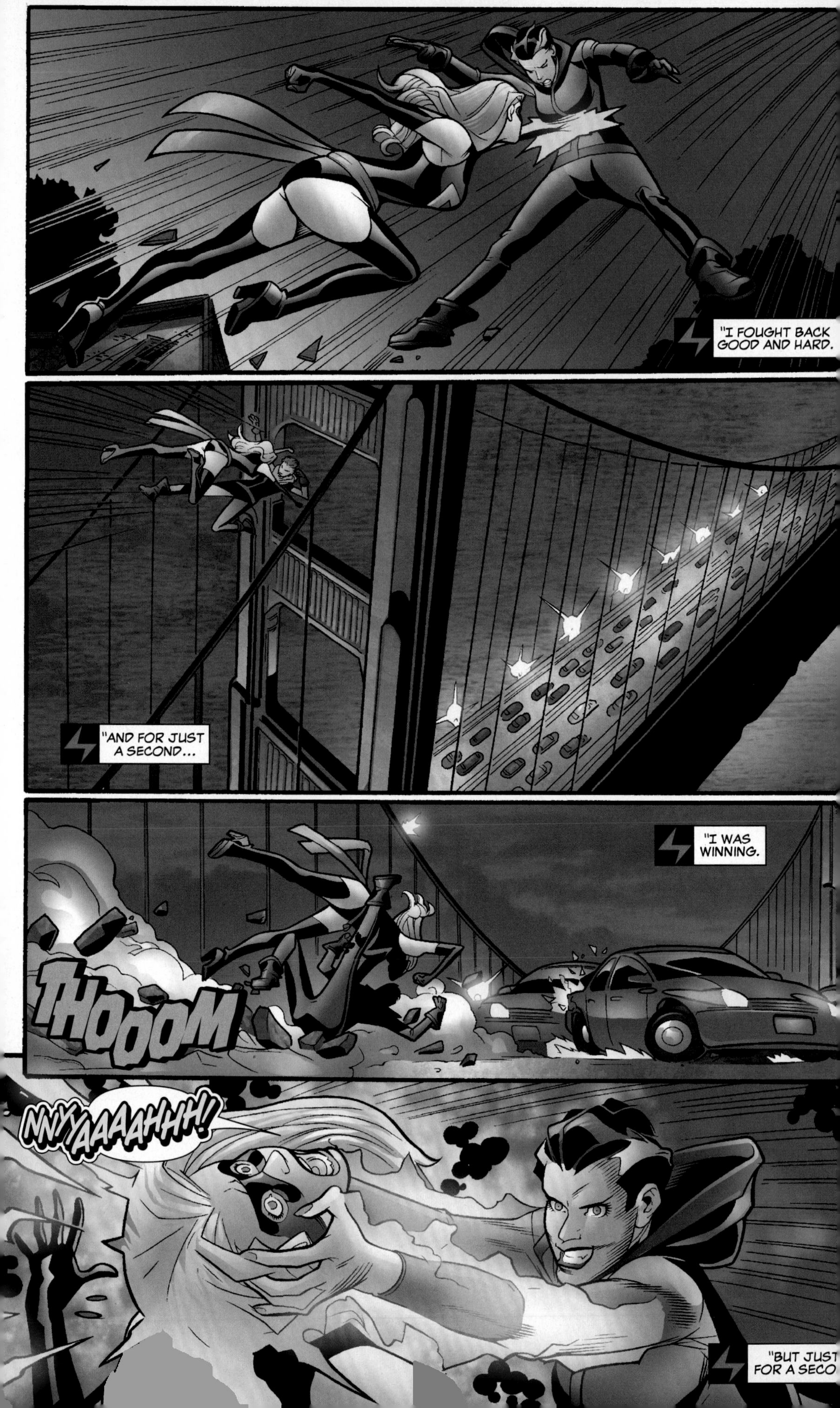

"I FOUGHT BACK GOOD AND HARD.
"AND FOR JUST A SECOND...
"I WAS WINNING.
THOOOM
NNYAAAAHHH!
"BUT JUST FOR A SECO

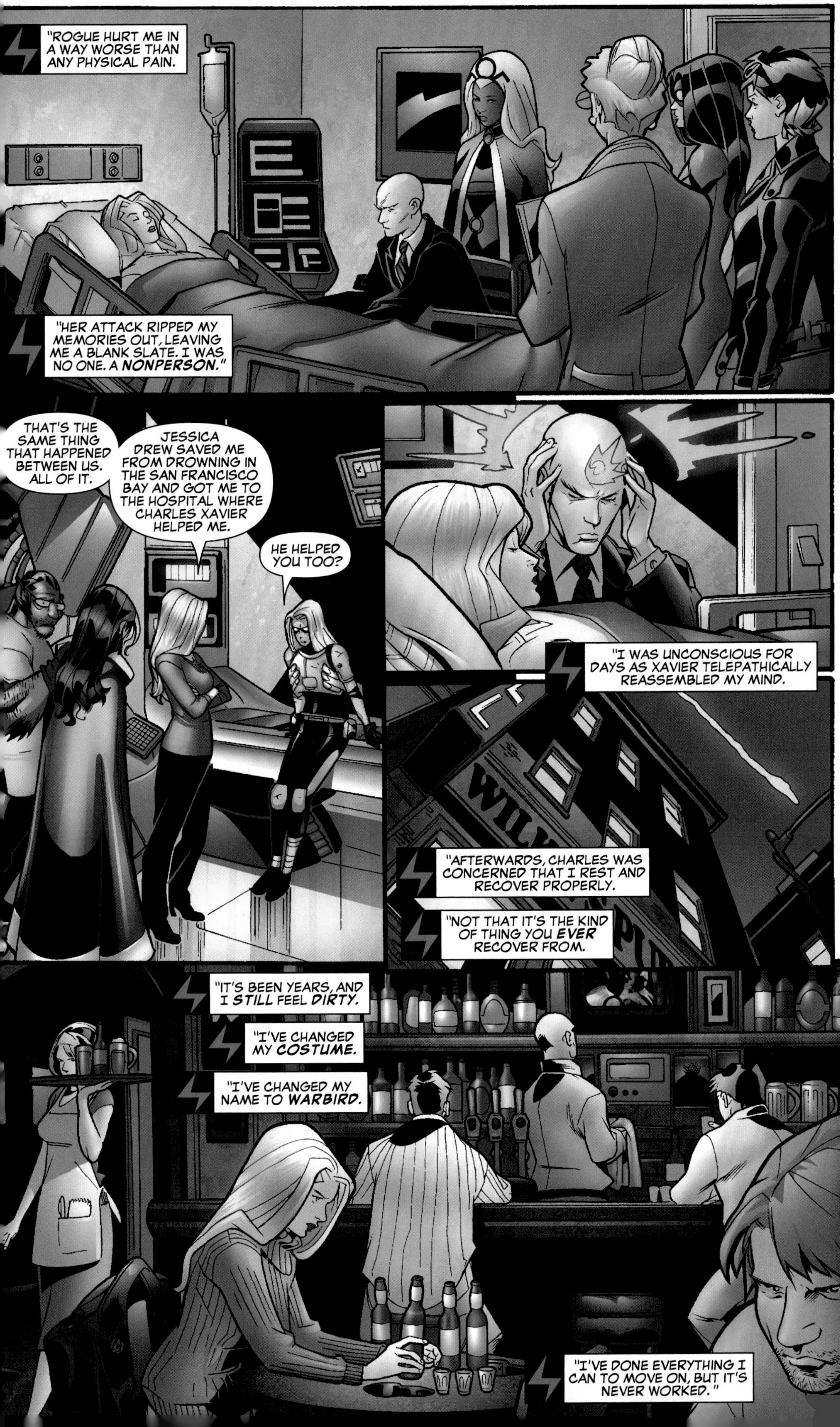
"ROGUE HURT ME IN A WAY WORSE THAN ANY PHYSICAL PAIN.
"HER ATTACK RIPPED MY MEMORIES OUT, LEAVING ME A BLANK SLATE. I WAS NO ONE. A NONPERSON."
THAT'S THE SAME THING THAT HAPPENED BETWEEN US. ALL OF IT.
JESSICA DREW SAVED ME FROM DROWNING IN THE SAN FRANCISCO BAY AND GOT ME TO THE HOSPITAL WHERE CHARLES XAVIER HELPED ME.
HE HELPED YOU TOO?
"I WAS UNCONSCIOUS FOR DAYS AS XAVIER TELEPATHICALLY REASSEMBLED MY MIND.
"AFTERWARDS, CHARLES WAS CONCERNED THAT I REST AND RECOVER PROPERLY.
"NOT THAT IT'S THE KIND OF THING YOU EVER RECOVER FROM.
"IT'S BEEN YEARS, AND I STILL FEEL DIRTY.
"I'VE CHANGED MY COSTUME.
"I'VE CHANGED MY NAME TO WARBIRD.
"I'VE DONE EVERYTHING I CAN TO MOVE ON, BUT IT'S NEVER WORKED."

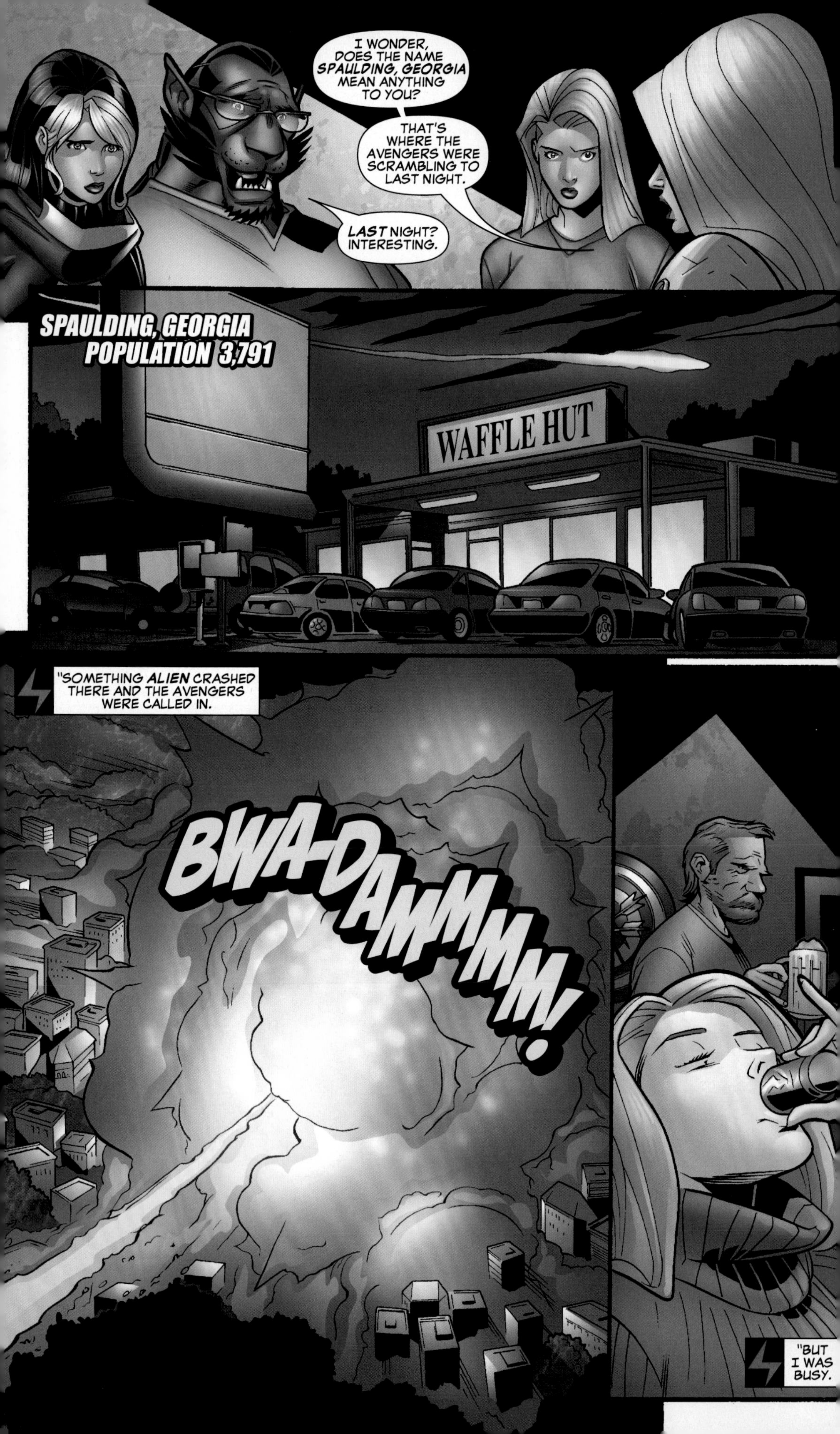
I WONDER, DOES THE NAME SPAULDING, GEORGIA MEAN ANYTHING TO YOU?
THAT'S WHERE THE AVENGERS WERE SCRAMBLING TO LAST NIGHT.
LAST NIGHT? INTERESTING.
SPAULDING, GEORGIA POPULATION 3,791
WAFFLE HUT
"SOMETHING ALIEN CRASHED THERE AND THE AVENGERS WERE CALLED IN.
BWA-DAMMMMM!
"BUT I WAS BUSY.

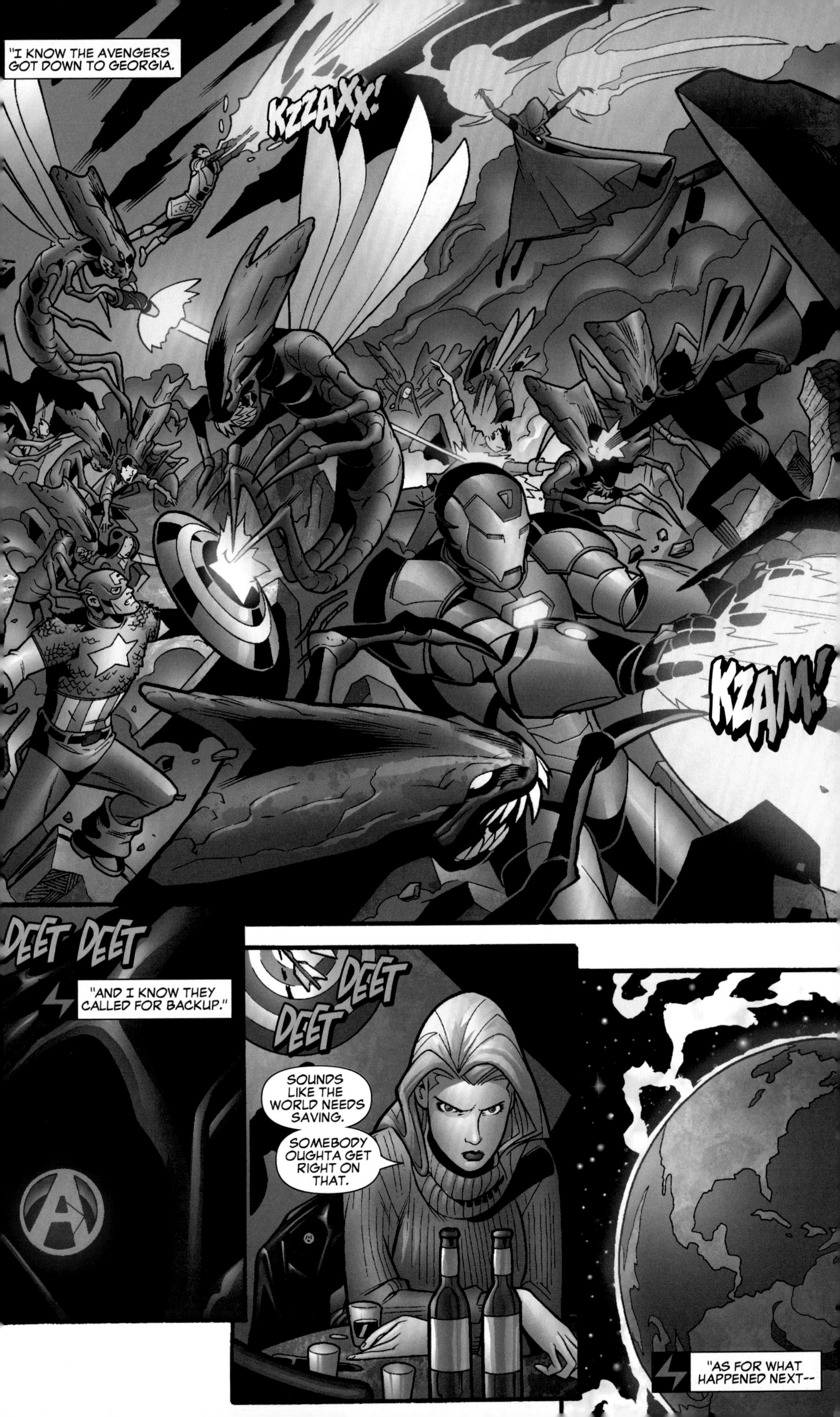
"I KNOW THE AVENGERS GOT DOWN TO GEORGIA.
KZZAXX!
KZAM!
DEET DEET
"AND I KNOW THEY CALLED FOR BACKUP."
DEET DEET
SOUNDS LIKE THE WORLD NEEDS SAVING.
SOMEBODY OUGHTA GET RIGHT ON THAT.
"AS FOR WHAT HAPPENED NEXT--

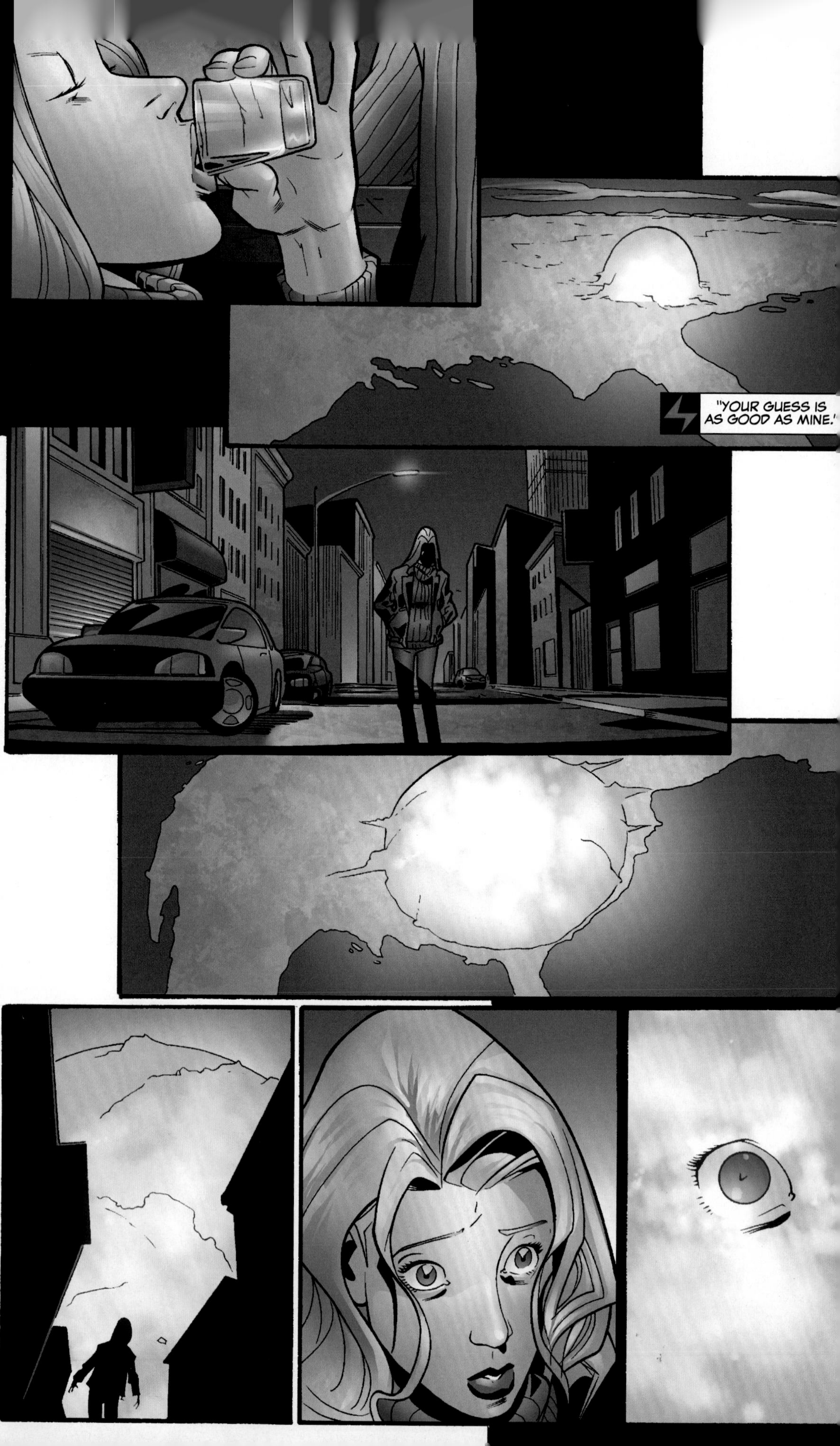
"YOUR GUESS IS AS GOOD AS MINE."

WELL, ME OF THIS EVENING'S CONUNDRUMS CERTAINLY MAKE MORE SENSE NOW.

YOU BET THEY DO.

SUCH AS?

WELL, I POSTULATE YOUR MEANS OF TRANSPORTATION FROM ONE UNIVERSE TO THE NEXT WAS A COMBINATION OF THE *SHOCKWAVE BLAST* FROM THE SPAULDING INCIDENT AND YOUR OWN ENERGY ABSORPTION POWERS.

YOU BOUNCED AROUND BETWEEN UNIVERSES FOR SEVERAL WEEKS BEFORE LANDING HERE.

OKAY. SO HOW DO WE GET HER BACK HOME?

OH, WELL, WE *DON'T.*

IT'S NOT THERE ANY MORE. JUDGING FROM THE READINGS TAKEN WHEN CAROL STOPPED SUCH AN EVENT IN *THIS* REALITY, I DOUBT EVEN THE SMALLEST MICROBE OF HER EARTH STILL EXISTS.

YOU STOPPED THIS FROM HAPPENING HERE?

SINGLE-HANDEDLY.

HOW?

I GOT OFF MY *BUTT* AND DID MY *JOB,* INSTEAD OF SITTING IN A BAR, HAVING A *PITY PARTY* FOR MYSELF.

DON'T GET ME WRONG, I DID MY TIME ON A BAR STOOL. I DRANK AWAY A LOT OF MY SORROWS.

BUT THEN I *GREW THE HELL UP.*

EXCUSE ME?

YOU HEARD ME.

DAMMIT! DO YOU KNOW THAT I'VE BEEN BEATING MYSELF UP LATELY? TOTALLY RIDING MYSELF ABOUT NOT DOING *ALL* I COULD BE DOING.

I'VE FELT LIKE I WAS A *FAILURE* AND AS IF I'D BEEN *WASTING* MY TALENTS, BUT YOU--

CAROL, I--

NOT RIGHT NOW, ROGUE! LITTLE MISS *"WARBIRD"* AND I HAVE SOME THINGS TO DISCUSS. THINGS LIKE--

YOU'D *BEST* THINK ABOUT WHAT YOU'RE GOING TO SAY NEXT.

YOU *SICKEN* ME.

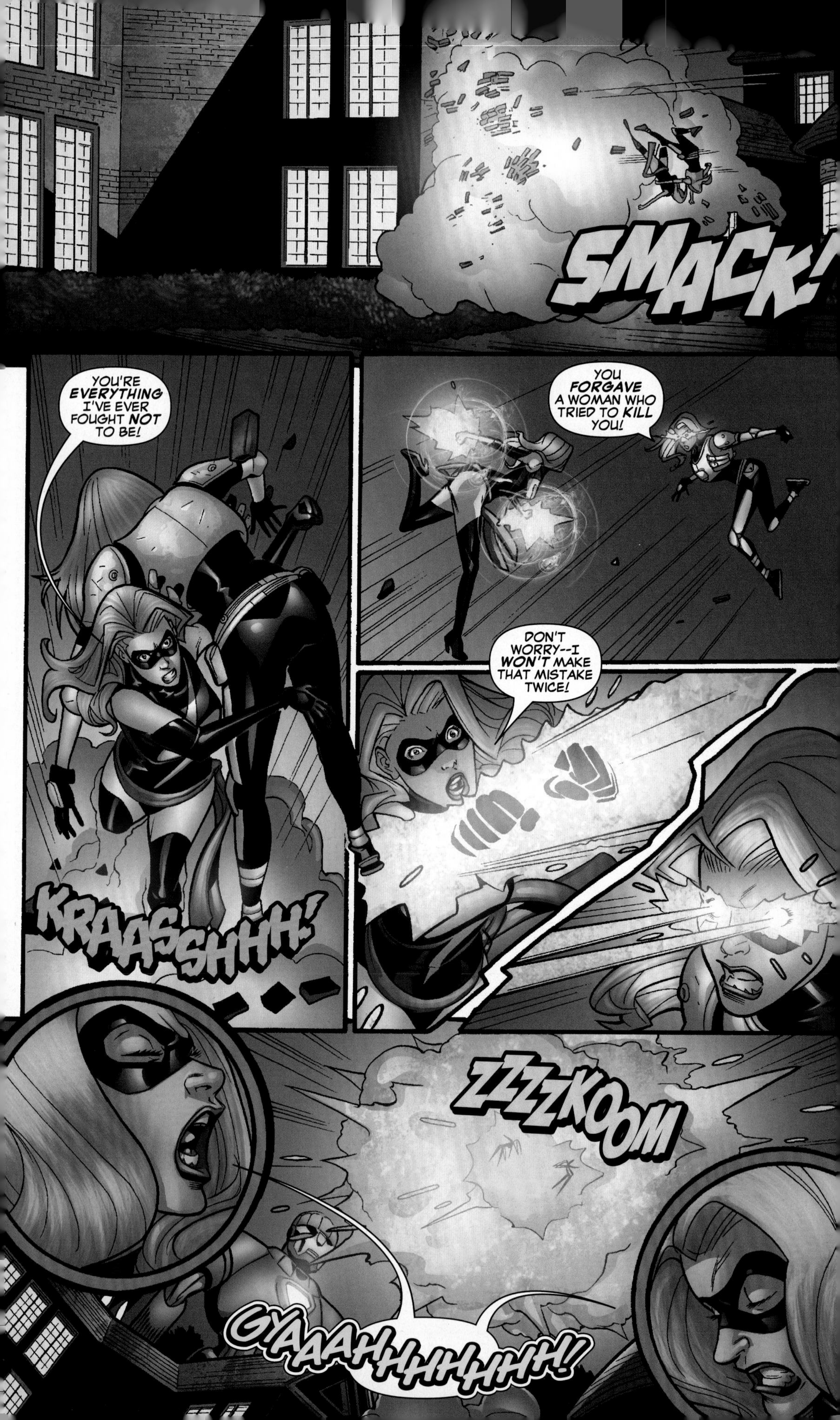
SMACK!
YOU'RE EVERYTHING I'VE EVER FOUGHT NOT TO BE!
KRAASSHHH!
YOU FORGAVE A WOMAN WHO TRIED TO KILL YOU!
DON'T WORRY--I WON'T MAKE THAT MISTAKE TWICE!
ZZZZKOOM
GYAAAHHHHHHHH!

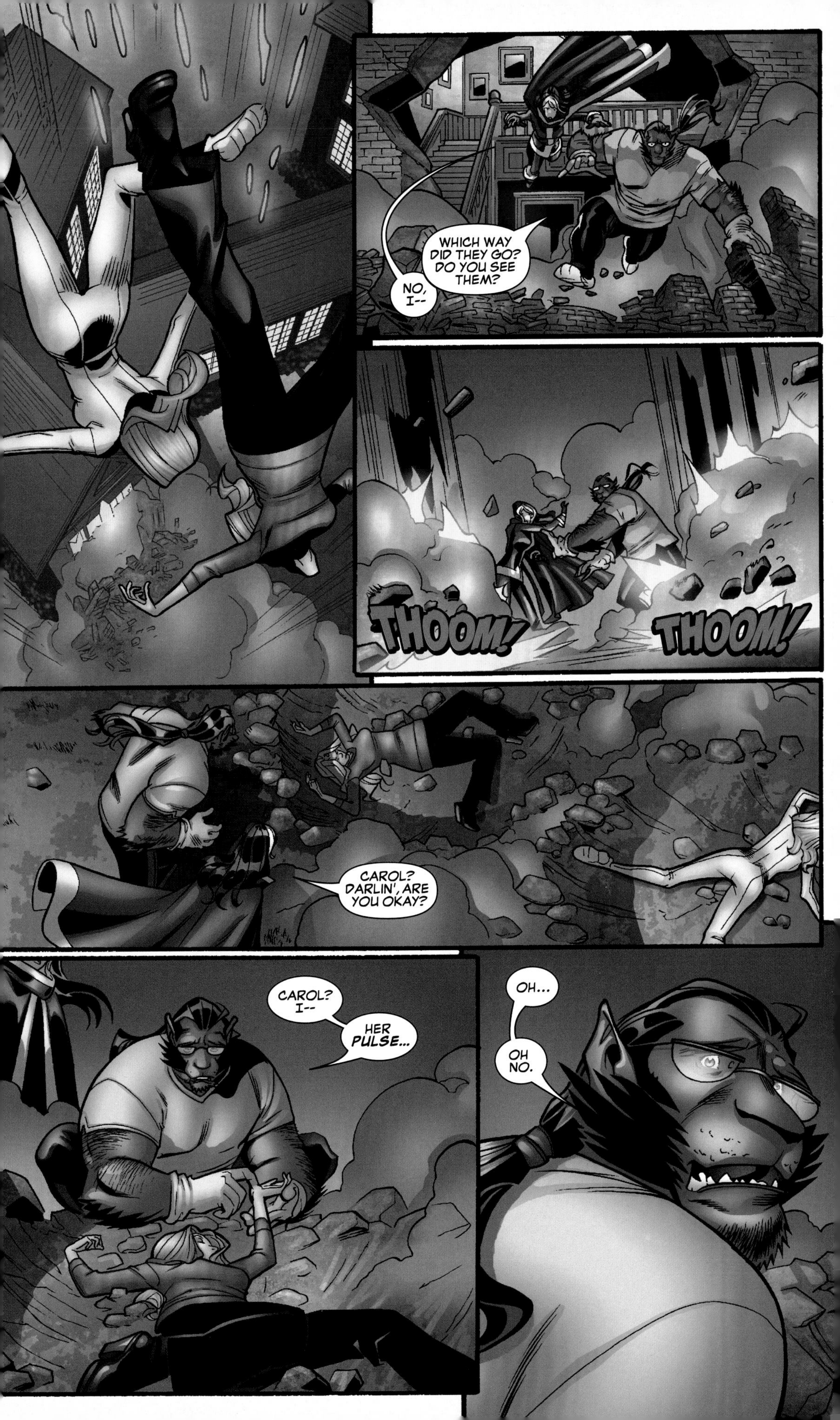
WHICH WAY DID THEY GO? DO YOU SEE THEM?
NO, I--
THOOM!
THOOM!
CAROL? DARLIN', ARE YOU OKAY?
CAROL? I--
HER PULSE...
OH...
OH NO.

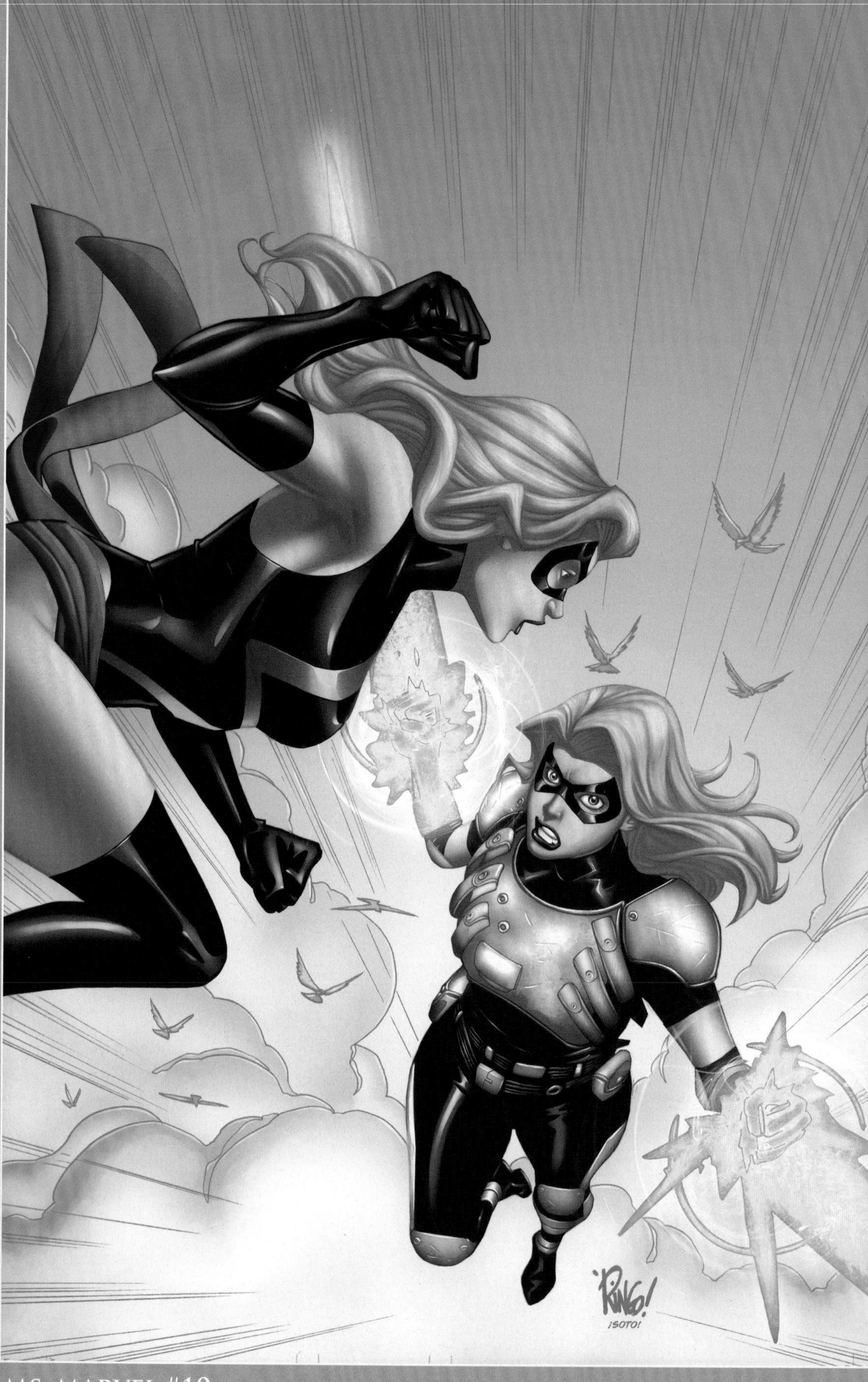
RINGO!
¡SOTO!

MS. MARVEL #10

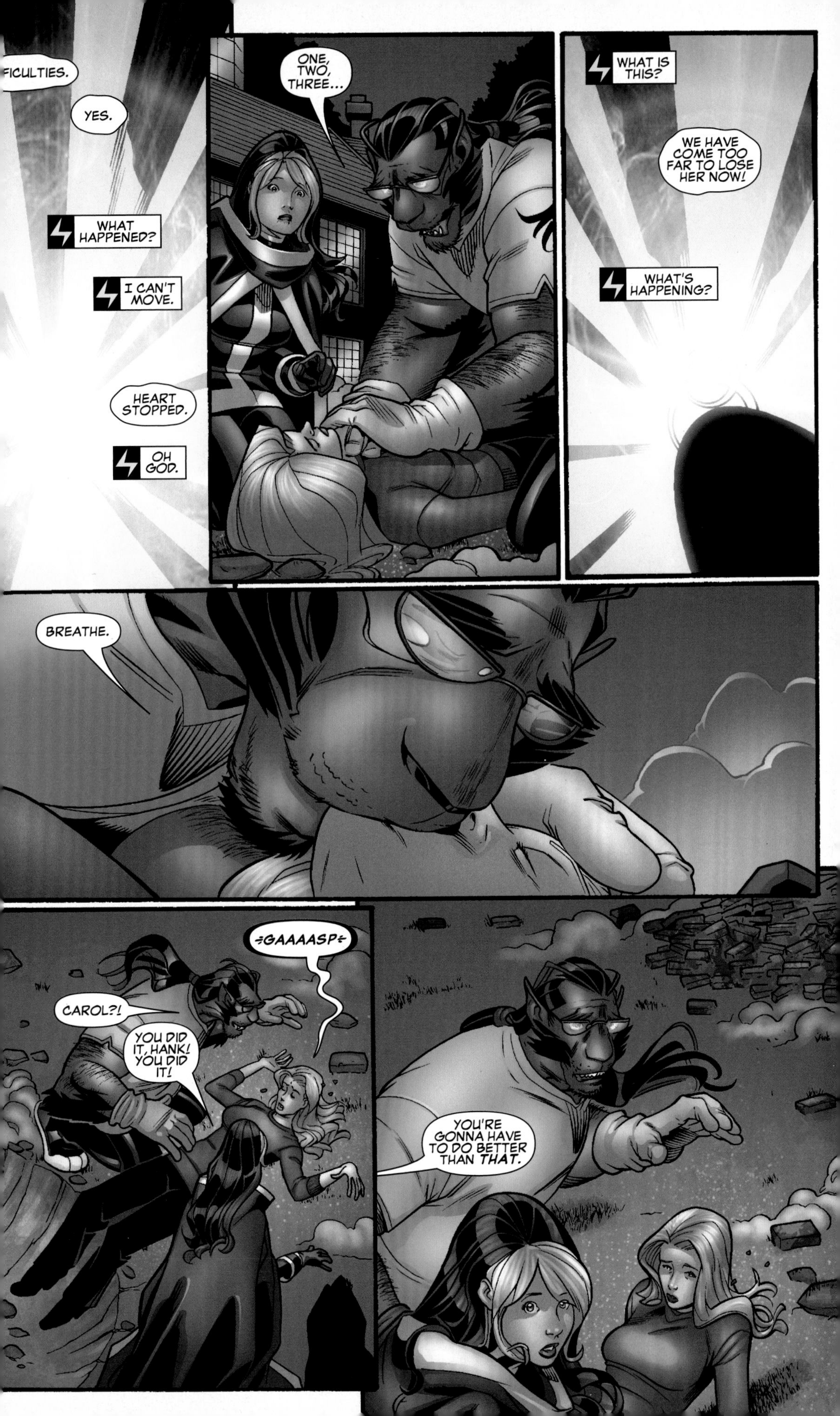
FICULTIES.
YES.
WHAT HAPPENED?
I CAN'T MOVE.
HEART STOPPED.
OH GOD.
ONE, TWO, THREE...
WHAT IS THIS?
WE HAVE COME TOO FAR TO LOSE HER NOW!
WHAT'S HAPPENING?
BREATHE.
CAROL?!
YOU DID IT, HANK! YOU DID IT!
GAAAASP
YOU'RE GONNA HAVE TO DO BETTER THAN THAT.

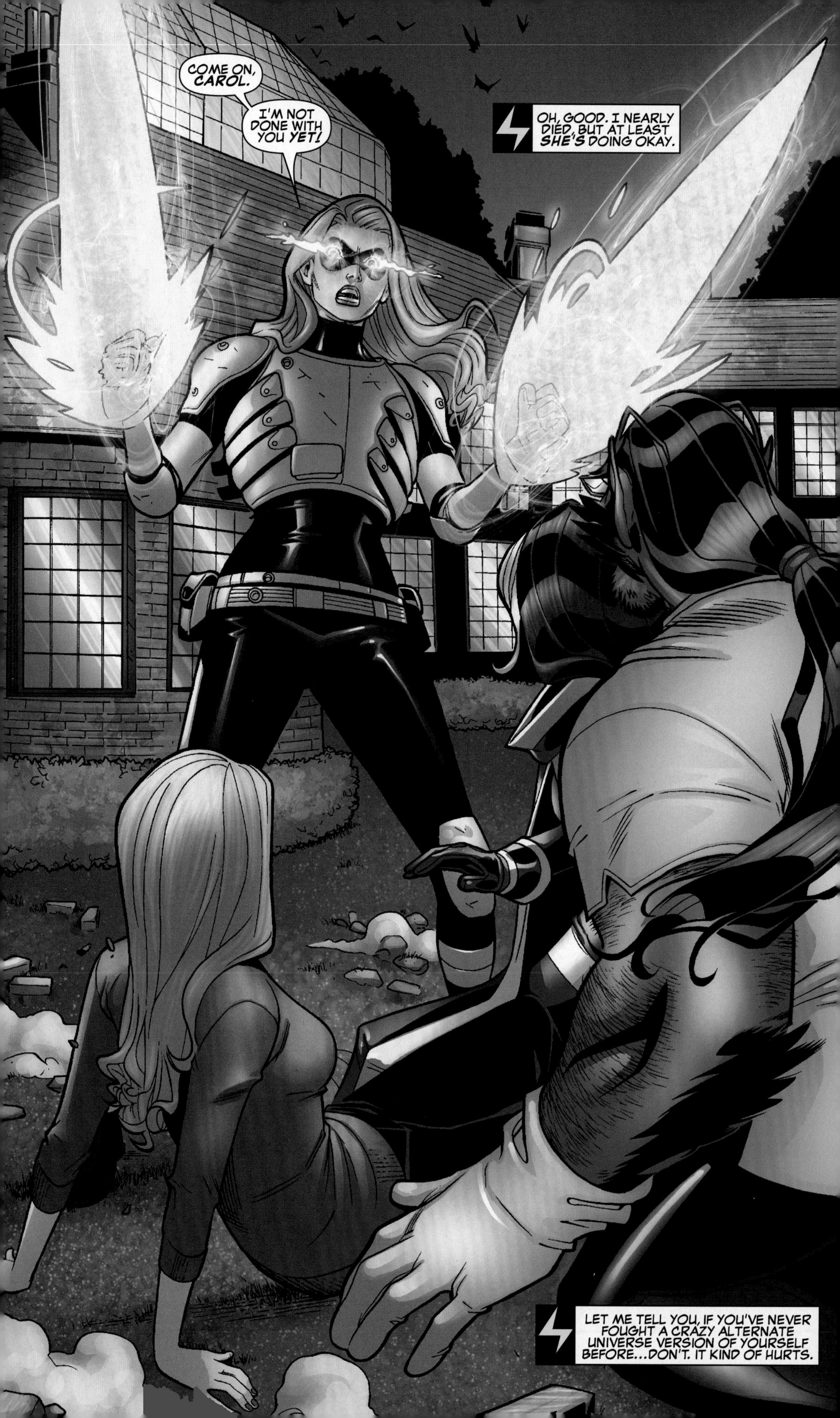
COME ON, CAROL.
I'M NOT DONE WITH YOU YET!
OH, GOOD. I NEARLY DIED, BUT AT LEAST SHE'S DOING OKAY.
LET ME TELL YOU, IF YOU'VE NEVER FOUGHT A CRAZY ALTERNATE UNIVERSE VERSION OF YOURSELF BEFORE...DON'T. IT KIND OF HURTS.

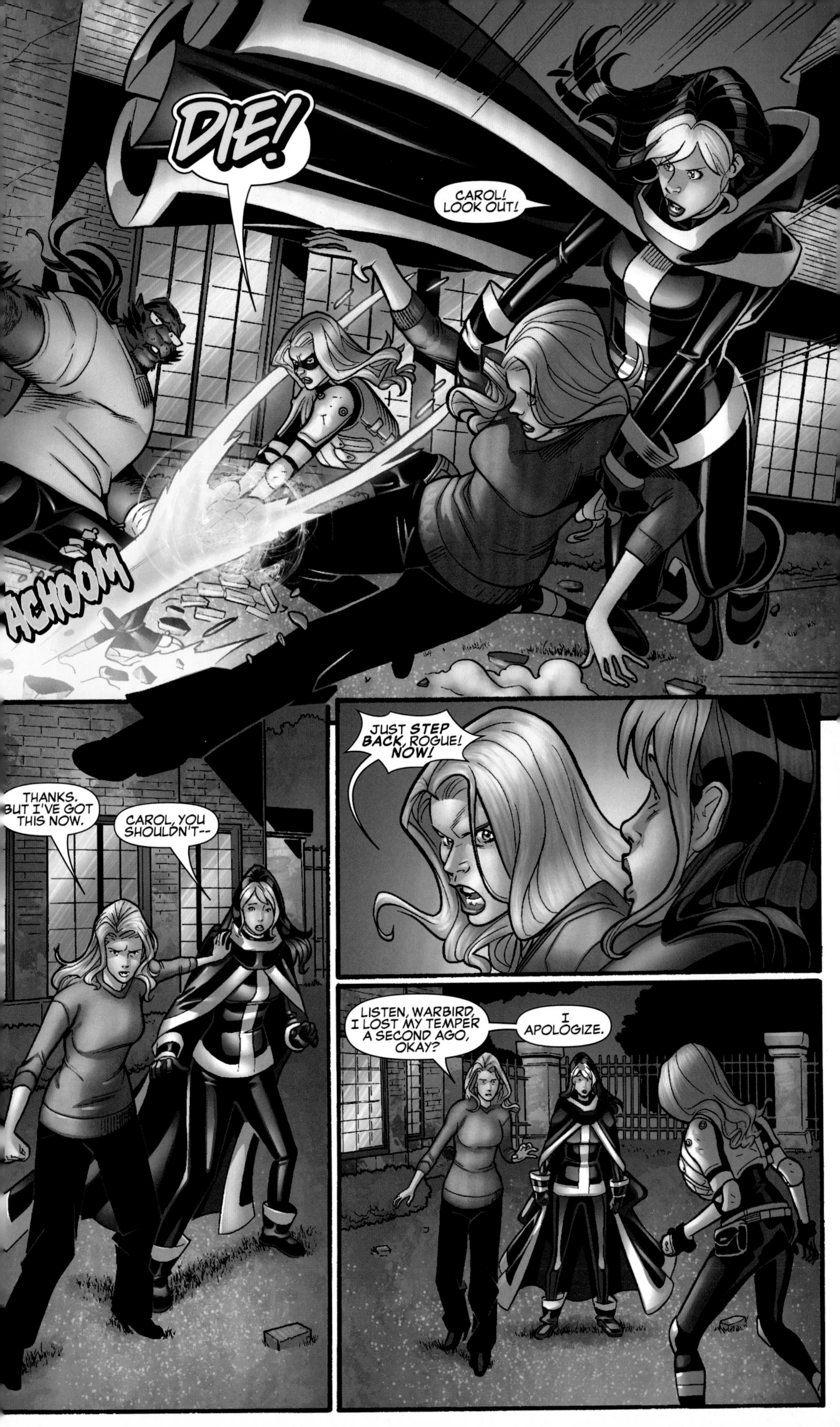
DIE!
CAROL! LOOK OUT!
ACHOOM
THANKS. BUT I'VE GOT THIS NOW.
CAROL, YOU SHOULDN'T--
JUST STEP BACK, ROGUE! NOW!
LISTEN, WARBIRD, I LOST MY TEMPER A SECOND AGO, OKAY?
I APOLOGIZE.

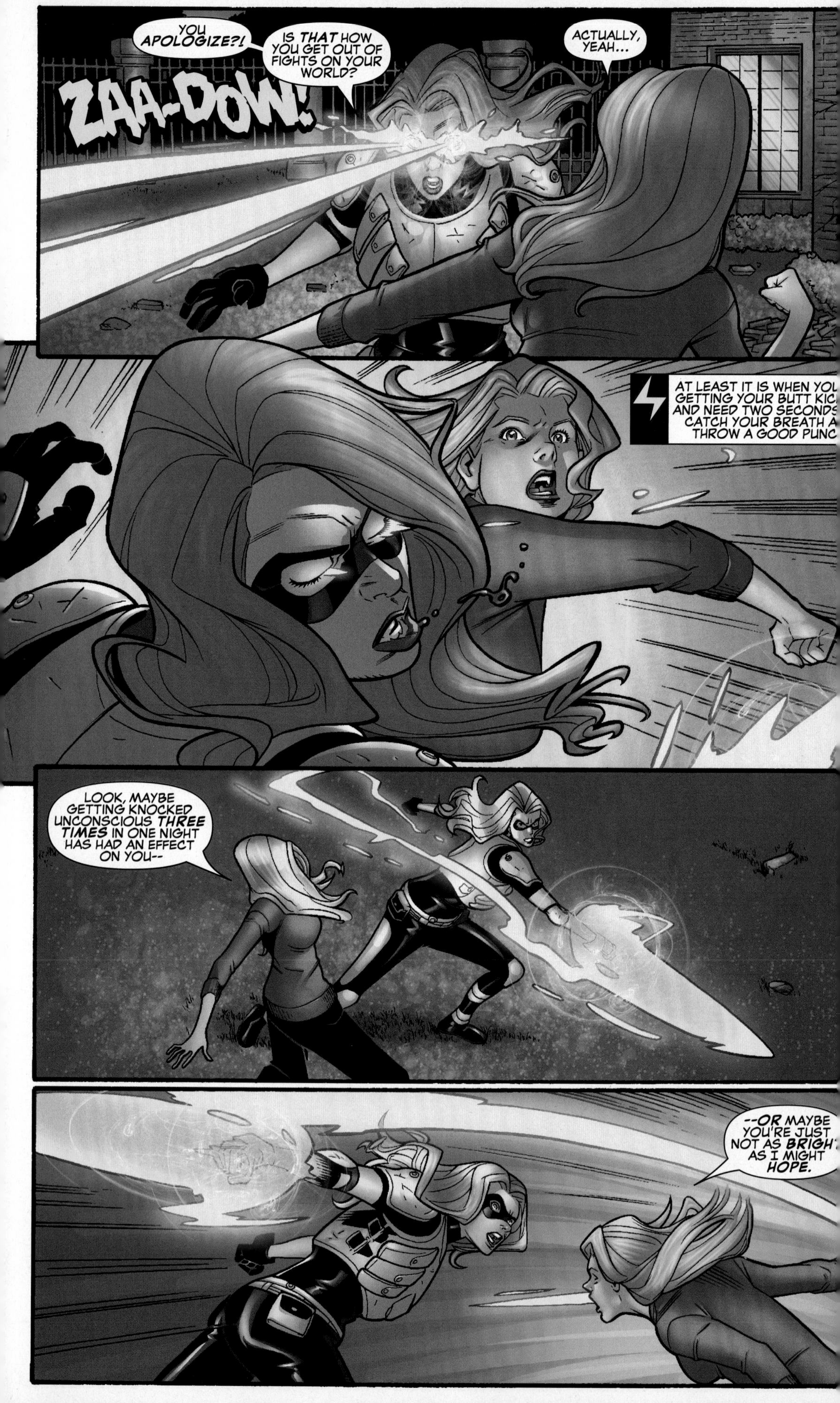
YOU APOLOGIZE?!
IS THAT HOW YOU GET OUT OF FIGHTS ON YOUR WORLD?
ZAA-DOW!
ACTUALLY, YEAH...
AT LEAST IT IS WHEN YOU GETTING YOUR BUTT KIC AND NEED TWO SECONDS CATCH YOUR BREATH A THROW A GOOD PUNC
LOOK, MAYBE GETTING KNOCKED UNCONSCIOUS THREE TIMES IN ONE NIGHT HAS HAD AN EFFECT ON YOU--
--OR MAYBE YOU'RE JUST NOT AS BRIGHT AS I MIGHT HOPE.

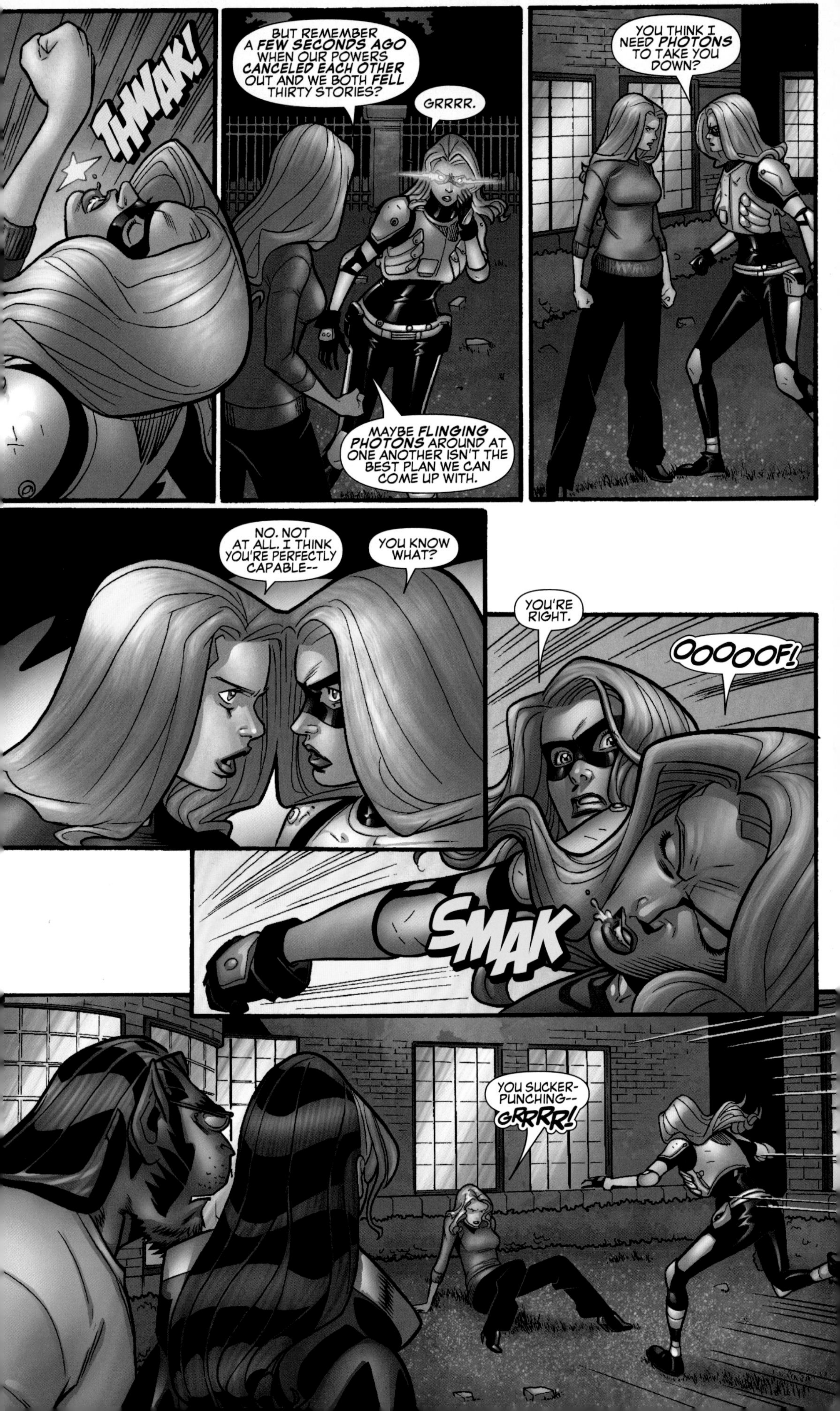
THWAK!
BUT REMEMBER A FEW SECONDS AGO WHEN OUR POWERS CANCELED EACH OTHER OUT AND WE BOTH FELL THIRTY STORIES?
GRRRR.
MAYBE FLINGING PHOTONS AROUND AT ONE ANOTHER ISN'T THE BEST PLAN WE CAN COME UP WITH.
YOU THINK I NEED PHOTONS TO TAKE YOU DOWN?
NO. NOT AT ALL. I THINK YOU'RE PERFECTLY CAPABLE--
YOU KNOW WHAT?
YOU'RE RIGHT.
OOOOOF!
SMAK
YOU SUCKER-PUNCHING-- GRRRR!

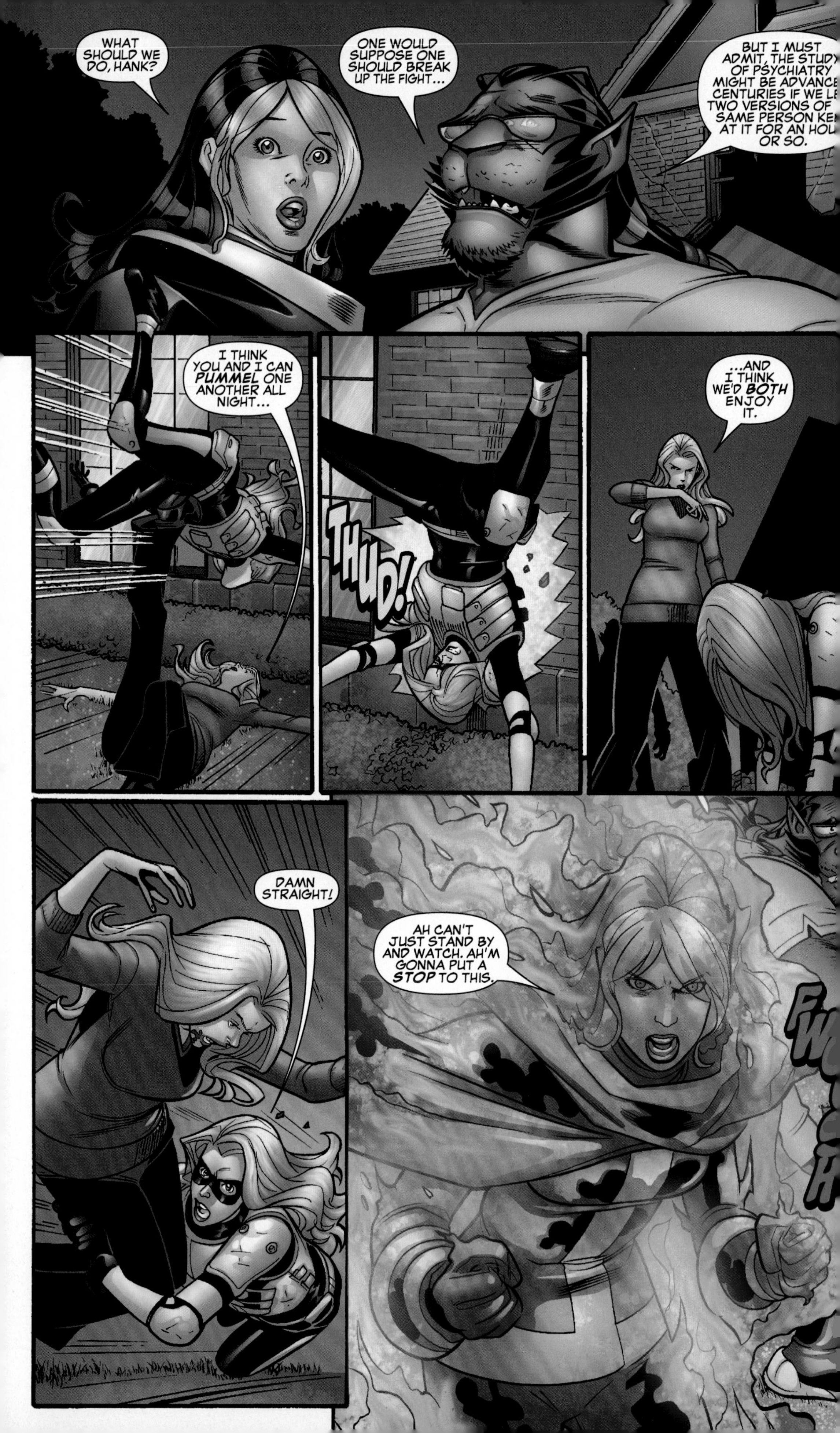
WHAT SHOULD WE DO, HANK?
ONE WOULD SUPPOSE ONE SHOULD BREAK UP THE FIGHT...
BUT I MUST ADMIT, THE STUDY OF PSYCHIATRY MIGHT BE ADVANCE CENTURIES IF WE LE TWO VERSIONS OF SAME PERSON KE AT IT FOR AN HOU OR SO.
I THINK YOU AND I CAN PUMMEL ONE ANOTHER ALL NIGHT...
THUD!
...AND I THINK WE'D BOTH ENJOY IT.
DAMN STRAIGHT!
AH CAN'T JUST STAND BY AND WATCH. AH'M GONNA PUT A STOP TO THIS.

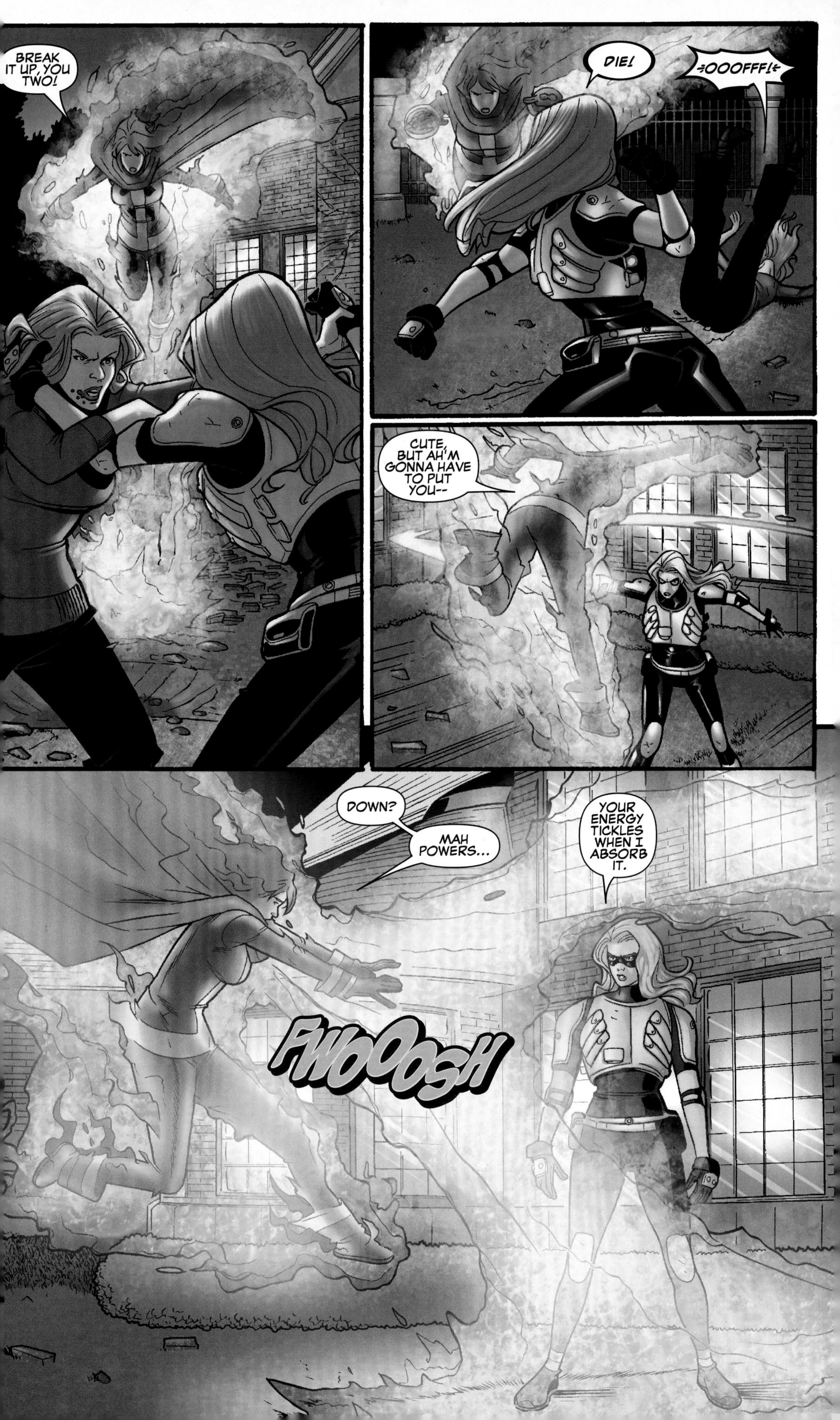
BREAK IT UP, YOU TWO!
DIE!
OOOFFF!
CUTE, BUT AH'M GONNA HAVE TO PUT YOU--
DOWN?
MAH POWERS...
YOUR ENERGY TICKLES WHEN I ABSORB IT.
FWOOOSH

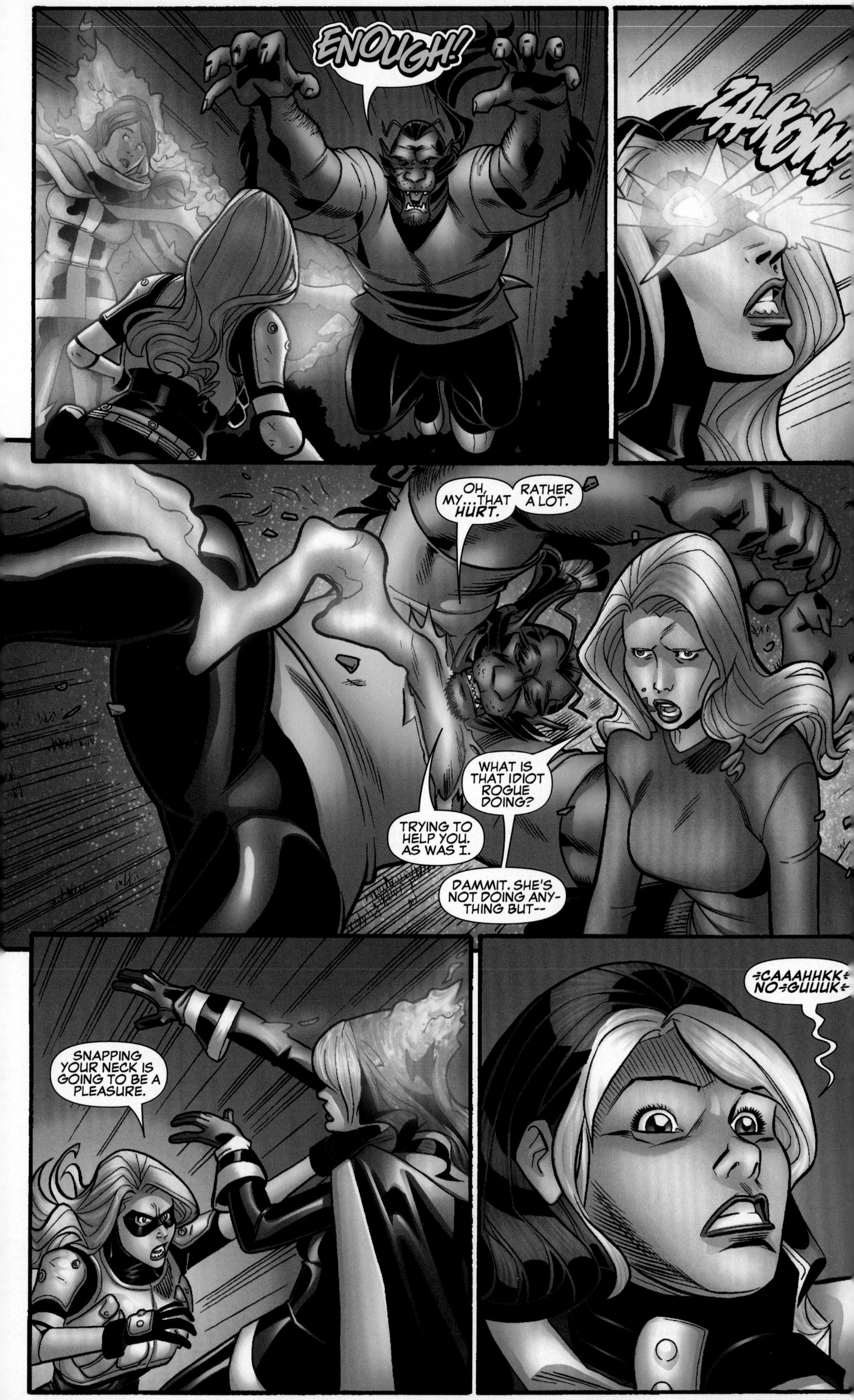
ENOUGH!
ZA-KOW!
OH, MY...THAT HÜRT.
RATHER A LOT.
WHAT IS THAT IDIOT ROGUE DOING?
TRYING TO HELP YOU. AS WAS I.
DAMMIT. SHE'S NOT DOING ANYTHING BUT--
SNAPPING YOUR NECK IS GOING TO BE A PLEASURE.
CAAAHHKK NO GUUUK

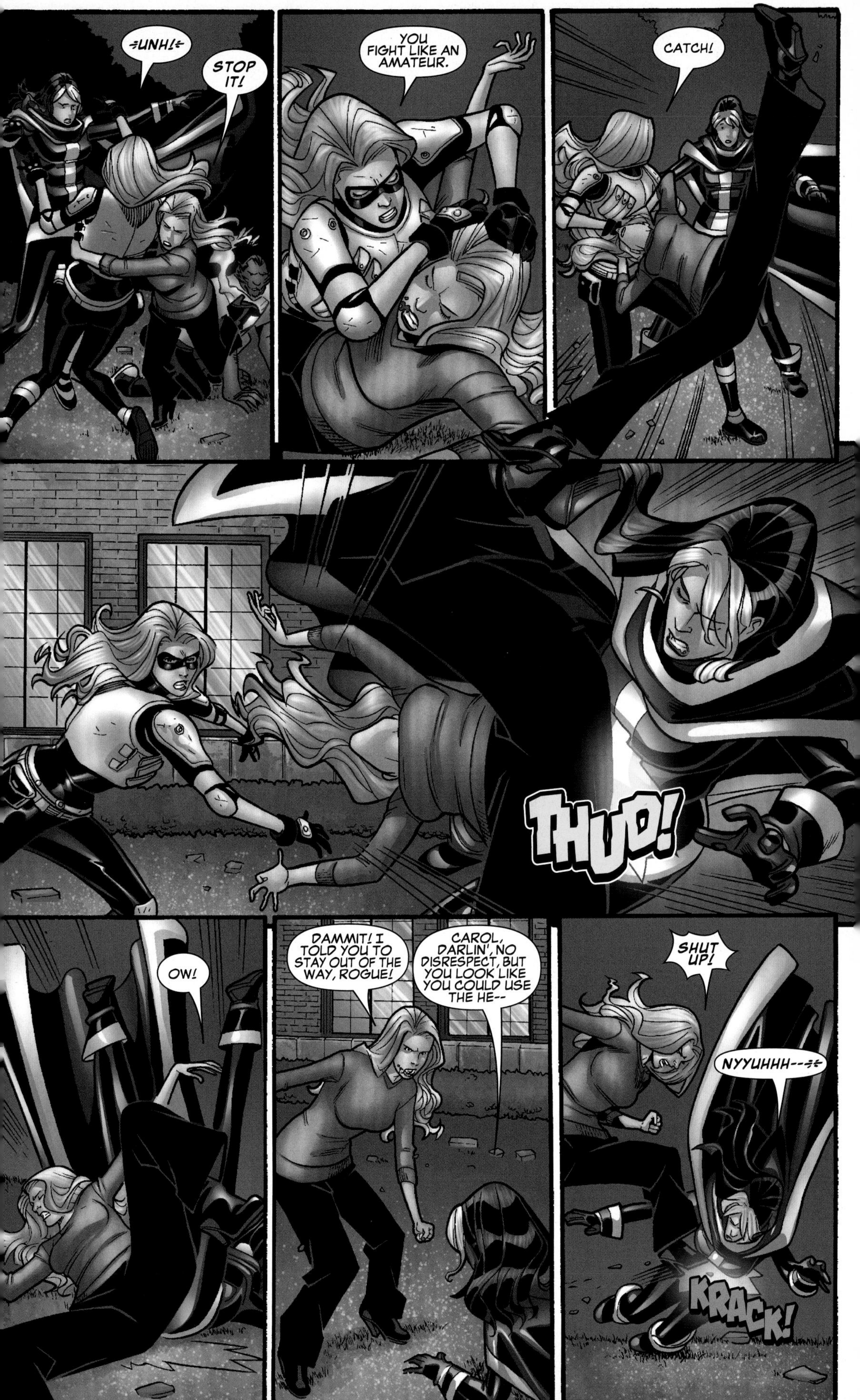
UNH!
STOP IT!
YOU FIGHT LIKE AN AMATEUR.
CATCH!
THUD!
OW!
DAMMIT! I TOLD YOU TO STAY OUT OF THE WAY, ROGUE!
CAROL, DARLIN', NO DISRESPECT, BUT YOU LOOK LIKE YOU COULD USE THE HE--
SHUT UP!
NYYUHHH--
KRACK!

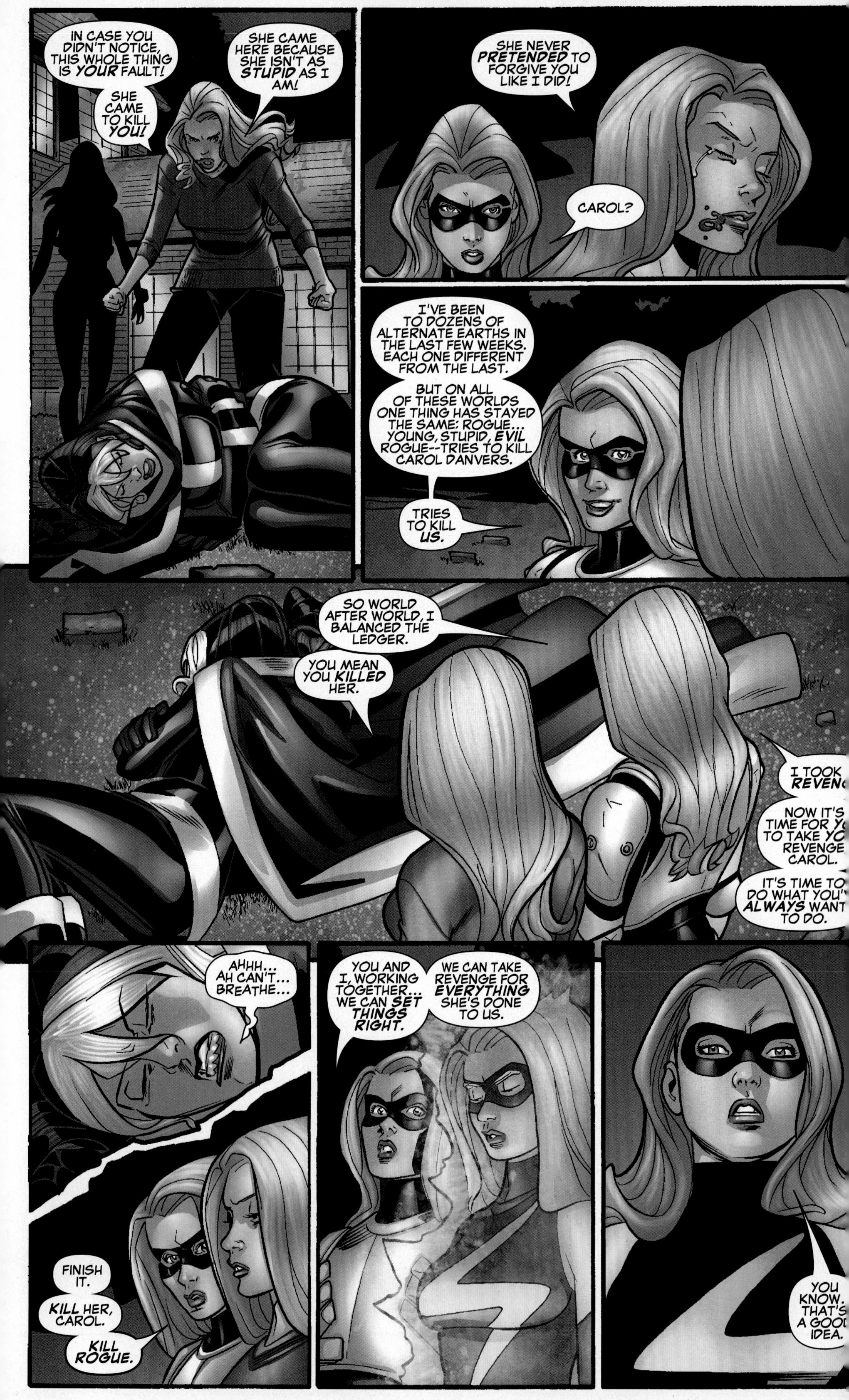
IN CASE YOU DIDN'T NOTICE, THIS WHOLE THING IS YOUR FAULT!
SHE CAME TO KILL YOU!
SHE CAME HERE BECAUSE SHE ISN'T AS STUPID AS I AM!
SHE NEVER PRETENDED TO FORGIVE YOU LIKE I DID!
CAROL?
I'VE BEEN TO DOZENS OF ALTERNATE EARTHS IN THE LAST FEW WEEKS. EACH ONE DIFFERENT FROM THE LAST.
BUT ON ALL OF THESE WORLDS ONE THING HAS STAYED THE SAME: ROGUE... YOUNG, STUPID, EVIL ROGUE--TRIES TO KILL CAROL DANVERS.
TRIES TO KILL US.
SO WORLD AFTER WORLD, I BALANCED THE LEDGER.
YOU MEAN YOU KILLED HER.
AHHH... AH CAN'T... BREATHE...
FINISH IT.
KILL HER, CAROL.
KILL ROGUE.
YOU AND I, WORKING TOGETHER... WE CAN SET THINGS RIGHT.
WE CAN TAKE REVENGE FOR EVERYTHING SHE'S DONE TO US.

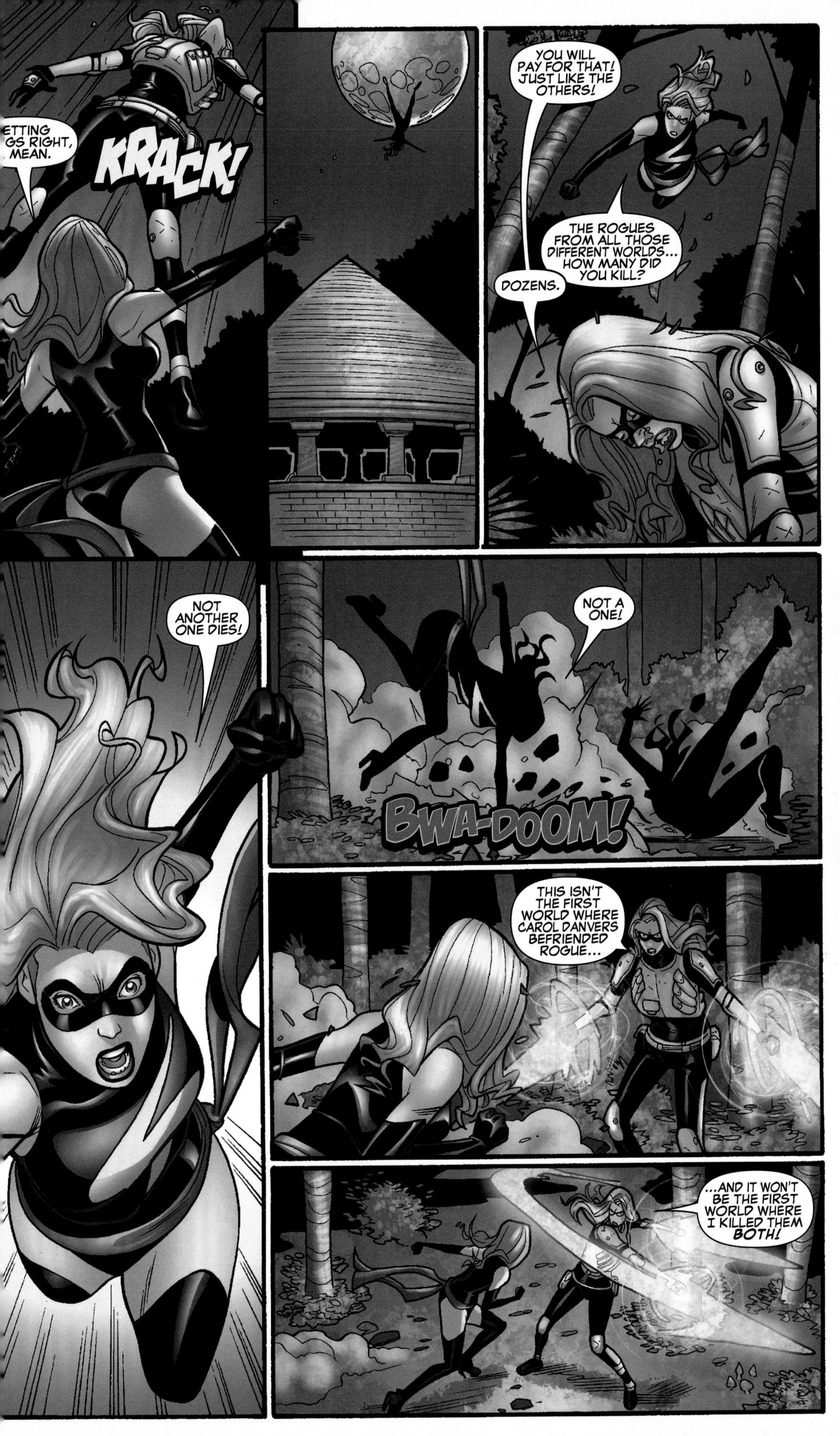

ETTING
GS RIGHT,
MEAN.
KRACK!
YOU WILL PAY FOR THAT! JUST LIKE THE OTHERS!
THE ROGUES FROM ALL THOSE DIFFERENT WORLDS... HOW MANY DID YOU KILL?
DOZENS.
NOT ANOTHER ONE DIES!
NOT A ONE!
BWA-DOOM!
THIS ISN'T THE FIRST WORLD WHERE CAROL DANVERS BEFRIENDED ROGUE...
...AND IT WON'T BE THE FIRST WORLD WHERE I KILLED THEM BOTH!

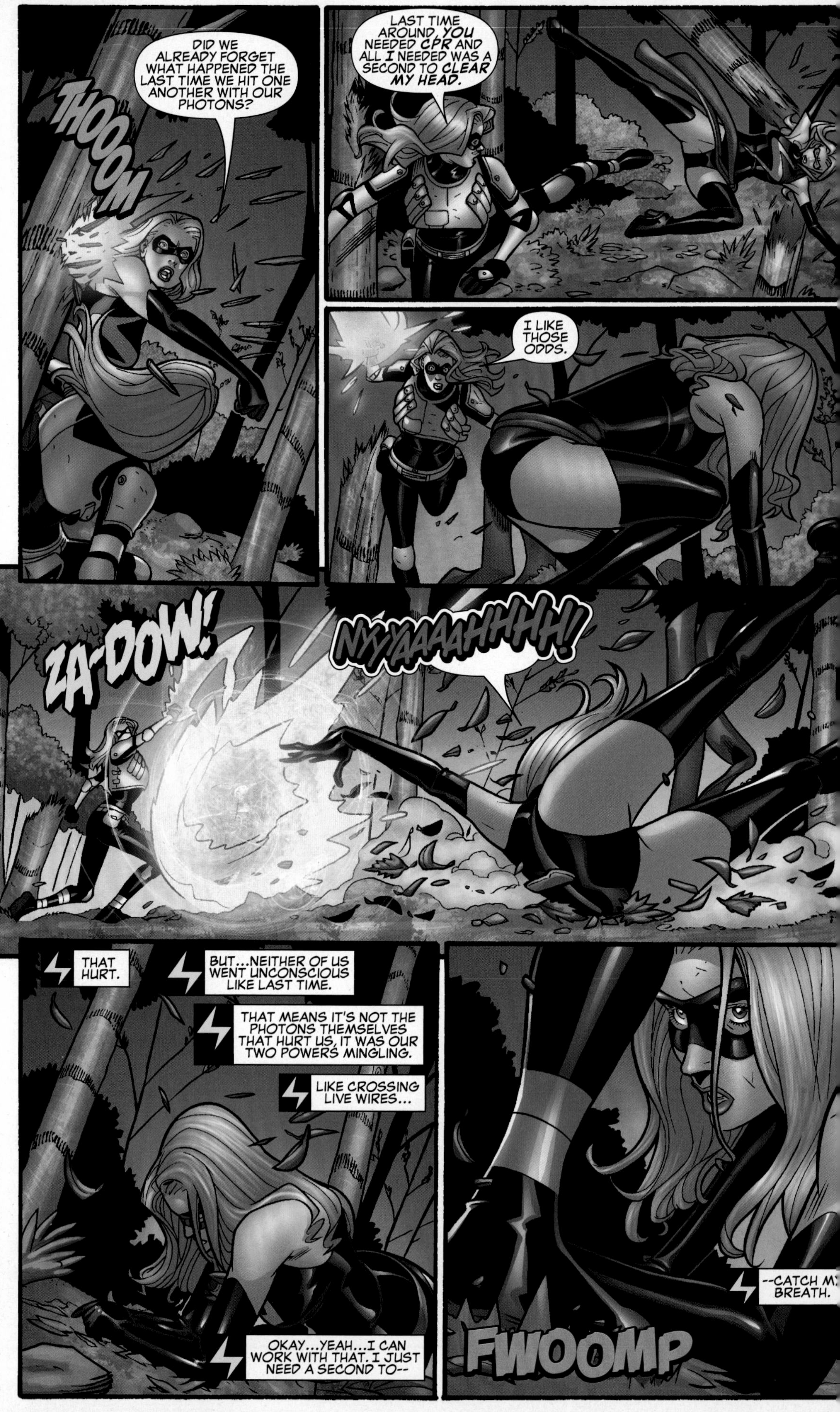
DID WE ALREADY FORGET WHAT HAPPENED THE LAST TIME WE HIT ONE ANOTHER WITH OUR PHOTONS?
THOOOM
LAST TIME AROUND, YOU NEEDED CPR AND ALL I NEEDED WAS A SECOND TO CLEAR MY HEAD.
I LIKE THOSE ODDS.
ZA-DOW!
NYYAAAAHHHH!
THAT HURT.
BUT...NEITHER OF US WENT UNCONSCIOUS LIKE LAST TIME.
THAT MEANS IT'S NOT THE PHOTONS THEMSELVES THAT HURT US, IT WAS OUR TWO POWERS MINGLING.
LIKE CROSSING LIVE WIRES...
OKAY...YEAH...I CAN WORK WITH THAT. I JUST NEED A SECOND TO--
--CATCH MY BREATH.
FWOOMP

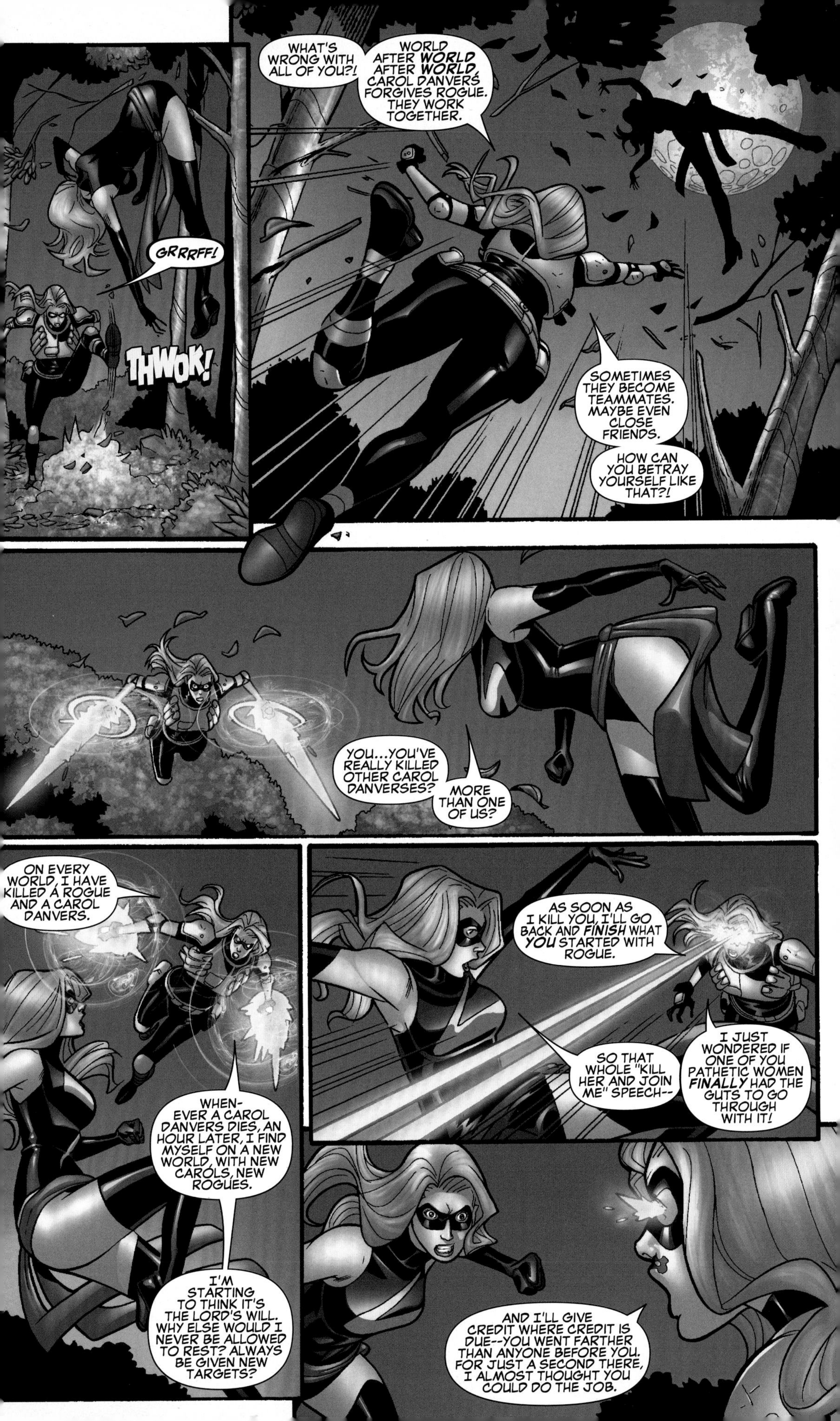
GRRRFF!
THWOK!
WHAT'S WRONG WITH ALL OF YOU?!
WORLD AFTER *WORLD* AFTER *WORLD*, CAROL DANVERS FORGIVES ROGUE. THEY WORK TOGETHER.
SOMETIMES THEY BECOME TEAMMATES. MAYBE EVEN CLOSE FRIENDS.
HOW CAN YOU BETRAY YOURSELF LIKE THAT?!
YOU...YOU'VE REALLY KILLED OTHER CAROL DANVERSES?
MORE THAN ONE OF US?
ON EVERY WORLD, I HAVE KILLED A ROGUE AND A CAROL DANVERS.
WHEN-EVER A CAROL DANVERS DIES, AN HOUR LATER, I FIND MYSELF ON A NEW WORLD, WITH NEW CAROLS, NEW ROGUES.
I'M STARTING TO THINK IT'S THE LORD'S WILL. WHY ELSE WOULD I NEVER BE ALLOWED TO REST? ALWAYS BE GIVEN NEW TARGETS?
AS SOON AS I KILL YOU, I'LL GO BACK AND *FINISH* WHAT *YOU* STARTED WITH ROGUE.
SO THAT WHOLE "KILL HER AND JOIN ME" SPEECH--
I JUST WONDERED IF ONE OF YOU PATHETIC WOMEN *FINALLY* HAD THE GUTS TO GO THROUGH WITH IT!
AND I'LL GIVE CREDIT WHERE CREDIT IS DUE--YOU WENT FARTHER THAN ANYONE BEFORE YOU. FOR JUST A SECOND THERE, I ALMOST THOUGHT YOU COULD DO THE JOB.

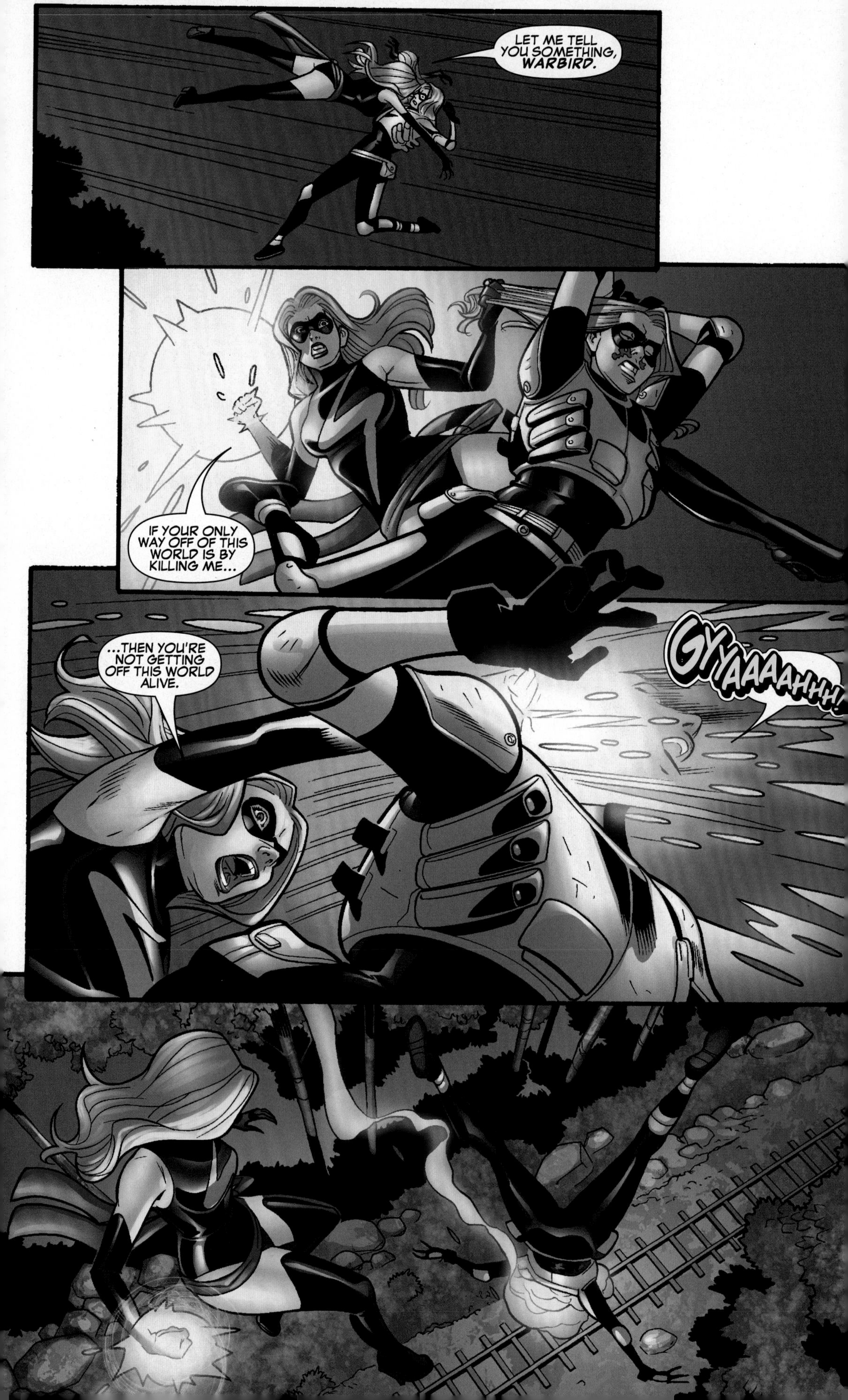
LET ME TELL YOU SOMETHING, WARBIRD.
IF YOUR ONLY WAY OFF OF THIS WORLD IS BY KILLING ME...
...THEN YOU'RE NOT GETTING OFF THIS WORLD ALIVE.
GYYAAAAHHH!

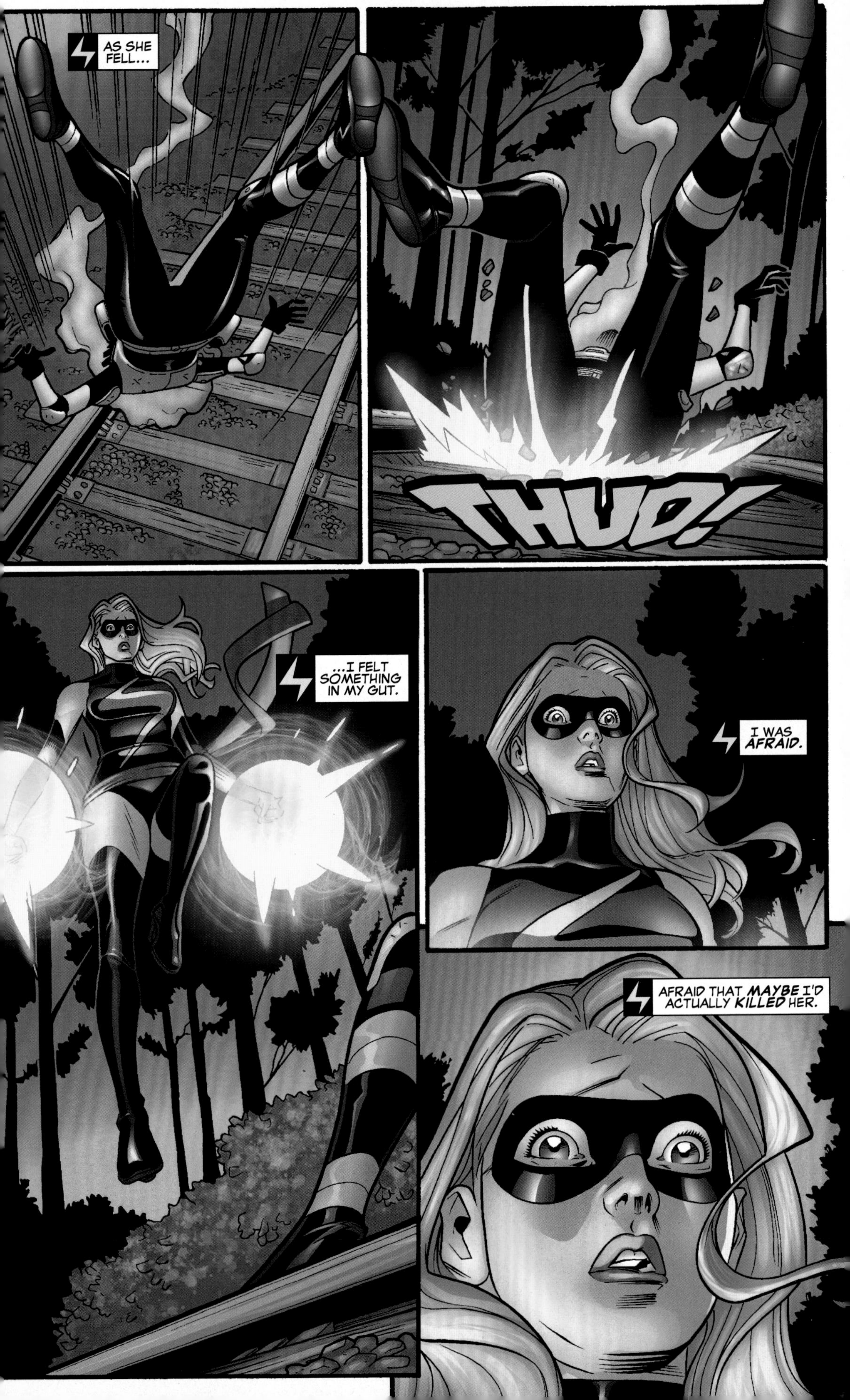
AS SHE FELL...
THUD!
...I FELT SOMETHING IN MY GUT.
I WAS *AFRAID*.
AFRAID THAT *MAYBE* I'D ACTUALLY *KILLED* HER.

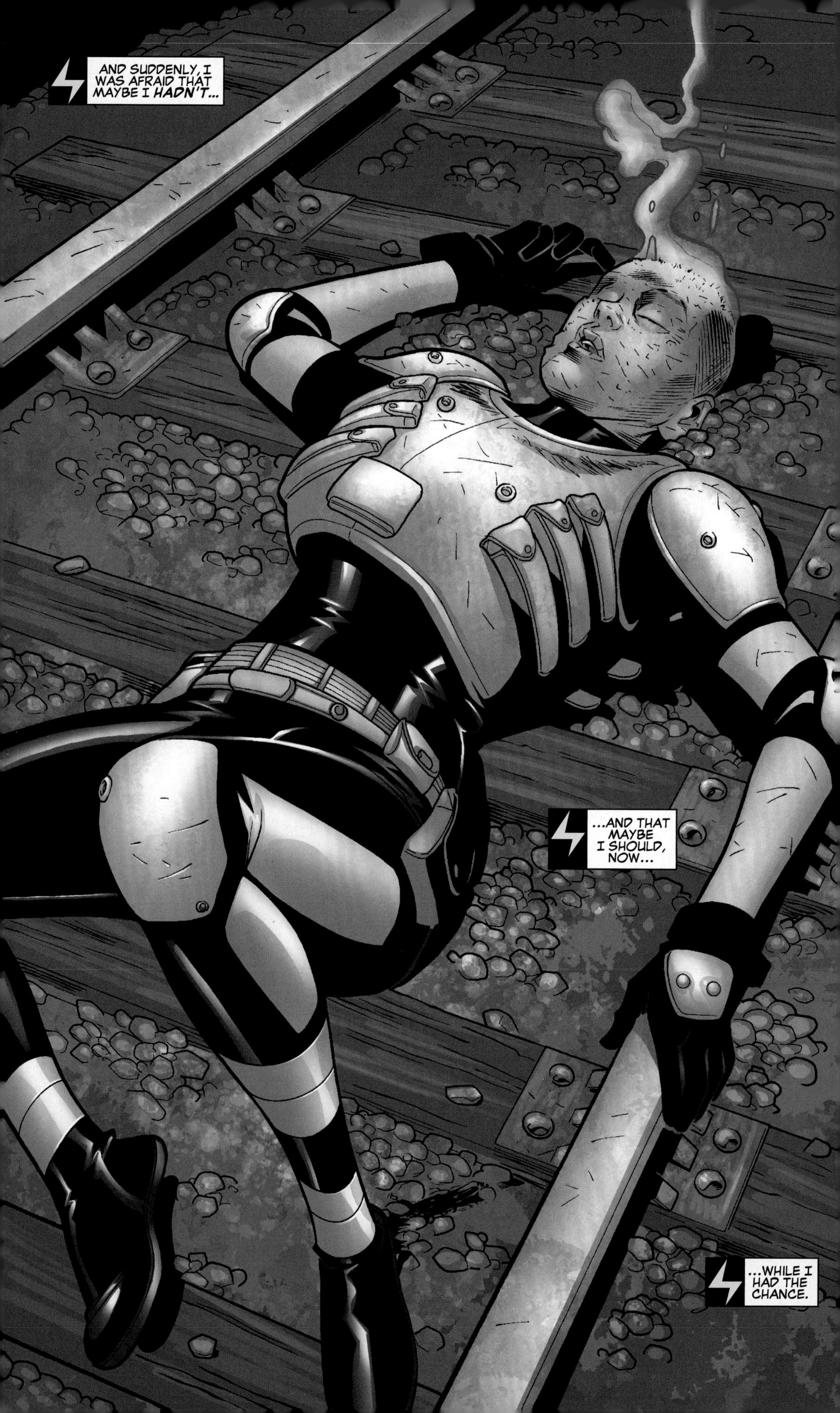
AND SUDDENLY, I WAS AFRAID THAT MAYBE I *HADN'T*...
...AND THAT MAYBE I SHOULD, NOW...
...WHILE I HAD THE CHANCE.

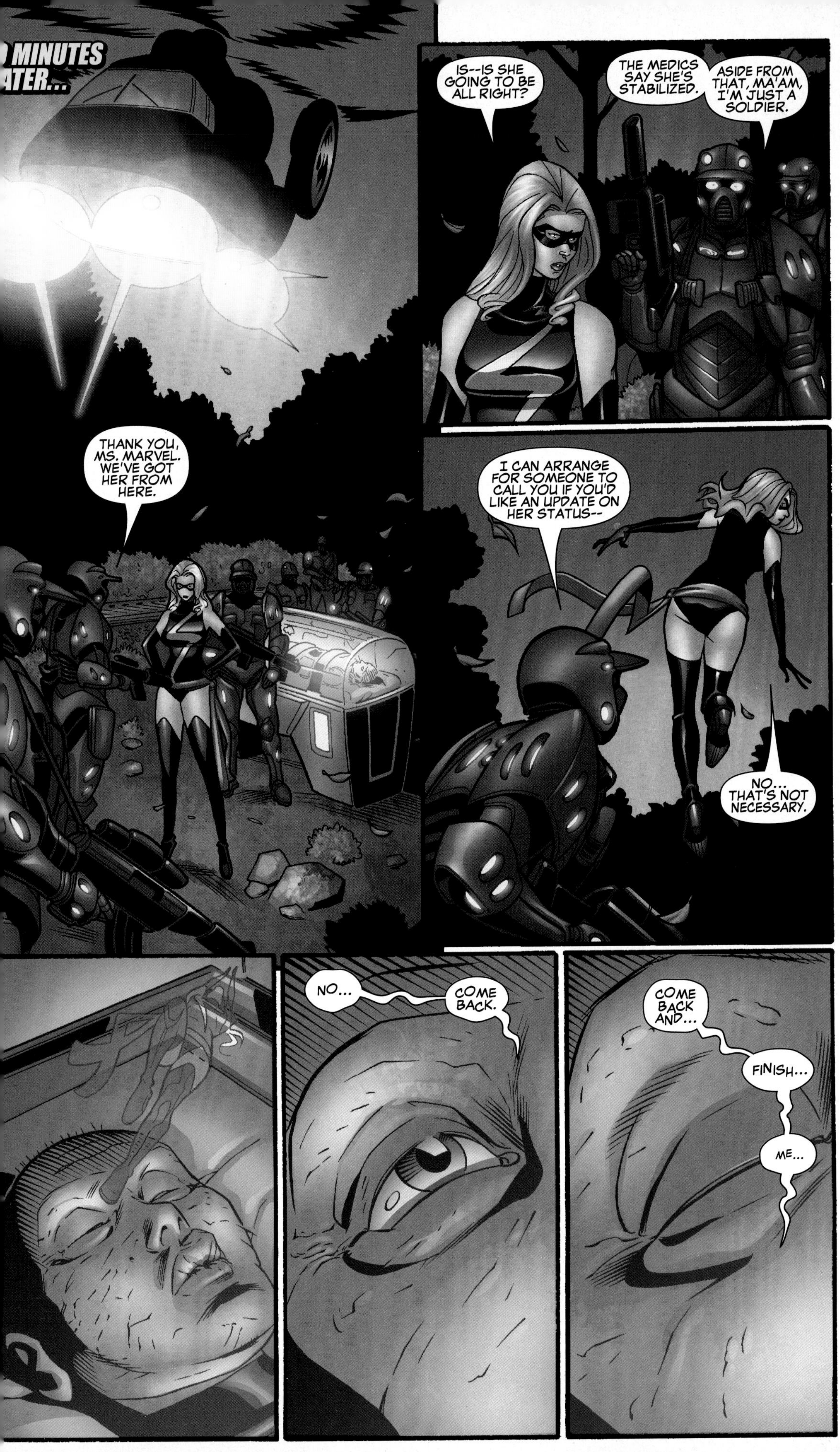

MINUTES
ATER...
IS--IS SHE GOING TO BE ALL RIGHT?
THE MEDICS SAY SHE'S STABILIZED.
ASIDE FROM THAT, MA'AM, I'M JUST A SOLDIER.
THANK YOU, MS. MARVEL. WE'VE GOT HER FROM HERE.
I CAN ARRANGE FOR SOMEONE TO CALL YOU IF YOU'D LIKE AN UPDATE ON HER STATUS--
NO... THAT'S NOT NECESSARY.
NO...
COME BACK.
COME BACK AND...
FINISH...
ME...

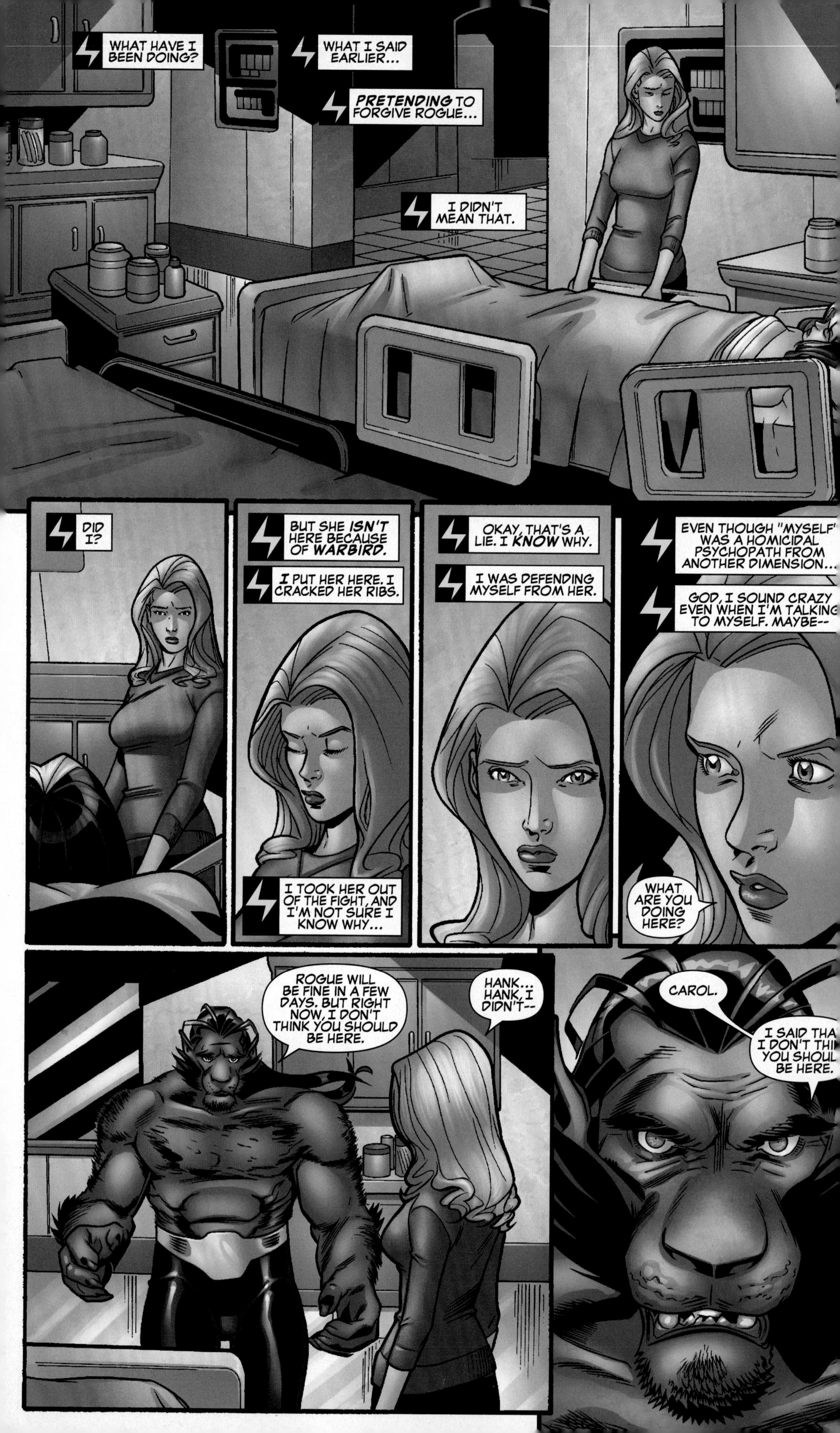
WHAT HAVE I BEEN DOING?
WHAT I SAID EARLIER...
PRETENDING TO FORGIVE ROGUE...
I DIDN'T MEAN THAT.
DID I?
BUT SHE ISN'T HERE BECAUSE OF WARBIRD.
I PUT HER HERE. I CRACKED HER RIBS.
I TOOK HER OUT OF THE FIGHT, AND I'M NOT SURE I KNOW WHY...
OKAY, THAT'S A LIE. I KNOW WHY.
I WAS DEFENDING MYSELF FROM HER.
EVEN THOUGH "MYSELF" WAS A HOMICIDAL PSYCHOPATH FROM ANOTHER DIMENSION...
GOD, I SOUND CRAZY EVEN WHEN I'M TALKING TO MYSELF. MAYBE--
WHAT ARE YOU DOING HERE?
ROGUE WILL BE FINE IN A FEW DAYS. BUT RIGHT NOW, I DON'T THINK YOU SHOULD BE HERE.
HANK... HANK, I DIDN'T--
CAROL.
I SAID THA I DON'T THI YOU SHOUL BE HERE.

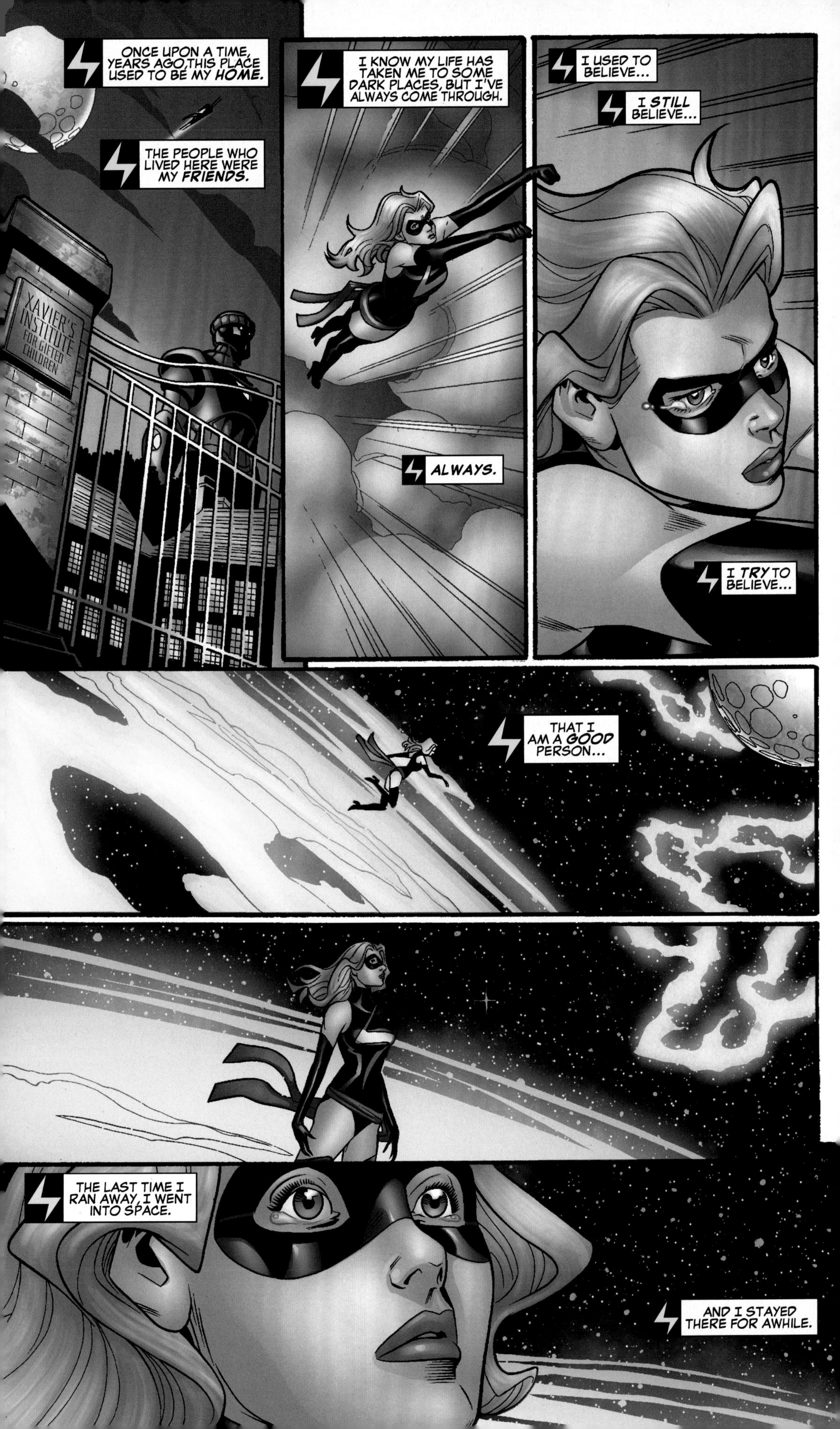
ONCE UPON A TIME, YEARS AGO, THIS PLACE USED TO BE MY HOME.
THE PEOPLE WHO LIVED HERE WERE MY FRIENDS.
XAVIER'S INSTITUTE FOR GIFTED CHILDREN
I KNOW MY LIFE HAS TAKEN ME TO SOME DARK PLACES, BUT I'VE ALWAYS COME THROUGH.
ALWAYS.
I USED TO BELIEVE...
I STILL BELIEVE...
I TRY TO BELIEVE...
THAT I AM A GOOD PERSON...
THE LAST TIME I RAN AWAY, I WENT INTO SPACE.
AND I STAYED THERE FOR AWHILE.

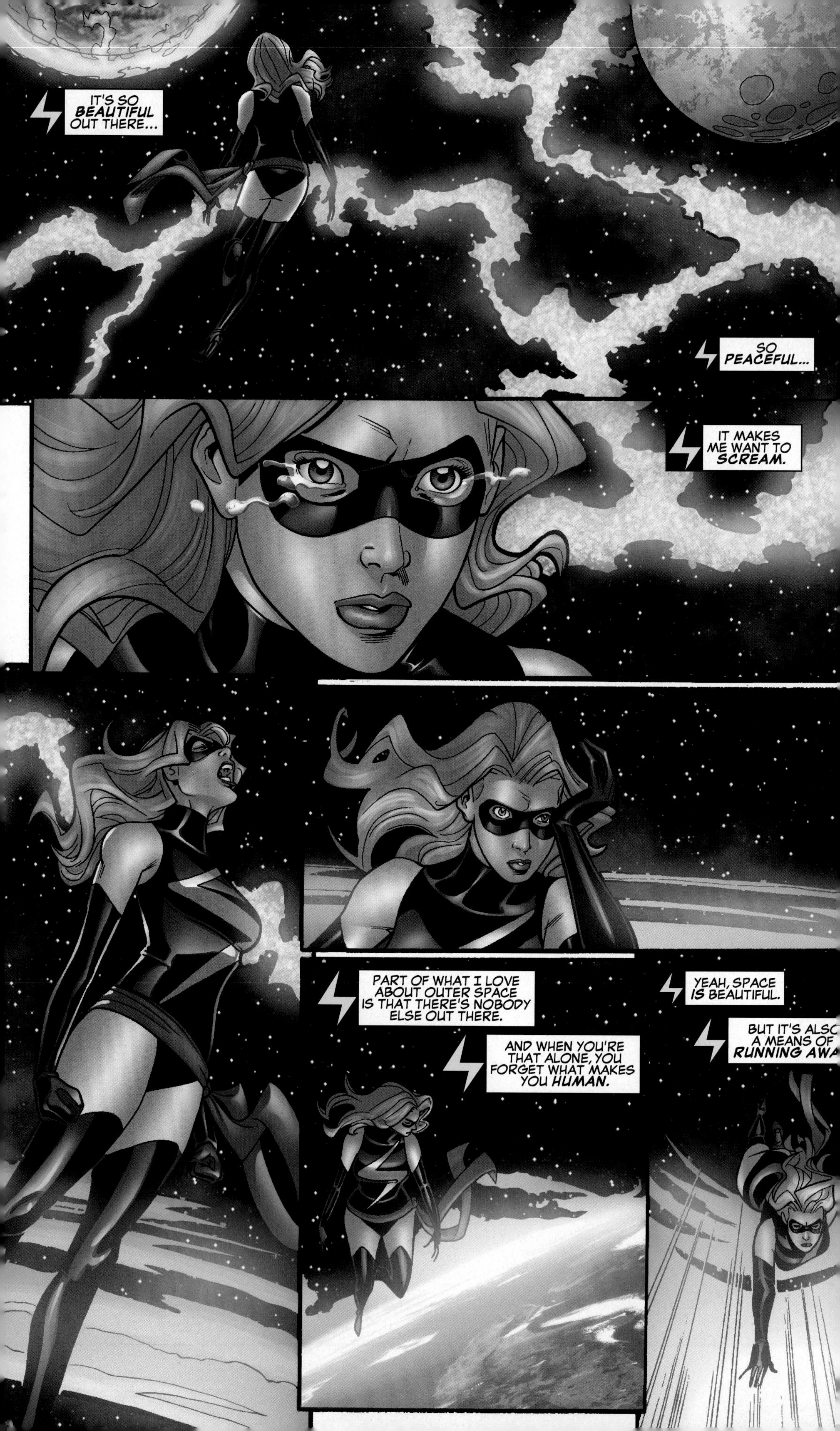
IT'S SO BEAUTIFUL OUT THERE...
SO PEACEFUL...
IT MAKES ME WANT TO SCREAM.
PART OF WHAT I LOVE ABOUT OUTER SPACE IS THAT THERE'S NOBODY ELSE OUT THERE.
AND WHEN YOU'RE THAT ALONE, YOU FORGET WHAT MAKES YOU HUMAN.
YEAH, SPACE IS BEAUTIFUL.

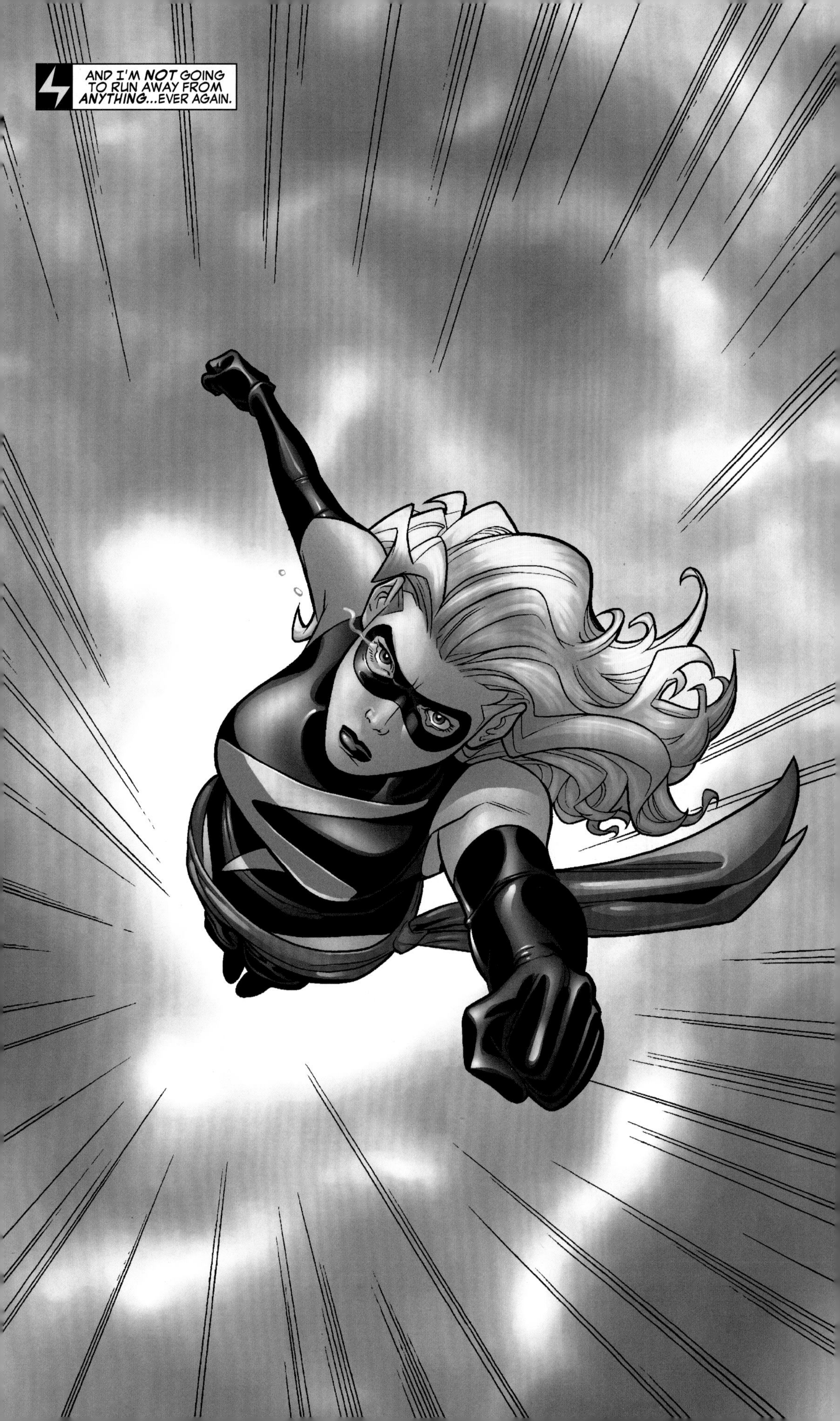
AND I'M **NOT** GOING TO RUN AWAY FROM ***ANYTHING***...EVER AGAIN.

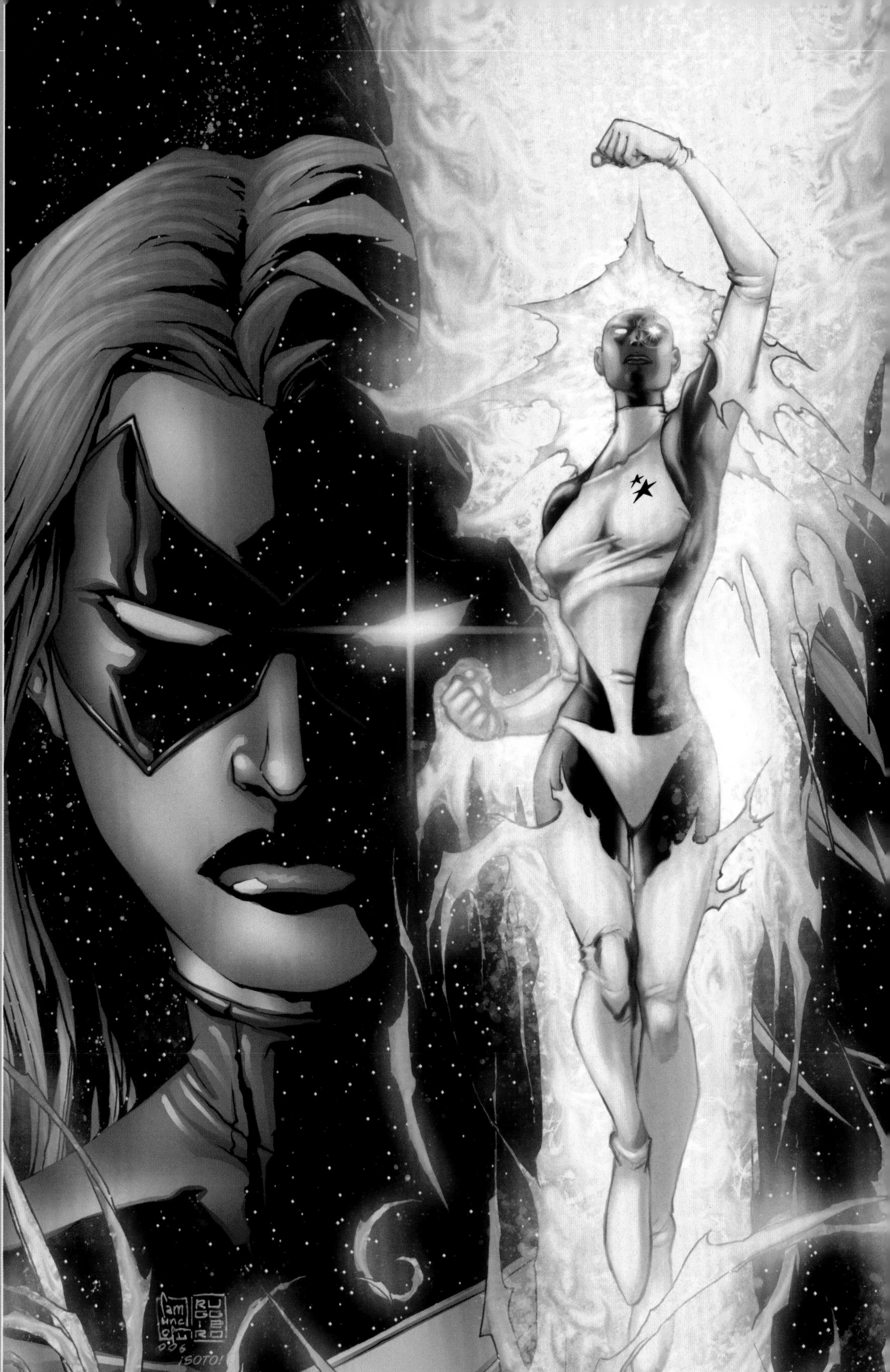
¡SOTO!

MS. MARVEL SPECIAL #1

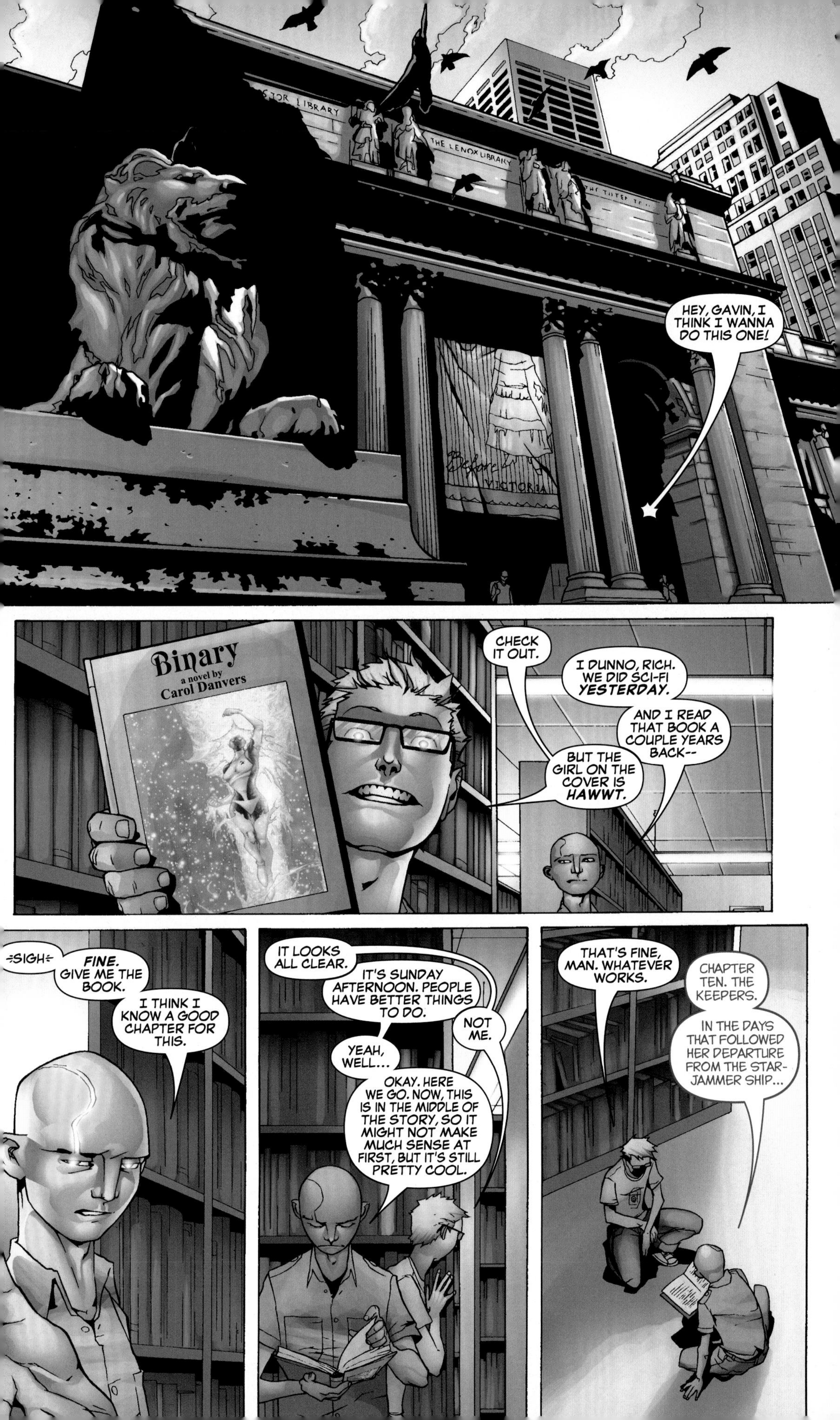

STOR LIBRARY
THE LENOX LIBRARY
Before VICTORIA
HEY, GAVIN, I THINK I WANNA DO THIS ONE!
Binary
a novel by
Carol Danvers
CHECK IT OUT.
I DUNNO, RICH. WE DID SCI-FI YESTERDAY.
AND I READ THAT BOOK A COUPLE YEARS BACK--
BUT THE GIRL ON THE COVER IS HAWWT.
=SIGH=
FINE. GIVE ME THE BOOK.
I THINK I KNOW A GOOD CHAPTER FOR THIS.
IT LOOKS ALL CLEAR.
IT'S SUNDAY AFTERNOON. PEOPLE HAVE BETTER THINGS TO DO.
NOT ME.
YEAH, WELL...
OKAY. HERE WE GO. NOW, THIS IS IN THE MIDDLE OF THE STORY, SO IT MIGHT NOT MAKE MUCH SENSE AT FIRST, BUT IT'S STILL PRETTY COOL.
THAT'S FINE, MAN. WHATEVER WORKS.
CHAPTER TEN. THE KEEPERS.
IN THE DAYS THAT FOLLOWED HER DEPARTURE FROM THE STAR-JAMMER SHIP...

Chapter 10:
The Keepers

In the days that followed her departure from the Starjammer ship, Binary traveled the galaxy aimlessly, lost in the great void of space and loving every moment of it. It was a simple matter for her to aim herself at a distant star and find new adventures along the way.

Yet, Binary realized that the moments of the day that made her feel "human" or "normal" were gone. Such routine moments as a simple "hello" to another member of the Starjammer crew, or something as mundane as following a schedule for waking and sleeping... In the depths of space, these things were lost. Time carried little meaning to Binary. Companionship was a thing of the past. The cosmos itself was her home now, and she found a certain comfort in its cold expanse.

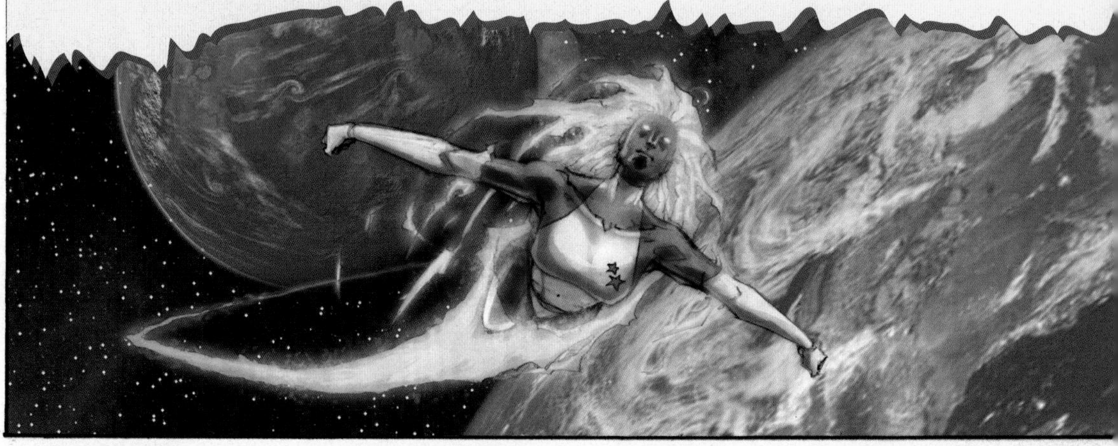

Binary was several months alone in the void before she encountered another living creature. At first, it was a gentle whisper in the back of her consciousness--

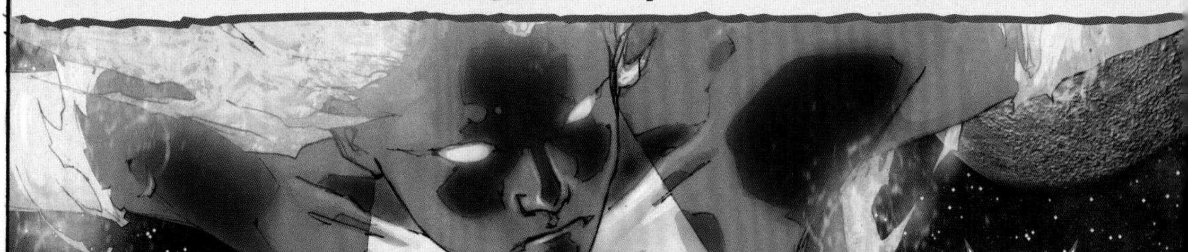

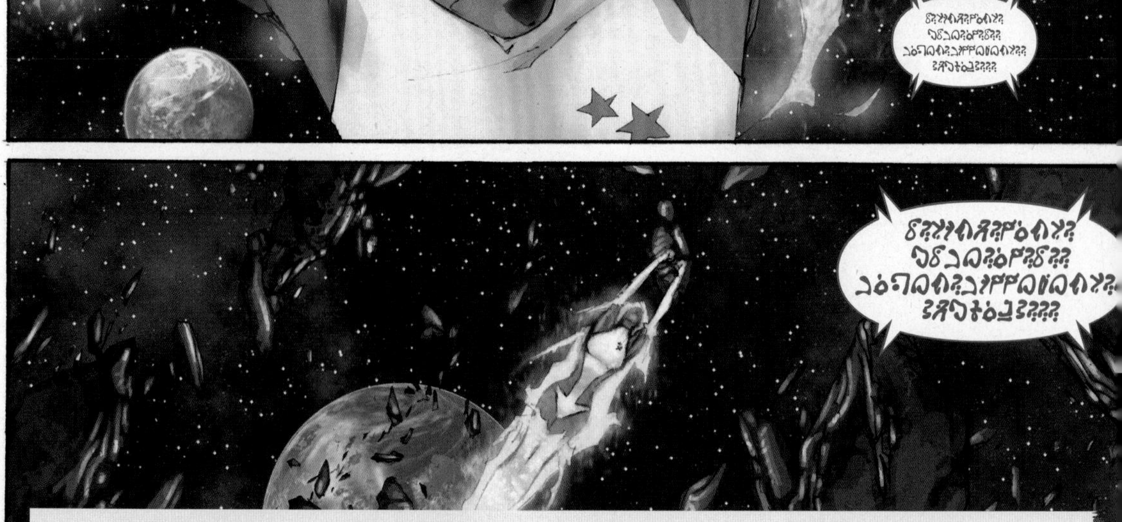
Binary followed the voice for days, getting closer and closer to the source with each passing moment.

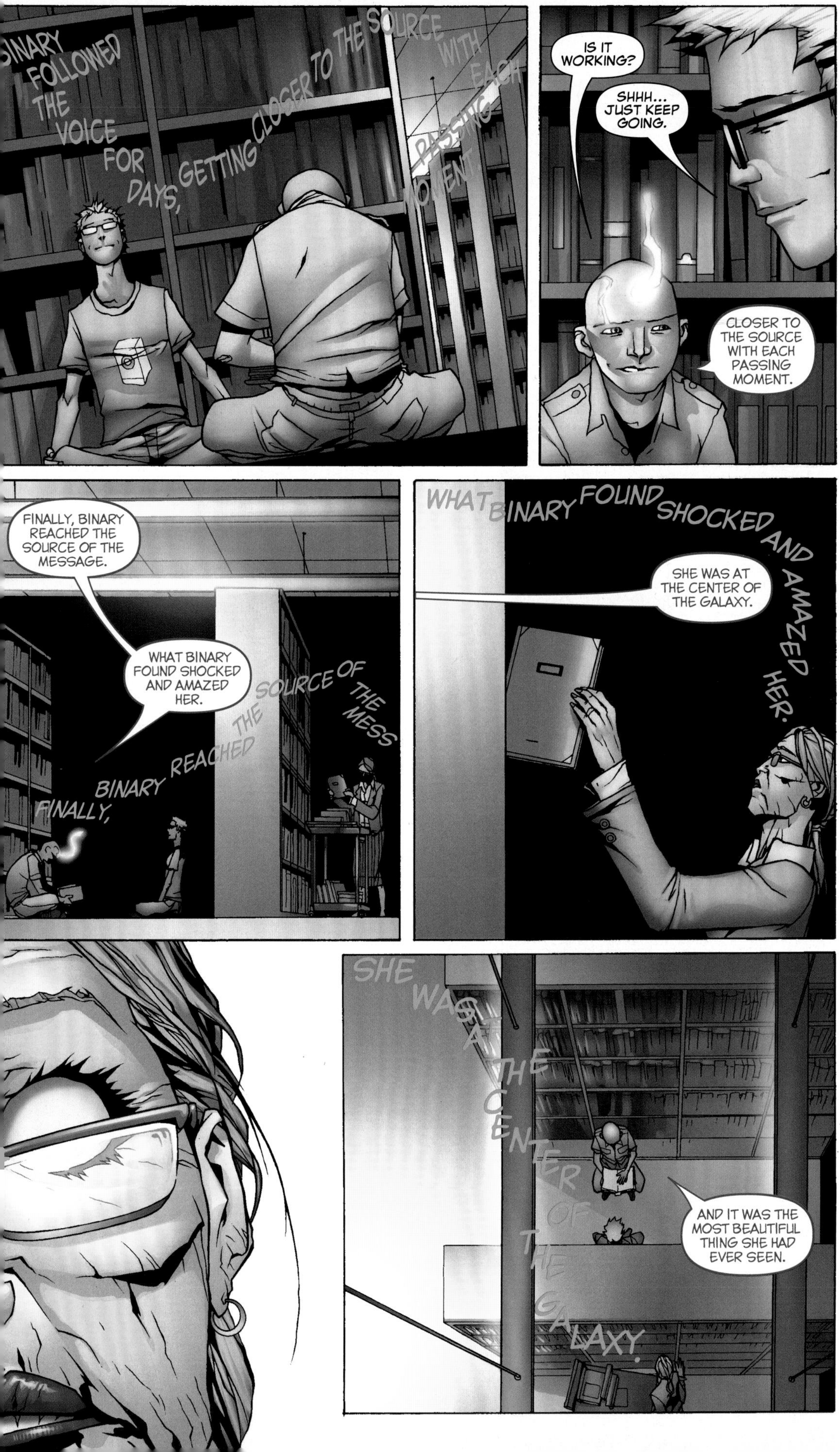
BINARY FOLLOWED THE VOICE FOR DAYS, GETTING CLOSER TO THE SOURCE WITH EACH PASSING MOMENT
IS IT WORKING?
SHHH... JUST KEEP GOING.
CLOSER TO THE SOURCE WITH EACH PASSING MOMENT.
FINALLY, BINARY REACHED THE SOURCE OF THE MESSAGE.
WHAT BINARY FOUND SHOCKED AND AMAZED HER.
FINALLY, BINARY REACHED THE SOURCE OF THE MESS
WHAT BINARY FOUND SHOCKED AND AMAZED HER.
SHE WAS AT THE CENTER OF THE GALAXY.
SHE WAS AT THE CENTER OF THE GALAXY.
AND IT WAS THE MOST BEAUTIFUL THING SHE HAD EVER SEEN.

The beauty of her surroundings was nothing compared to the awesomeness of the source of the telepathic transmissions.

ⵔⵣⵙⵓⵙⴲⴲⵔⵙⵙ
ⵙⴲⵔⵛⴲⴲⵔⴲⵣⵙⵙ
ⵡⵙⵔⵣⵓⵔⵣⵙⴲⴲⵙⵔⵙ
ⵣⴲⴲⵙⵔⵙⵝⵔ

I DON'T UNDERSTAND.

OH MY--

YES.

‹YOU UNDERSTAND NOW.›

‹YOUR HELP. REQUIRED. I AM ENDING. TH KEEPERS. ARE ENDING.›

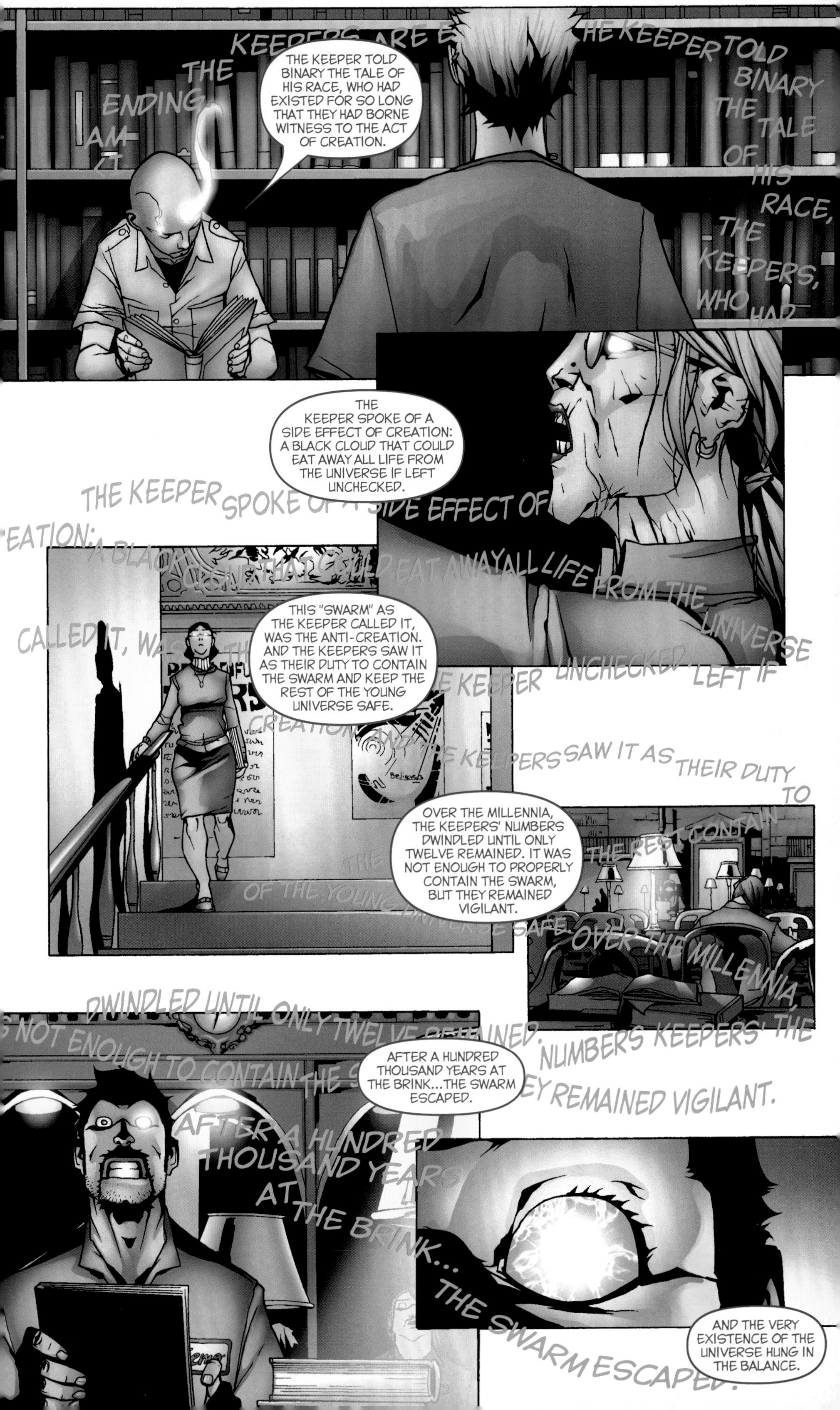
THE KEEPER TOLD BINARY THE TALE OF HIS RACE, WHO HAD EXISTED FOR SO LONG THAT THEY HAD BORNE WITNESS TO THE ACT OF CREATION.
THE KEEPER SPOKE OF A SIDE EFFECT OF CREATION: A BLACK CLOUD THAT COULD EAT AWAY ALL LIFE FROM THE UNIVERSE IF LEFT UNCHECKED.
THIS "SWARM" AS THE KEEPER CALLED IT, WAS THE ANTI-CREATION. AND THE KEEPERS SAW IT AS THEIR DUTY TO CONTAIN THE SWARM AND KEEP THE REST OF THE YOUNG UNIVERSE SAFE.
OVER THE MILLENNIA, THE KEEPERS' NUMBERS DWINDLED UNTIL ONLY TWELVE REMAINED. IT WAS NOT ENOUGH TO PROPERLY CONTAIN THE SWARM, BUT THEY REMAINED VIGILANT.
AFTER A HUNDRED THOUSAND YEARS AT THE BRINK...THE SWARM ESCAPED.
AND THE VERY EXISTENCE OF THE UNIVERSE HUNG IN THE BALANCE.

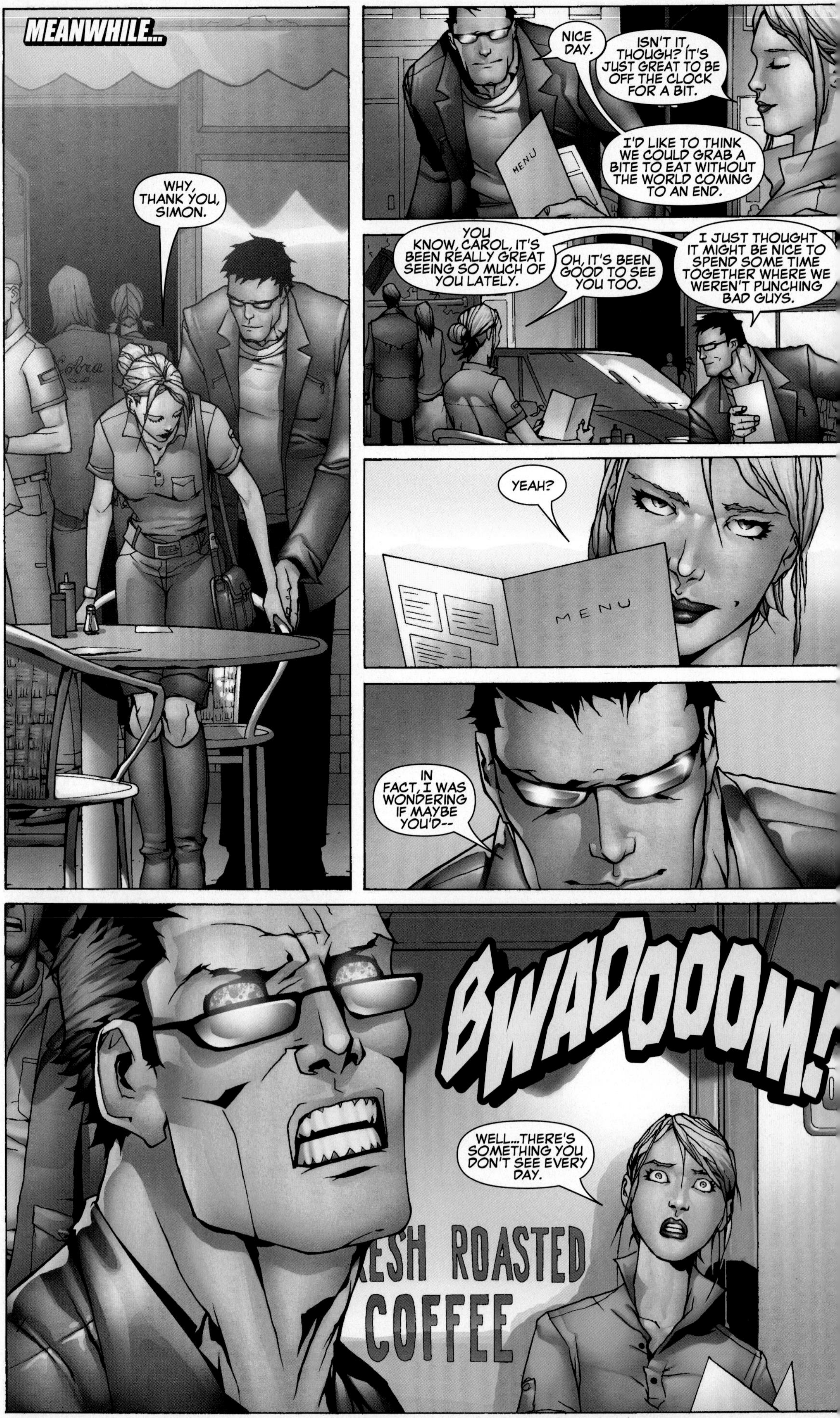
MEANWHILE...
WHY, THANK YOU, SIMON.
NICE DAY.
ISN'T IT, THOUGH? IT'S JUST GREAT TO BE OFF THE CLOCK FOR A BIT.
MENU
I'D LIKE TO THINK WE COULD GRAB A BITE TO EAT WITHOUT THE WORLD COMING TO AN END.
YOU KNOW, CAROL, IT'S BEEN REALLY GREAT SEEING SO MUCH OF YOU LATELY.
OH, IT'S BEEN GOOD TO SEE YOU TOO.
I JUST THOUGHT IT MIGHT BE NICE TO SPEND SOME TIME TOGETHER WHERE WE WEREN'T PUNCHING BAD GUYS.
YEAH?
MENU
IN FACT, I WAS WONDERING IF MAYBE YOU'D--
BWADOOOM!
WELL...THERE'S SOMETHING YOU DON'T SEE EVERY DAY.
RESH ROASTED
COFFEE

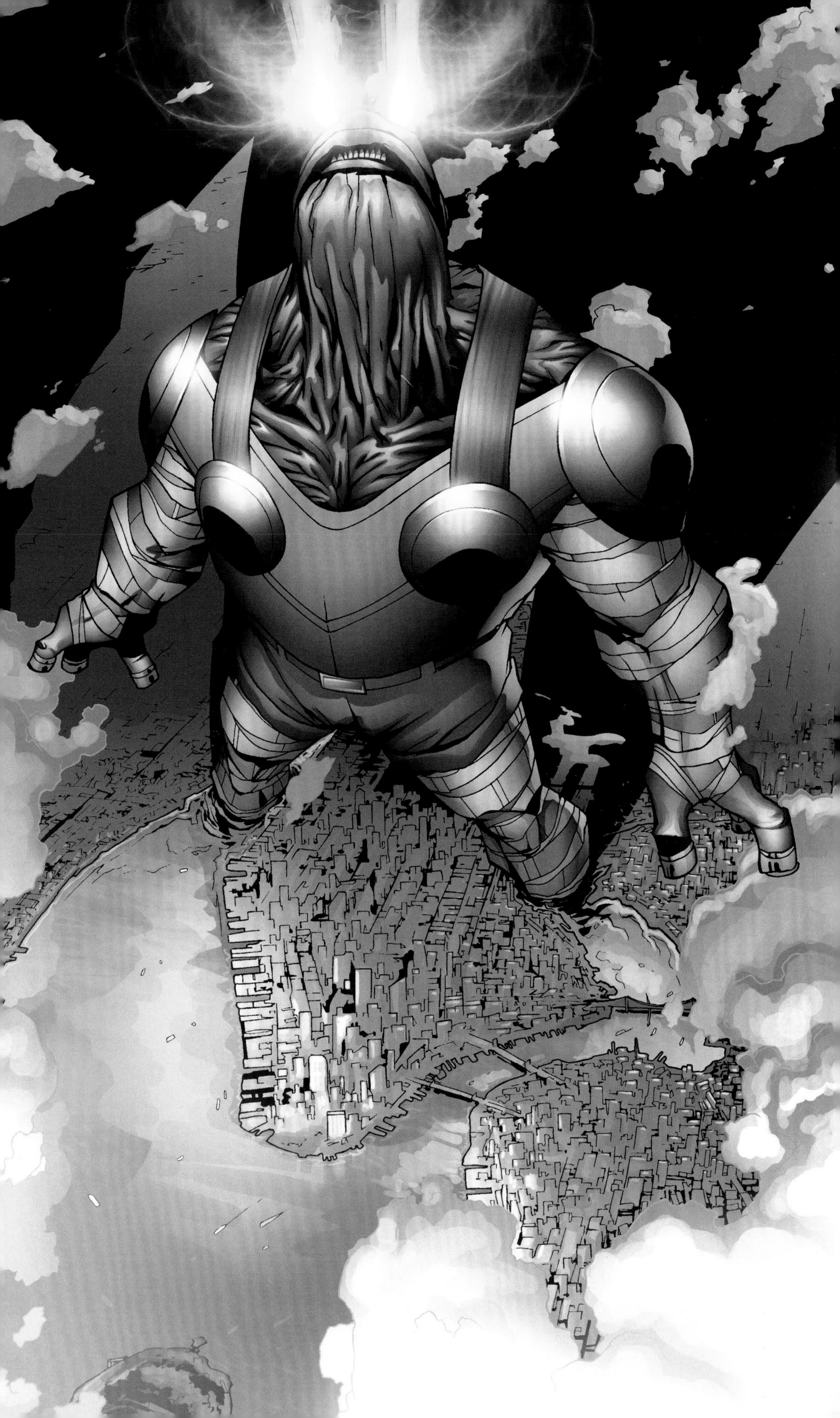

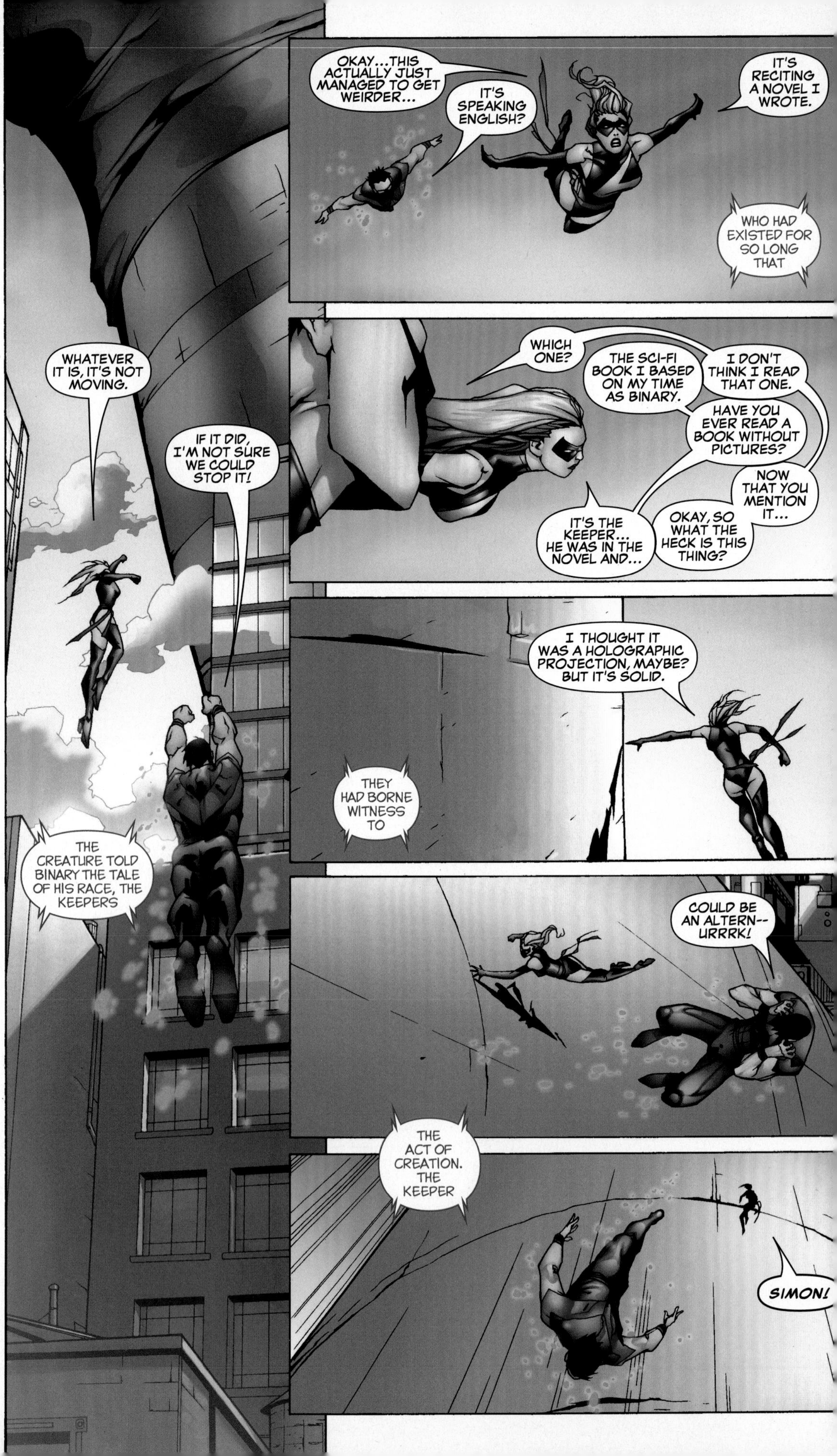
WHATEVER IT IS, IT'S NOT MOVING.
IF IT DID, I'M NOT SURE WE COULD STOP IT!
THE CREATURE TOLD BINARY THE TALE OF HIS RACE, THE KEEPERS
OKAY...THIS ACTUALLY JUST MANAGED TO GET WEIRDER...
IT'S SPEAKING ENGLISH?
IT'S RECITING A NOVEL I WROTE.
WHO HAD EXISTED FOR SO LONG THAT
WHICH ONE?
THE SCI-FI BOOK I BASED ON MY TIME AS BINARY.
I DON'T THINK I READ THAT ONE.
HAVE YOU EVER READ A BOOK WITHOUT PICTURES?
NOW THAT YOU MENTION IT...
IT'S THE KEEPER... HE WAS IN THE NOVEL AND...
OKAY, SO WHAT THE HECK IS THIS THING?
I THOUGHT IT WAS A HOLOGRAPHIC PROJECTION, MAYBE? BUT IT'S SOLID.
THEY HAD BORNE WITNESS TO
COULD BE AN ALTERN-- URRRK!
THE ACT OF CREATION. THE KEEPER
SIMON!

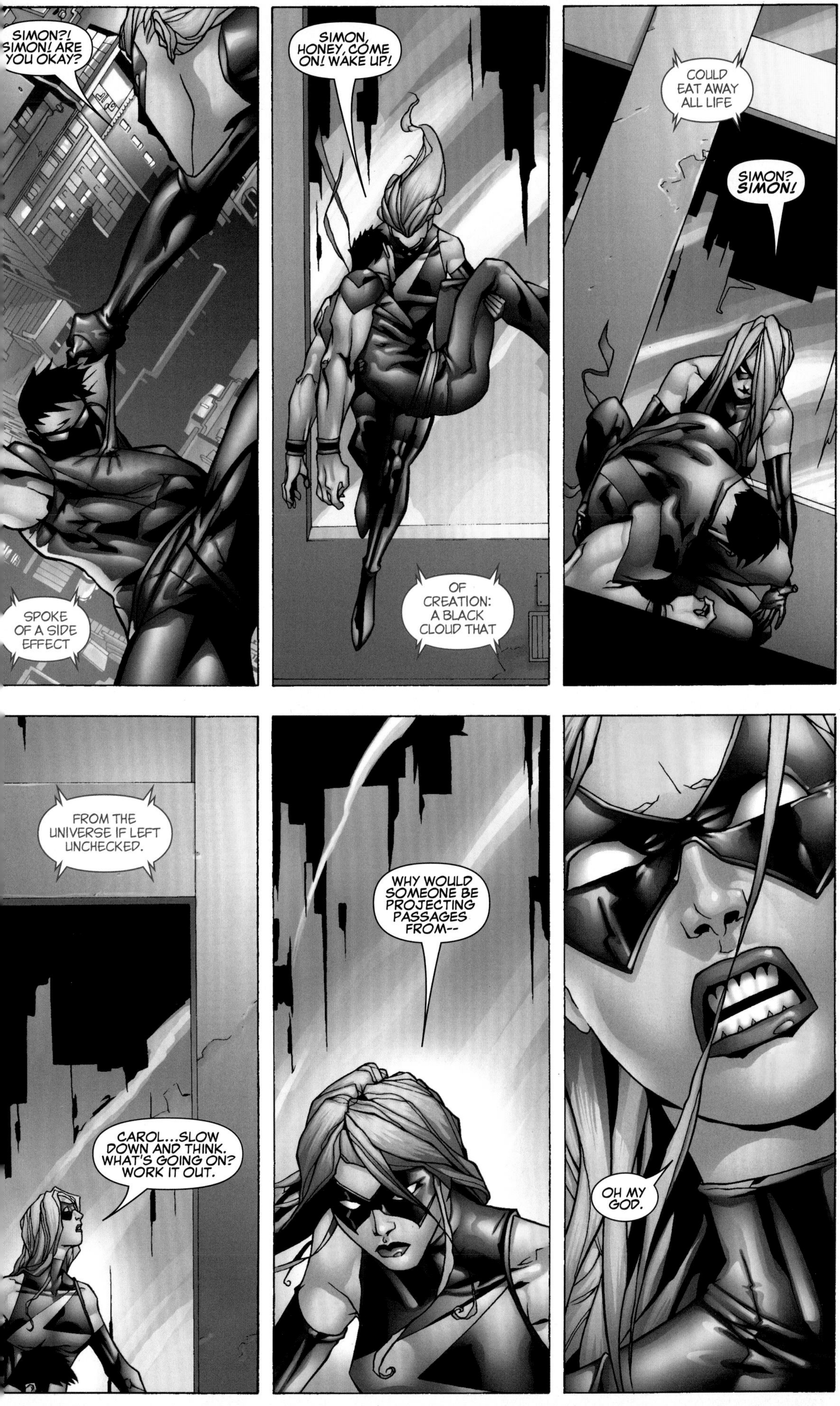
SIMON?! SIMON! ARE YOU OKAY?
SPOKE OF A SIDE EFFECT
SIMON, HONEY, COME ON! WAKE UP!
OF CREATION: A BLACK CLOUD THAT
COULD EAT AWAY ALL LIFE
SIMON? SIMON!
FROM THE UNIVERSE IF LEFT UNCHECKED.
CAROL...SLOW DOWN AND THINK. WHAT'S GOING ON? WORK IT OUT.
WHY WOULD SOMEONE BE PROJECTING PASSAGES FROM--
OH MY GOD.

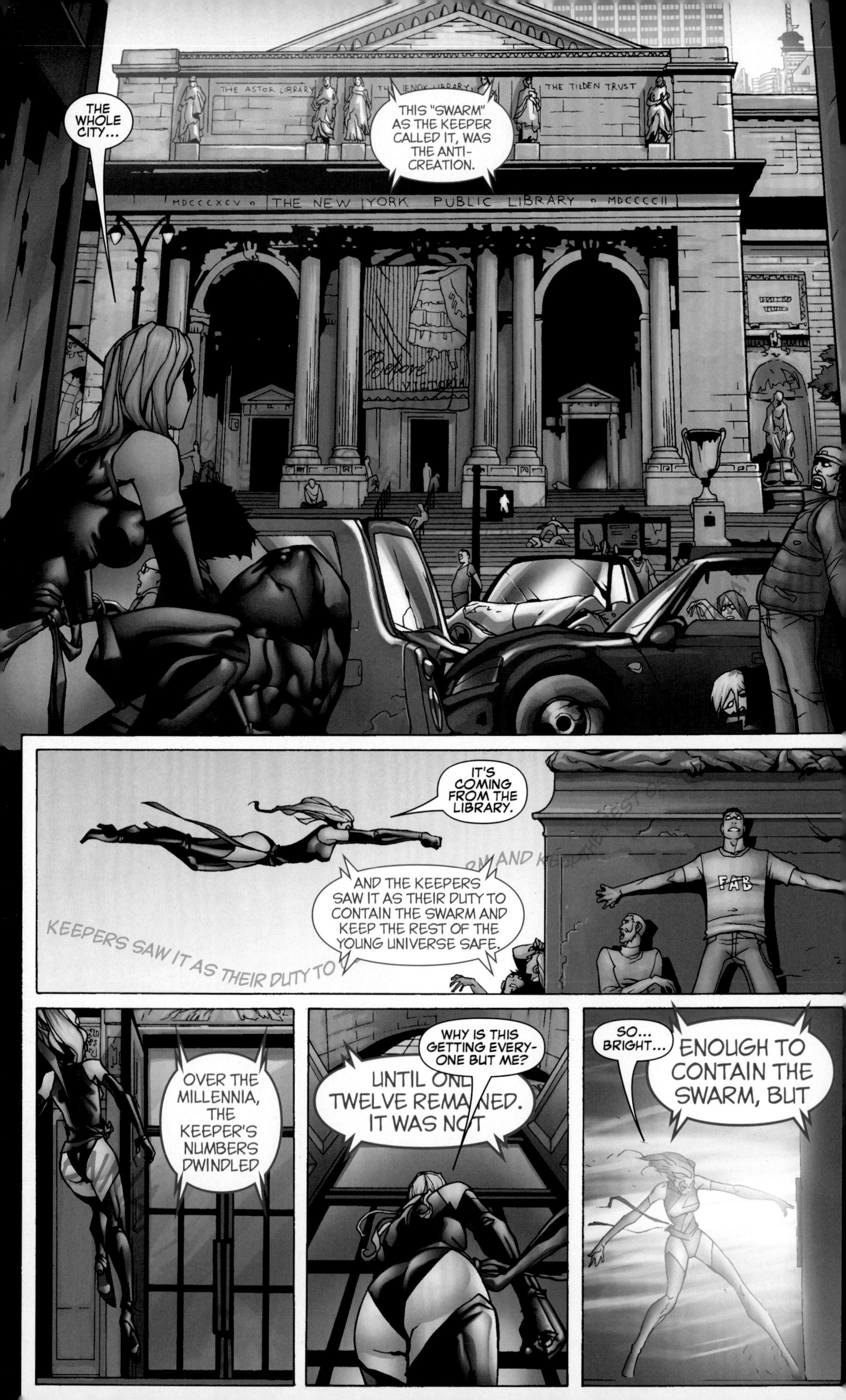
THE WHOLE CITY...
THE ASTOR LIBRARY
THE TILDEN TRUST
THIS "SWARM" AS THE KEEPER CALLED IT, WAS THE ANTI-CREATION.
MDCCCXCV THE NEW YORK PUBLIC LIBRARY MDCCCCII
IT'S COMING FROM THE LIBRARY.
AND THE KEEPERS SAW IT AS THEIR DUTY TO CONTAIN THE SWARM AND KEEP THE REST OF THE YOUNG UNIVERSE SAFE.
KEEPERS SAW IT AS THEIR DUTY TO
FAB
OVER THE MILLENNIA, THE KEEPER'S NUMBERS DWINDLED
WHY IS THIS GETTING EVERY-ONE BUT ME?
UNTIL ONL TWELVE REMA NED. IT WAS NOT
SO... BRIGHT...
ENOUGH TO CONTAIN THE SWARM, BUT

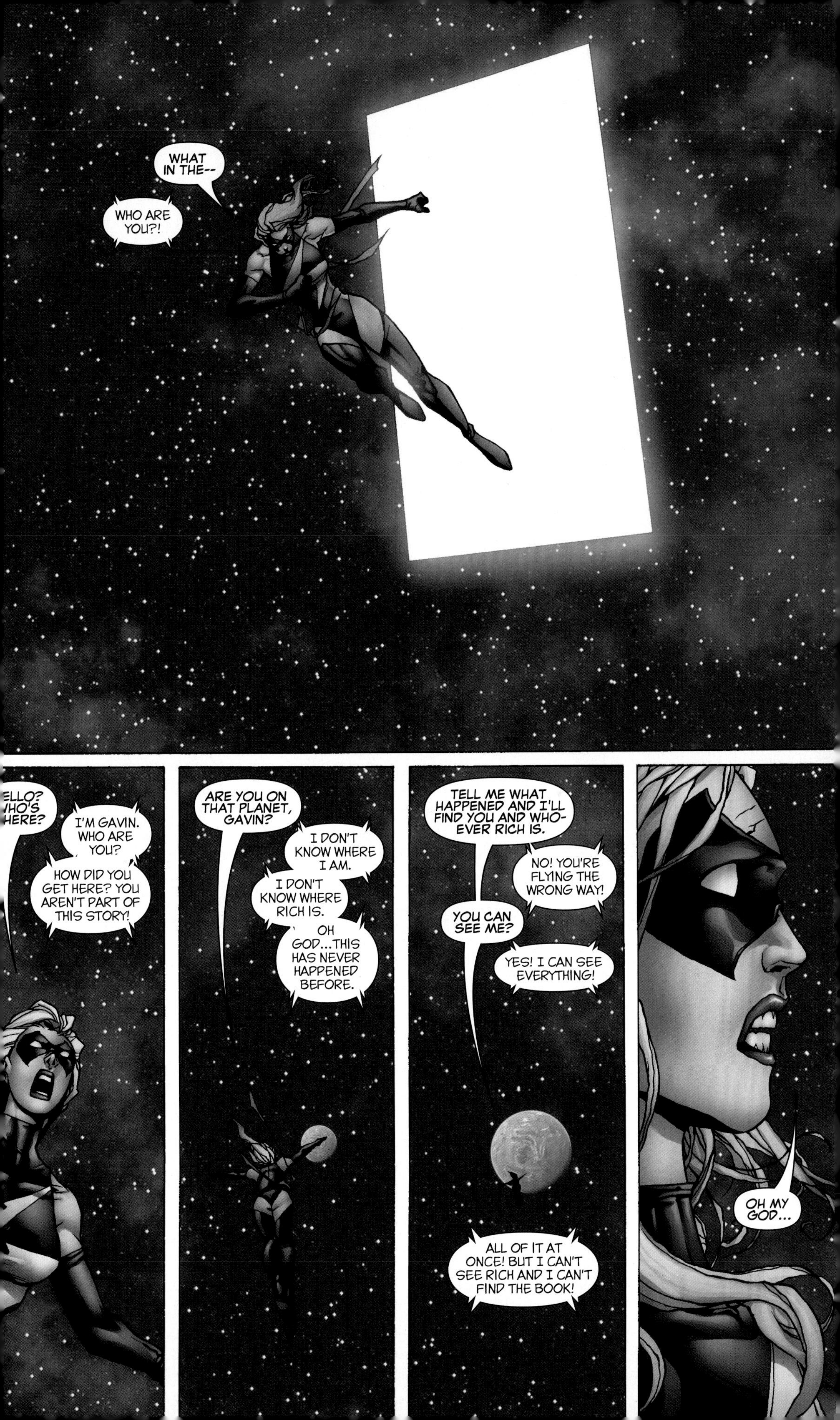

WHAT IN THE--
WHO ARE YOU?!
ELLO? WHO'S HERE?
I'M GAVIN. WHO ARE YOU?
HOW DID YOU GET HERE? YOU AREN'T PART OF THIS STORY!
ARE YOU ON THAT PLANET, GAVIN?
I DON'T KNOW WHERE I AM.
I DON'T KNOW WHERE RICH IS.
OH GOD...THIS HAS NEVER HAPPENED BEFORE.
TELL ME WHAT HAPPENED AND I'LL FIND YOU AND WHO-EVER RICH IS.
NO! YOU'RE FLYING THE WRONG WAY!
YOU CAN SEE ME?
YES! I CAN SEE EVERYTHING!
ALL OF IT AT ONCE! BUT I CAN'T SEE RICH AND I CAN'T FIND THE BOOK!
OH MY GOD...

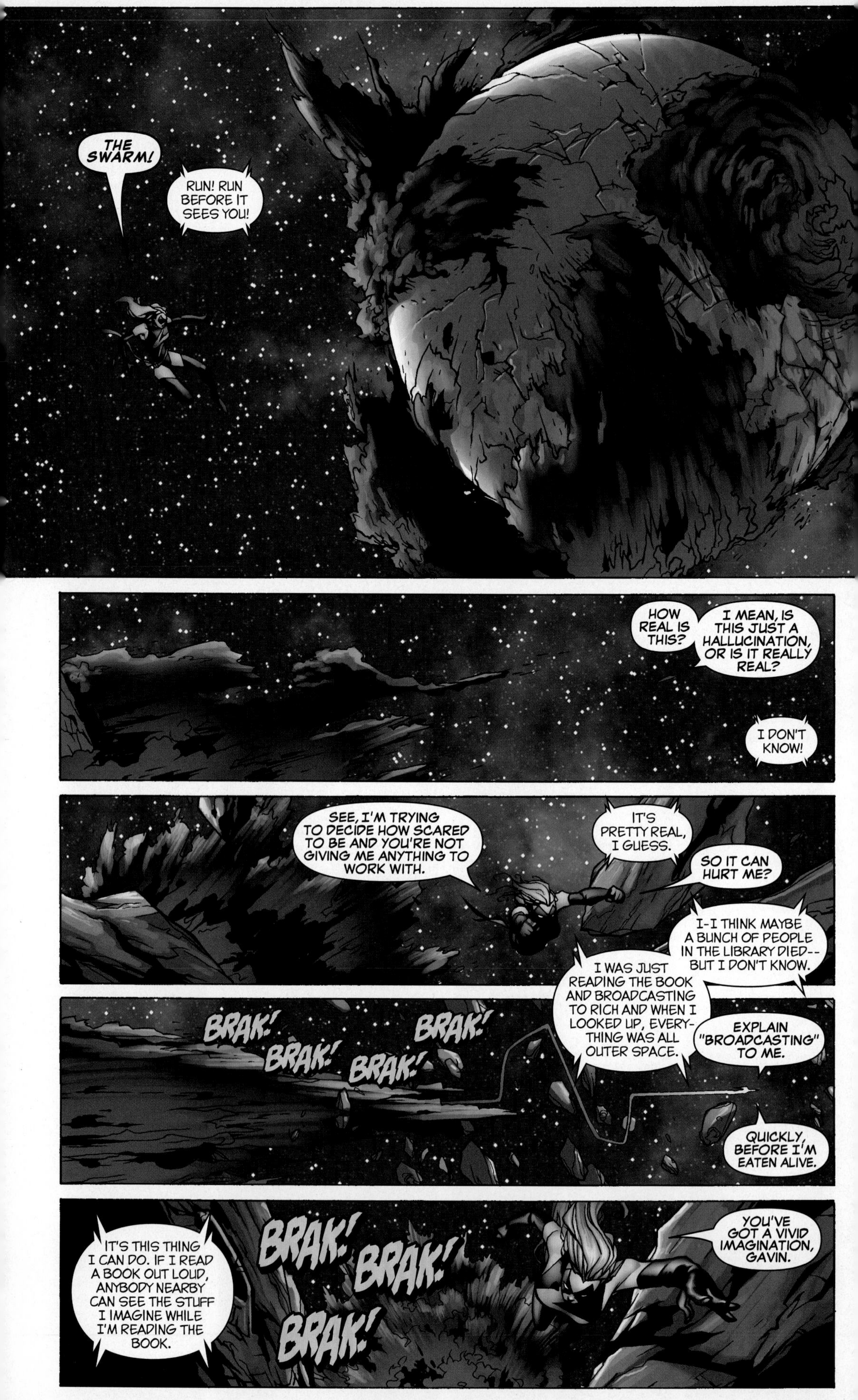
THE SWARM!
RUN! RUN BEFORE IT SEES YOU!
HOW REAL IS THIS?
I MEAN, IS THIS JUST A HALLUCINATION, OR IS IT REALLY REAL?
I DON'T KNOW!
SEE, I'M TRYING TO DECIDE HOW SCARED TO BE AND YOU'RE NOT GIVING ME ANYTHING TO WORK WITH.
IT'S PRETTY REAL, I GUESS.
SO IT CAN HURT ME?
I-I THINK MAYBE A BUNCH OF PEOPLE IN THE LIBRARY DIED--BUT I DON'T KNOW.
I WAS JUST READING THE BOOK AND BROADCASTING TO RICH AND WHEN I LOOKED UP, EVERYTHING WAS ALL OUTER SPACE.
BRAK! BRAK! BRAK! BRAK!
EXPLAIN "BROADCASTING" TO ME.
QUICKLY, BEFORE I'M EATEN ALIVE.
IT'S THIS THING I CAN DO. IF I READ A BOOK OUT LOUD, ANYBODY NEARBY CAN SEE THE STUFF I IMAGINE WHILE I'M READING THE BOOK.
BRAK! BRAK! BRAK!
YOU'VE GOT A VIVID IMAGINATION, GAVIN.

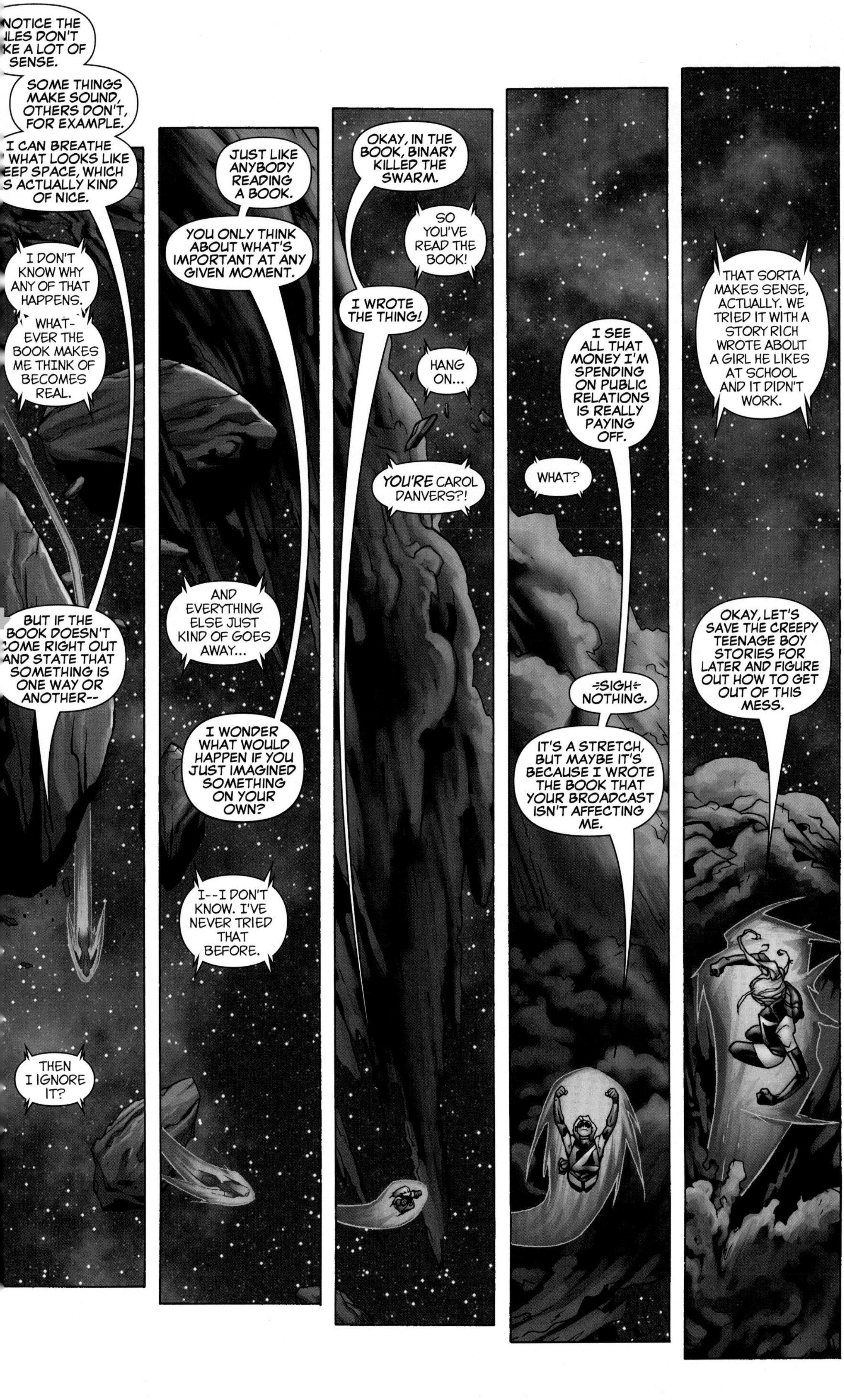
NOTICE THE
ILES DON'T
KE A LOT OF
SENSE.
SOME THINGS MAKE SOUND, OTHERS DON'T, FOR EXAMPLE.
I CAN BREATHE
WHAT LOOKS LIKE
EEP SPACE, WHICH
S ACTUALLY KIND
OF NICE.
I DON'T KNOW WHY ANY OF THAT HAPPENS.
WHAT-EVER THE BOOK MAKES ME THINK OF BECOMES REAL.
BUT IF THE BOOK DOESN'T
COME RIGHT OUT
AND STATE THAT SOMETHING IS ONE WAY OR ANOTHER--
THEN I IGNORE IT?
JUST LIKE ANYBODY READING A BOOK.
YOU ONLY THINK ABOUT WHAT'S IMPORTANT AT ANY GIVEN MOMENT.
AND EVERYTHING ELSE JUST KIND OF GOES AWAY...
I WONDER WHAT WOULD HAPPEN IF YOU JUST IMAGINED SOMETHING ON YOUR OWN?
I--I DON'T KNOW. I'VE NEVER TRIED THAT BEFORE.
OKAY, IN THE BOOK, BINARY KILLED THE SWARM.
SO YOU'VE READ THE BOOK!
I WROTE THE THING!
HANG ON...
YOU'RE CAROL DANVERS?!
I SEE ALL THAT MONEY I'M SPENDING ON PUBLIC RELATIONS IS REALLY PAYING OFF.
WHAT?
=SIGH= NOTHING.
IT'S A STRETCH, BUT MAYBE IT'S BECAUSE I WROTE THE BOOK THAT YOUR BROADCAST ISN'T AFFECTING ME.
THAT SORTA MAKES SENSE, ACTUALLY. WE TRIED IT WITH A STORY RICH WROTE ABOUT A GIRL HE LIKES AT SCHOOL AND IT DIDN'T WORK.
OKAY, LET'S SAVE THE CREEPY TEENAGE BOY STORIES FOR LATER AND FIGURE OUT HOW TO GET OUT OF THIS MESS.

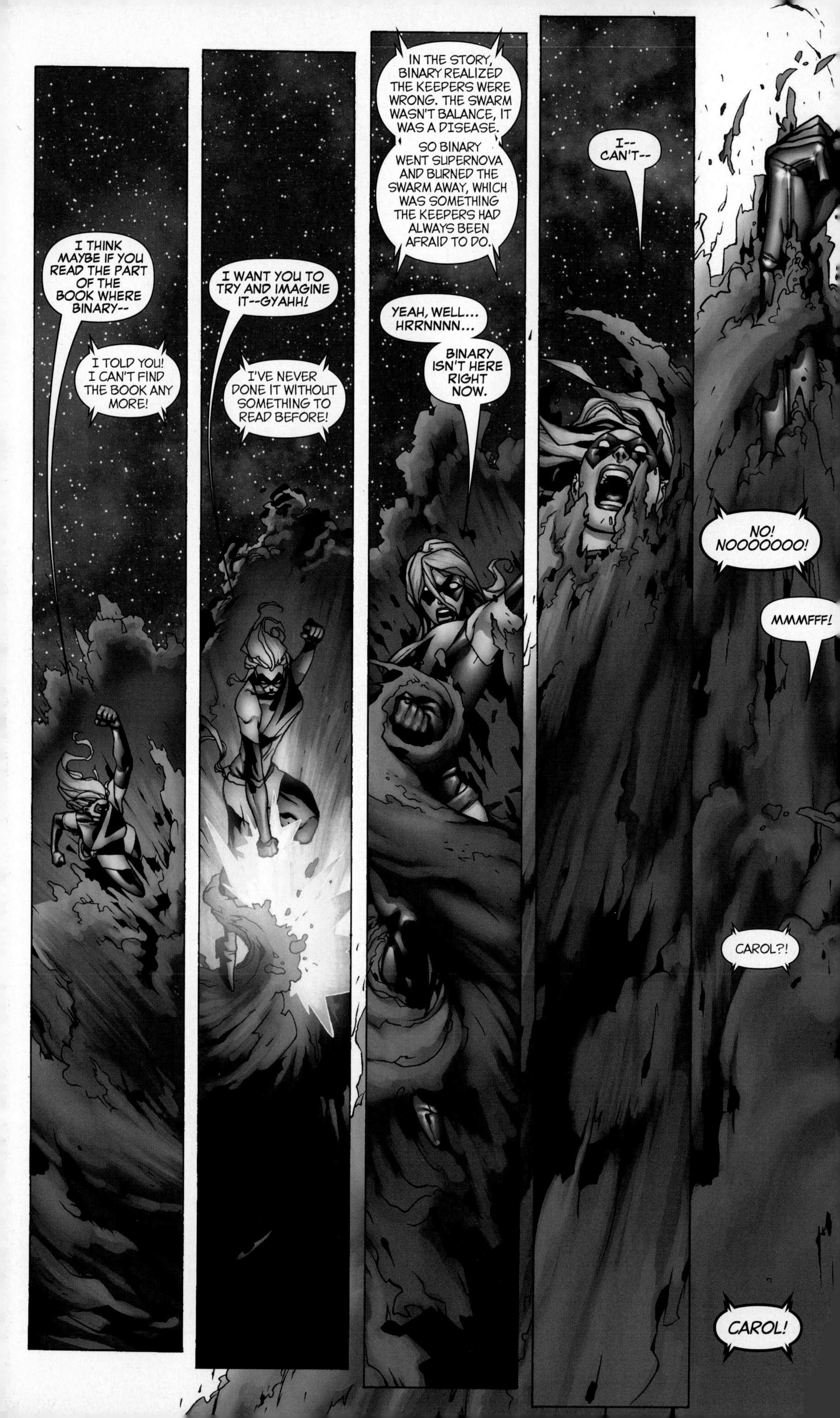
I THINK MAYBE IF YOU READ THE PART OF THE BOOK WHERE BINARY--
I TOLD YOU! I CAN'T FIND THE BOOK ANY MORE!
I WANT YOU TO TRY AND IMAGINE IT--GYAHH!
I'VE NEVER DONE IT WITHOUT SOMETHING TO READ BEFORE!
IN THE STORY, BINARY REALIZED THE KEEPERS WERE WRONG. THE SWARM WASN'T BALANCE, IT WAS A DISEASE.
SO BINARY WENT SUPERNOVA AND BURNED THE SWARM AWAY, WHICH WAS SOMETHING THE KEEPERS HAD ALWAYS BEEN AFRAID TO DO.
YEAH, WELL... HRRNNNN...
BINARY ISN'T HERE RIGHT NOW.
I-- CAN'T--
NO! NOOOOOOO!
MMMFFF!
CAROL?!
CAROL!

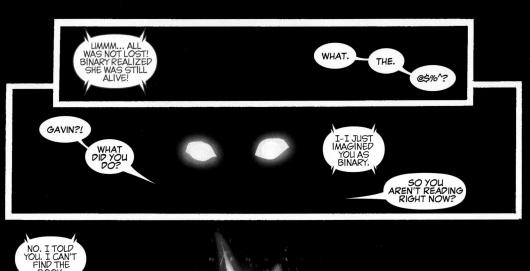

UMMM... ALL WAS NOT LOST! BINARY REALIZED SHE WAS STILL ALIVE!

WHAT. THE. @$%^?

GAVIN?! WHAT DID YOU DO?

I-I JUST IMAGINED YOU AS BINARY.

SO YOU AREN'T READING RIGHT NOW?

NO. I TOLD YOU. I CAN'T FIND THE BOOK.

OKAY. YEAH.

WOW...

WOW.

YOU KNOW WHAT? WE CAN DO THIS, GAVIN. ME AND YOU.

I'M GOING TO START POWERING UP AND I WANT YOU TO IMAGINE THE SWARM BURNING AWAY. OKAY?

I--I DON'T--

YOU CAN DO IT, GAVIN... COME ON NOW. IN 3...2...1...

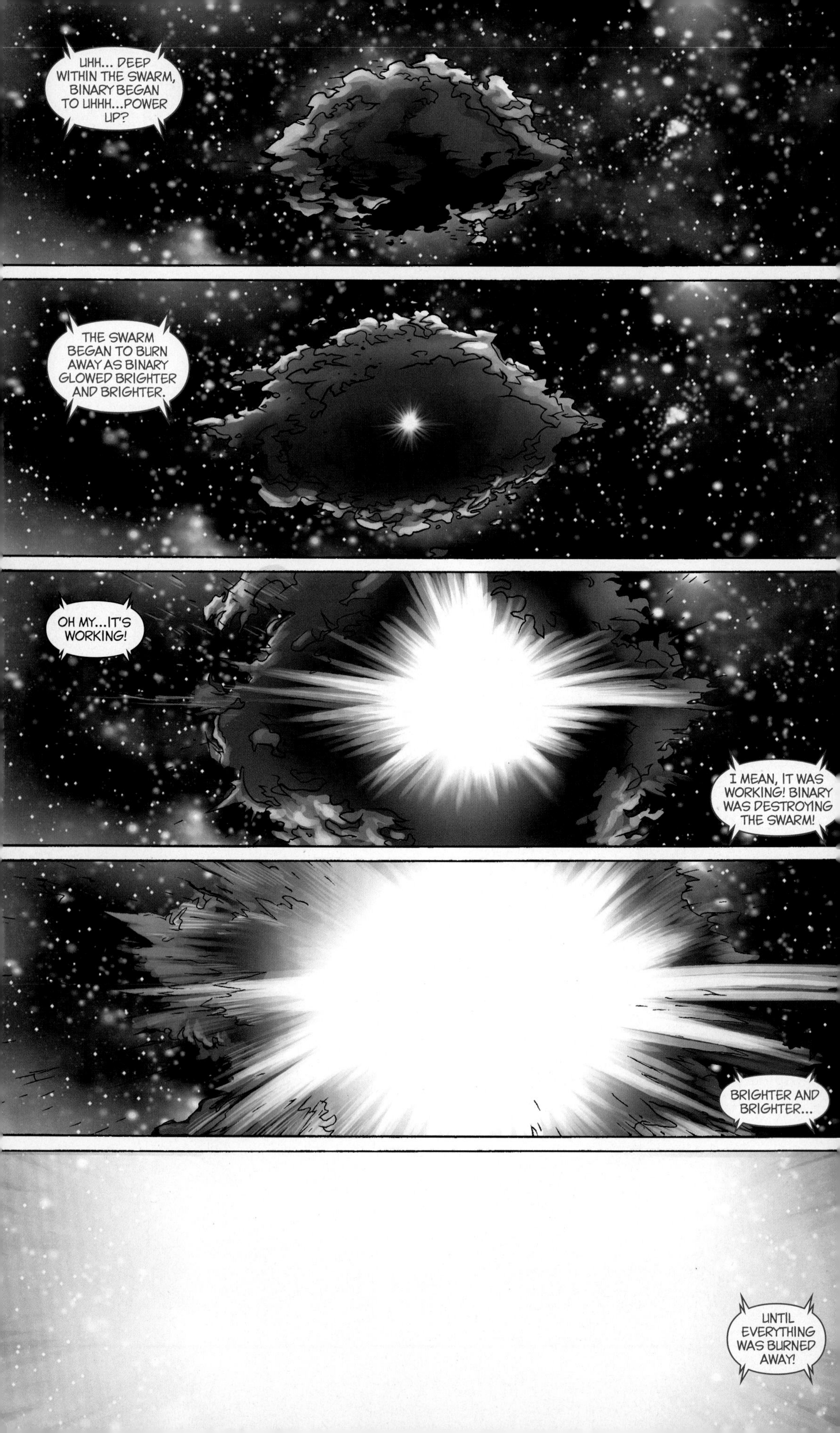
UHH... DEEP WITHIN THE SWARM, BINARY BEGAN TO UHHH...POWER UP?
THE SWARM BEGAN TO BURN AWAY AS BINARY GLOWED BRIGHTER AND BRIGHTER.
OH MY...IT'S WORKING!
I MEAN, IT WAS WORKING! BINARY WAS DESTROYING THE SWARM!
BRIGHTER AND BRIGHTER...
UNTIL EVERYTHING WAS BURNED AWAY!

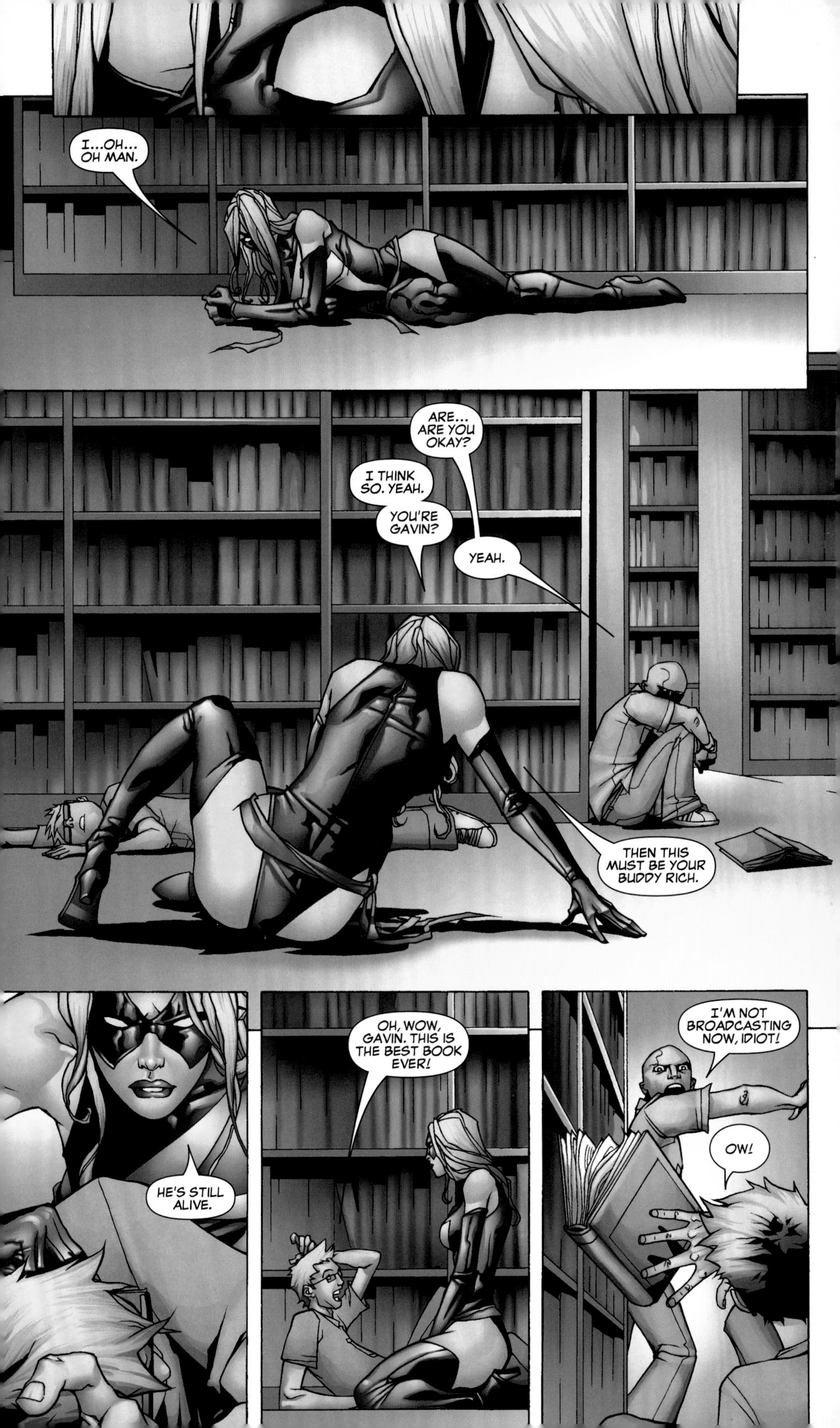
I...OH...
OH MAN.
ARE...
ARE YOU
OKAY?
I THINK
SO. YEAH.
YOU'RE
GAVIN?
YEAH.
THEN THIS
MUST BE YOUR
BUDDY RICH.
HE'S STILL
ALIVE.
OH, WOW,
GAVIN. THIS IS
THE BEST BOOK
EVER!
I'M NOT
BROADCASTING
NOW, IDIOT!
OW!

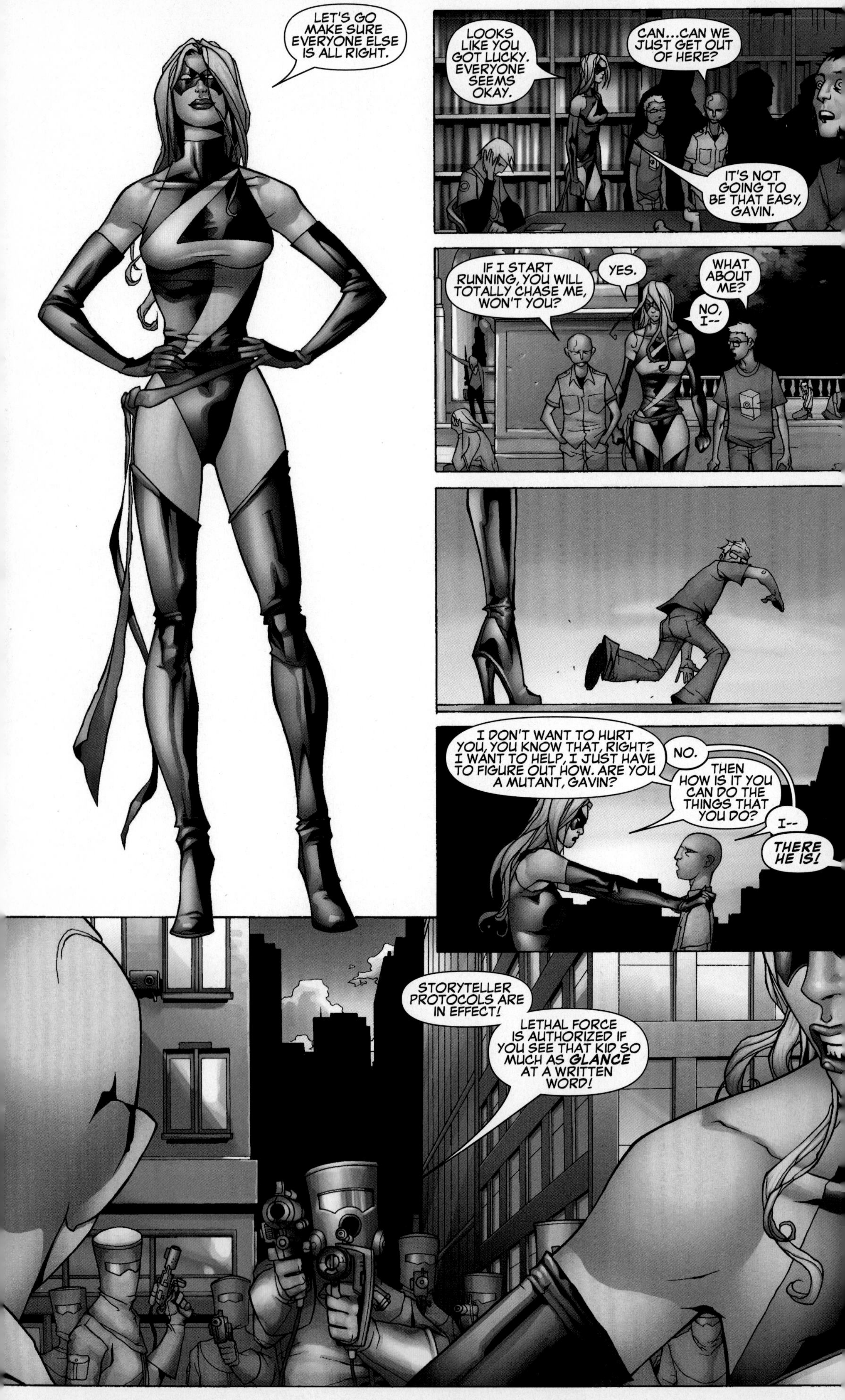
LET'S GO MAKE SURE EVERYONE ELSE IS ALL RIGHT.
LOOKS LIKE YOU GOT LUCKY. EVERYONE SEEMS OKAY.
CAN...CAN WE JUST GET OUT OF HERE?
IT'S NOT GOING TO BE THAT EASY, GAVIN.
IF I START RUNNING, YOU WILL TOTALLY CHASE ME, WON'T YOU?
YES.
WHAT ABOUT ME?
NO, I--
I DON'T WANT TO HURT YOU, YOU KNOW THAT, RIGHT? I WANT TO HELP, I JUST HAVE TO FIGURE OUT HOW. ARE YOU A MUTANT, GAVIN?
NO.
THEN HOW IS IT YOU CAN DO THE THINGS THAT YOU DO?
I--
THERE HE IS!
STORYTELLER PROTOCOLS ARE IN EFFECT!
LETHAL FORCE IS AUTHORIZED IF YOU SEE THAT KID SO MUCH AS GLANCE AT A WRITTEN WORD!

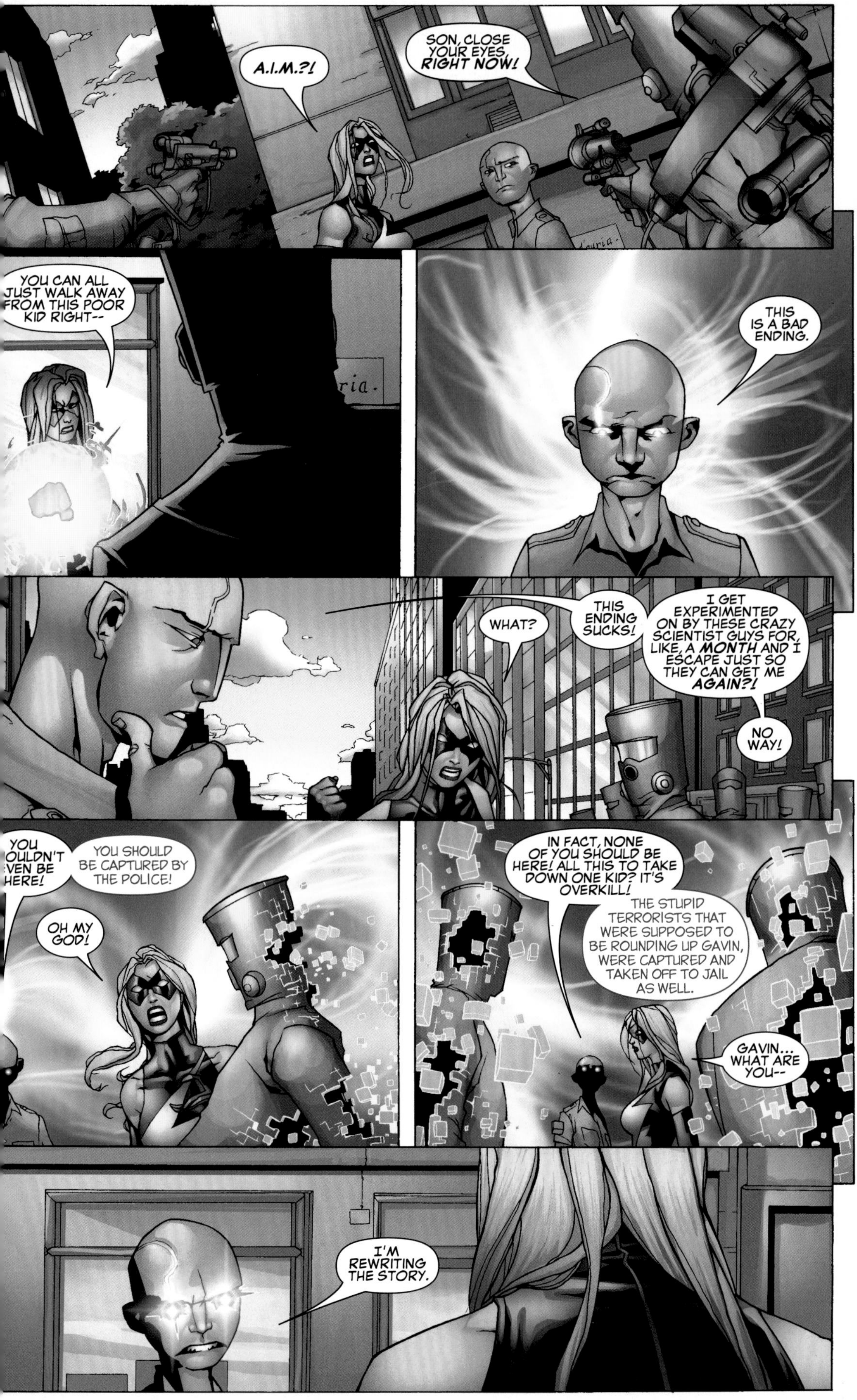
A.I.M.?!
SON, CLOSE YOUR EYES, RIGHT NOW!
YOU CAN ALL JUST WALK AWAY FROM THIS POOR KID RIGHT--
THIS IS A BAD ENDING.
THIS ENDING SUCKS!
WHAT?
I GET EXPERIMENTED ON BY THESE CRAZY SCIENTIST GUYS FOR, LIKE, A MONTH AND I ESCAPE JUST SO THEY CAN GET ME AGAIN?!
NO WAY!
YOU SHOULD BE CAPTURED BY THE POLICE!
OH MY GOD!
IN FACT, NONE OF YOU SHOULD BE HERE! ALL THIS TO TAKE DOWN ONE KID? IT'S OVERKILL!
THE STUPID TERRORISTS THAT WERE SUPPOSED TO BE ROUNDING UP GAVIN, WERE CAPTURED AND TAKEN OFF TO JAIL AS WELL.
GAVIN... WHAT ARE YOU--
I'M REWRITING THE STORY.

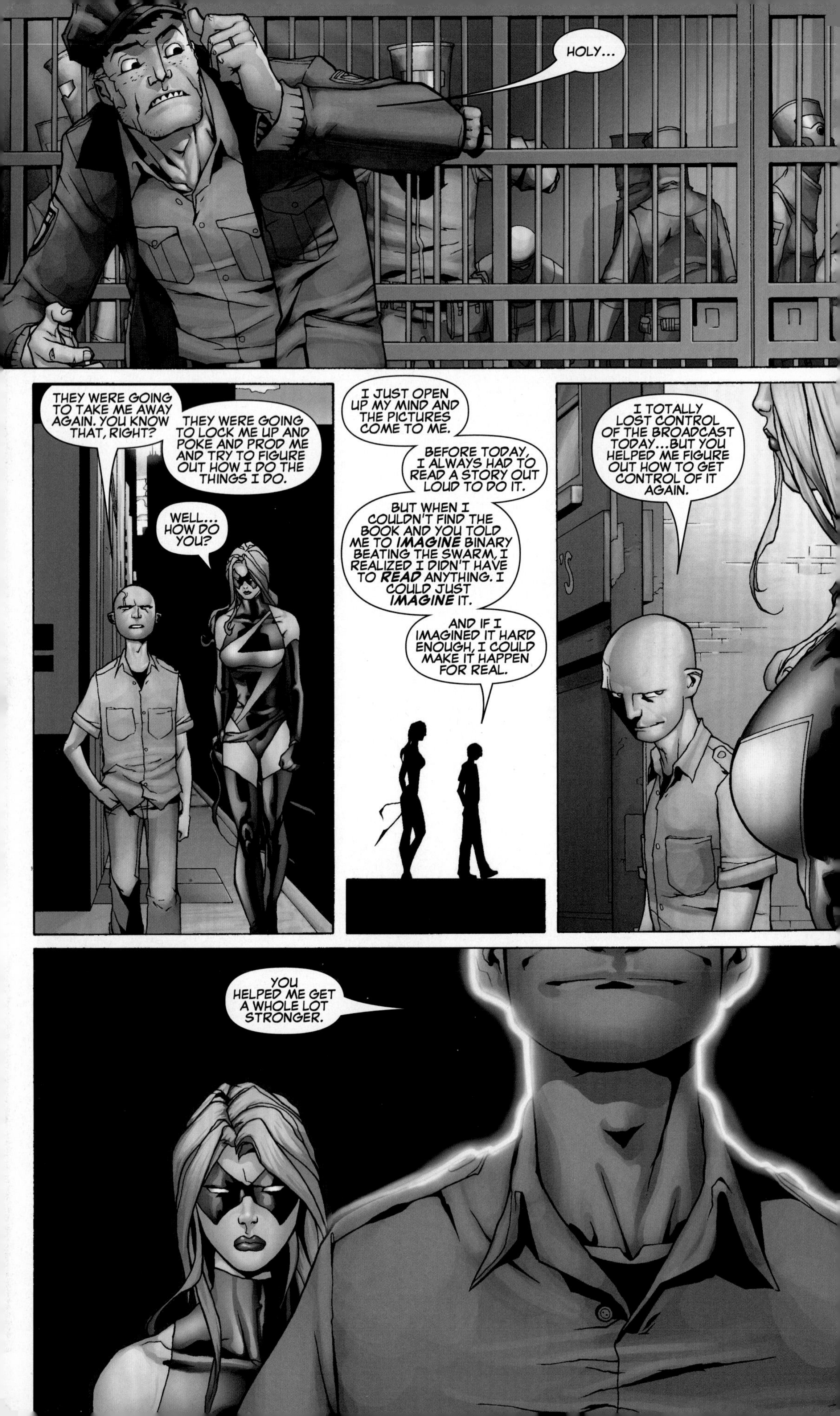
HOLY...
THEY WERE GOING TO TAKE ME AWAY AGAIN. YOU KNOW THAT, RIGHT?
THEY WERE GOING TO LOCK ME UP AND POKE AND PROD ME AND TRY TO FIGURE OUT HOW I DO THE THINGS I DO.
WELL... HOW DO YOU?
I JUST OPEN UP MY MIND AND THE PICTURES COME TO ME.
BEFORE TODAY, I ALWAYS HAD TO READ A STORY OUT LOUD TO DO IT.
BUT WHEN I COULDN'T FIND THE BOOK AND YOU TOLD ME TO *IMAGINE* BINARY BEATING THE SWARM, I REALIZED I DIDN'T HAVE TO *READ* ANYTHING. I COULD JUST *IMAGINE* IT.
AND IF I IMAGINED IT HARD ENOUGH, I COULD MAKE IT HAPPEN FOR REAL.
I TOTALLY LOST CONTROL OF THE BROADCAST TODAY...BUT YOU HELPED ME FIGURE OUT HOW TO GET CONTROL OF IT AGAIN.
YOU HELPED ME GET A WHOLE LOT STRONGER.

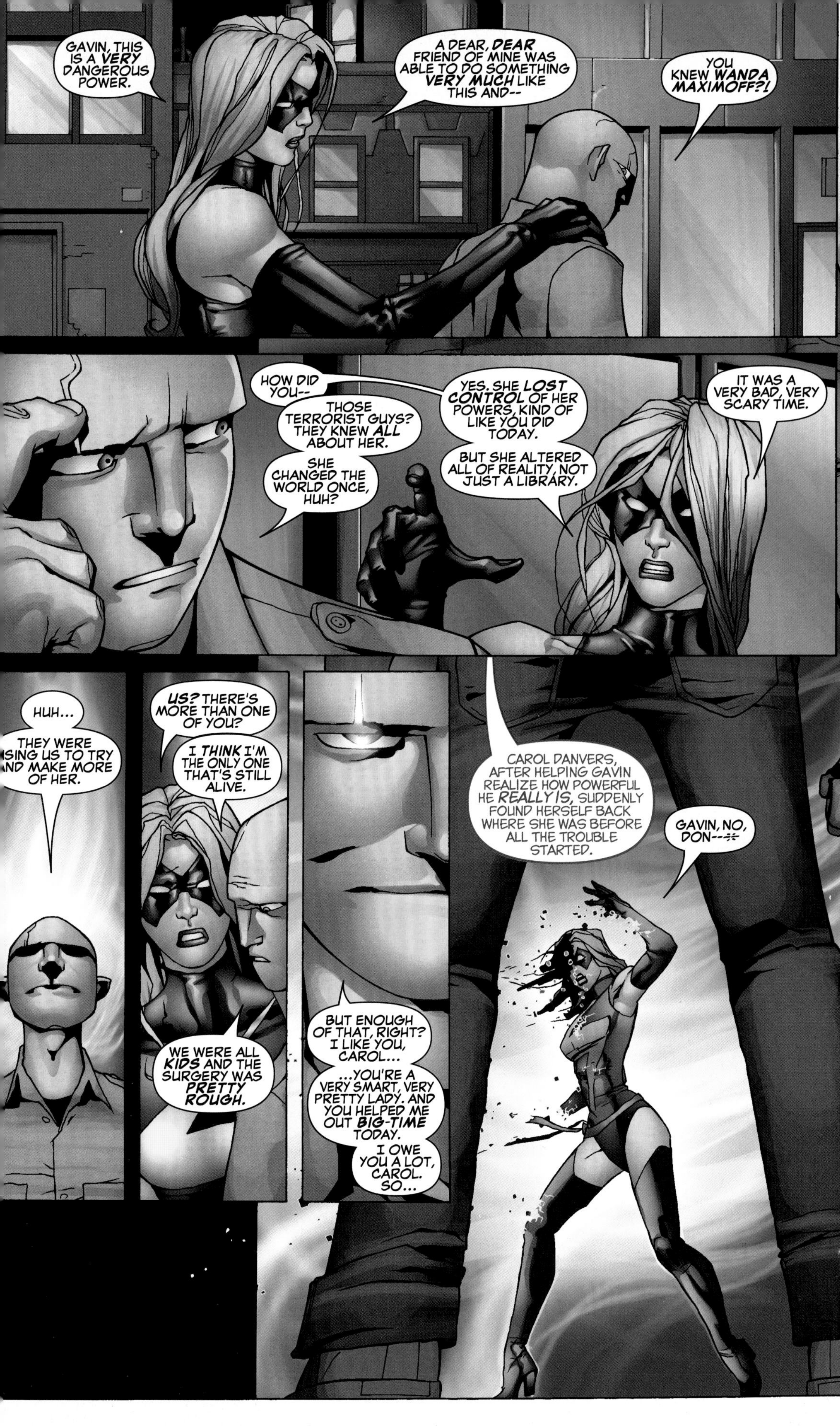
GAVIN, THIS IS A VERY DANGEROUS POWER.
A DEAR, DEAR FRIEND OF MINE WAS ABLE TO DO SOMETHING VERY MUCH LIKE THIS AND--
YOU KNEW WANDA MAXIMOFF?!
HOW DID YOU--
YES. SHE LOST CONTROL OF HER POWERS, KIND OF LIKE YOU DID TODAY.
BUT SHE ALTERED ALL OF REALITY, NOT JUST A LIBRARY.
IT WAS A VERY BAD, VERY SCARY TIME.
THOSE TERRORIST GUYS? THEY KNEW ALL ABOUT HER.
SHE CHANGED THE WORLD ONCE, HUH?
HUH...
THEY WERE USING US TO TRY AND MAKE MORE OF HER.
US? THERE'S MORE THAN ONE OF YOU?
I THINK I'M THE ONLY ONE THAT'S STILL ALIVE.
WE WERE ALL KIDS AND THE SURGERY WAS PRETTY ROUGH.
BUT ENOUGH OF THAT, RIGHT? I LIKE YOU, CAROL...
...YOU'RE A VERY SMART, VERY PRETTY LADY. AND YOU HELPED ME OUT BIG-TIME TODAY.
I OWE YOU A LOT, CAROL. SO...
CAROL DANVERS, AFTER HELPING GAVIN REALIZE HOW POWERFUL HE REALLY IS, SUDDENLY FOUND HERSELF BACK WHERE SHE WAS BEFORE ALL THE TROUBLE STARTED.
GAVIN, NO, DON--

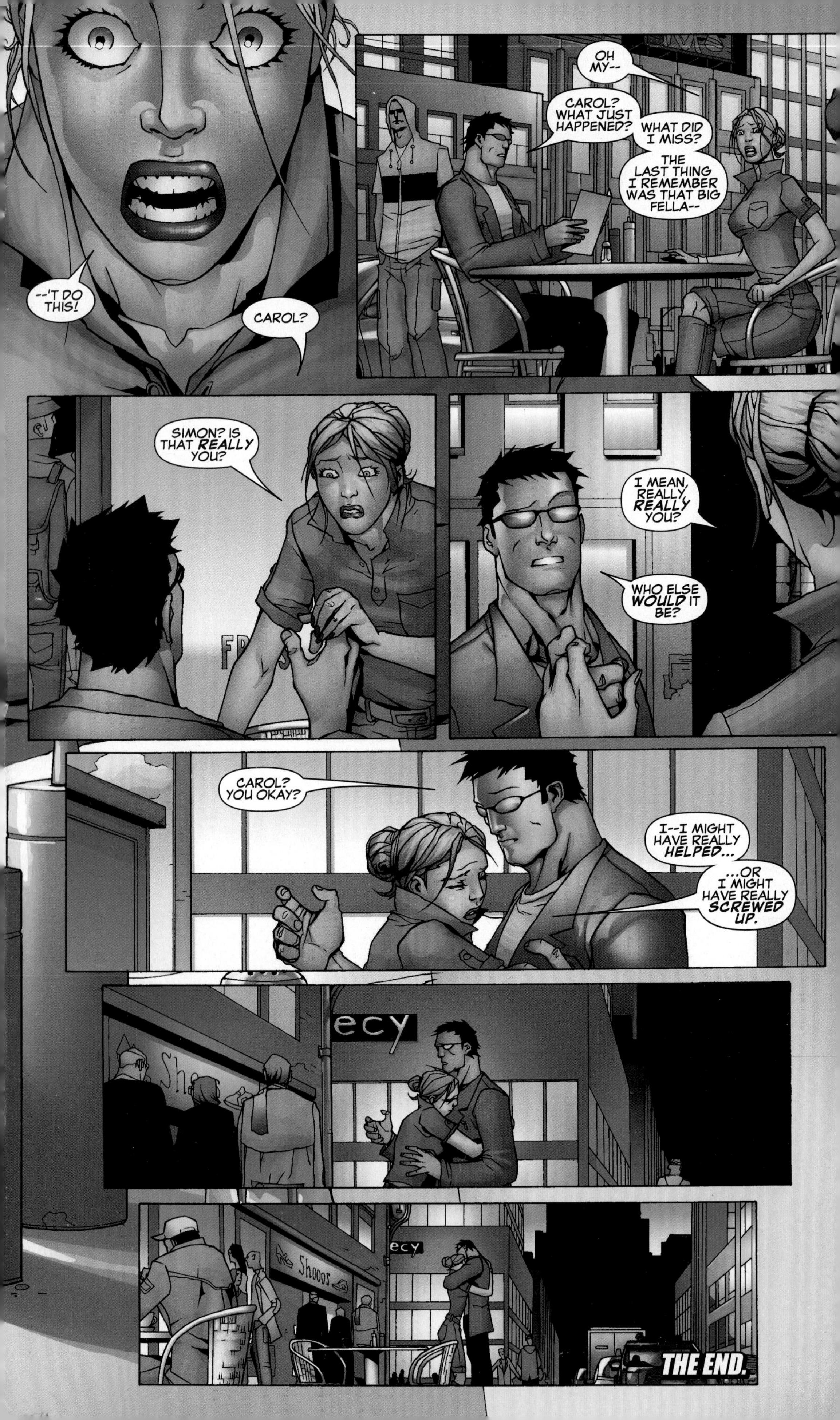
--'T DO THIS!
CAROL?
OH MY--
CAROL? WHAT JUST HAPPENED?
WHAT DID I MISS?
THE LAST THING I REMEMBER WAS THAT BIG FELLA--
SIMON? IS THAT REALLY YOU?
I MEAN, REALLY, REALLY YOU?
WHO ELSE WOULD IT BE?
CAROL? YOU OKAY?
I--I MIGHT HAVE REALLY HELPED...
...OR I MIGHT HAVE REALLY SCREWED UP.
ecy
THE END.